# Building the Ultimate Game PC



Loyd Case

QUE®
A Division of Macmillan USA
201 West 103rd Street, Indianapolis, Indiana 46290

# Building the Ultimate Game PC



International Standard Book Number:0-7897-2204-6

Library of Congress Catalog Card Number: 99-65442

Printed in the United States of America

First Printing: October 1999

01 00 99 4 3 2 1

## Trademarks

All terms mentioned in this book that are known to be trademarks or service marks have been appropriately capitalized. Que cannot attest to the accuracy of this information. Use of a term in this book should not be regarded as affecting the validity of any trademark or service mark.

## Warning and Disclaimer

Every effort has been made to make this book as complete and as accurate as possible, but no warranty or fitness is implied. The information provided is on an "as is" basis. The author and the publisher shall have neither liability nor responsibility to any person or entity with respect to any loss or damages arising from the information contained in this book.

BRADYGAMES
TAKE YOUR GAME FURTHER

An imprint of Macmillan USA
201 West 103rd Street, Indianapolis, Indiana 46290

### Publisher
Jim Minatel

### Acquisitions Editor
Jill Byus

### Senior Development Editor
Rick Kughen

### Managing Editor
Lisa Wilson

### Project Editor
Linda Seifert

### Copy Editor
Kate Givens

### Indexer
Amy Bowling

### Proofreaders
Bob LaRoche
Megan Wade

### Technical Editor
Dave Salvator

### Team Coordinator
Vicki Harding

### Interior Design
Kevin Spear

### Cover Design
Kevin Spear

### Production
Stacey DeRome
Ayanna Lacey
Heather Hiatt Miller

# Contents

## II Technology Issues

## III Software

# About the Author

**Loyd Case** is contributing editor for technology to *Computer Gaming World* magazine and its sister Web site, Gamespot. A full-time writer, he has written for other leading industry publications, including *PC Magazine* and *Computer Shopper*. Loyd pioneered the field of PC hardware testing and reviews related to game performance, beginning with the first graphics card roundup for *Computer Gaming World* seven years ago.

When he's not up to his elbows inside a computer chassis, you can find him playing networked computer games, skiing with his wife and two daughters, or reading.

# Dedication

***This book is dedicated to my parents, who let me read anything I wanted when I was growing up.***

***It's also dedicated to my wife, Jan, and my two daughters, Elizabeth and Emily. Without their support and encouragement, this book would not have happened.***

# Acknowledgments

There are many people who make a work like this possible. Thanks goes to my family, who put up with my long days and nights at the keyboard. Then, there's the Friday Night Follies gaming crew, including Ron Talbot, Scott Gardner, Scott Crandall, Gary Moshofsky, and Max Heim. They helped me troubleshoot and test many a multiplayer gaming title.

A special tip of the hat goes to Chris Lombardi, managing editor of *Computer Gaming World*. He gave me my first hardware writing assignment many years ago, writing the first-ever gaming graphics card roundup. I also want to thank the editors, including Rick Kughen, Jill Byus, and Dave Salvator, who pulled me through my first book with good humor and patience.

# Tell Us What You Think!

As the reader of this book, *you* are our most important critic and commentator. We value your opinion and want to know what we're doing right, what we could do better, what areas you'd like to see us publish in, and any other words of wisdom you're willing to pass our way.

As a Publisher for Que, I welcome your comments. You can fax, email, or write me directly to let me know what you did or didn't like about this book—as well as what we can do to make our books stronger.

*Please note that I cannot help you with technical problems related to the topic of this book, and that due to the high volume of mail I receive, I might not be able to reply to every message.*

When you write, please be sure to include this book's title and author as well as your name and phone or fax number. I will carefully review your comments and share them with the author and editors who worked on the book.


Fax: 317-581-4666

Email: `opsys@mcp.com`

Mail: Publisher
Que
201 West 103rd Street
Indianapolis, IN 46290 USA

# Introduction

## What's In This Book?

Computer games can be exhilarating, thought-provoking, absorbing adrenaline pumping, or all of the above at the same time. They can also be frustrating and annoying if they don't run properly on your PC. This book can help you tweak your existing PC or create an "ultimate" gaming rig that will run the latest cool new PC titles smoothly and without hassles. Here's just a taste of what you'll find between these covers:

- Understand the inner workings of PC technology as it applies to games, including 3D graphics, positional sound, DirectX, and Windows.
- Discover new tips, tricks, and tweaks to smooth out your gaming experience.
- Learn how to build your own hotrod gaming rig using components that *you* choose.
- Explore the brave new world of Internet gaming.
- Install, set up, and configure your own local area network for multiplayer gaming thrills.
- Understand once and for all how game controllers work and how to get the best performance out of them.

## Who Should Buy This Book?

Have you ever wondered how a joystick works?

Are you curious about the inner workings of a 3D game?

Did you ever want to put together a gaming PC built to your specifications?

Are you tired of playing against the computer, and want to set up a network to game with your friends?

Have you stared at the specs on the side of a 3D graphics card or sound card and wondered what it all meant?

Are you frustrated with the performance of new games on your almost-new PC?

If the answer to any or all of the questions above is "yes," then this book is for you. Whether you are a hard-core PC game player or just occasionally boot up a game, this book can help you understand how to wring out the maximum performance from your PC. Along the way, you'll develop an understanding and appreciation of 3D graphics, positional audio, and network gaming. Finally, you'll be able to develop a cost-effective upgrade strategy to maximize your PC hardware investment.

# Special Elements

As you read this book, you'll come across special highlighted notes.

Commands, directions, and explanations in this book are presented in the clearest format possible. The following items are some of the features that will make this book easier for you to use:

- **Commands that you must enter.** Commands that you'll need to type are easily identified by underline format. For example, if I direct you to delete the d3d directory in the Windows Registry, I'll do it like so: `DEL d3d*.*` This tells you that you'll need to enter this command exactly as it is shown.
- **Cross-references.** If there's a related topic that is prerequisite to the section or steps you are reading, or a topic that builds further on what you are reading, you'll find the cross-reference to it after the steps or at the end of the section, like this:

For a walkthrough of how to set up Windows, see page 261, Chapter 21.

## Tips, Notes, and Cautions

### Tips

Tips suggest alternate methods for accomplishing a task or provide additional information that will help you learn a concept or complete a task more easily.

### Notes

Notes provide additional information about the current topic that is either ancillary to the topic at hand or is designed to provide additional insight into a topic.

## Cautions

Cautions point out actions that could be counterproductive, at the least, and downright dangerous, at the most. When you see one of these, be sure to read it!

Some of these are just additional tidbits of knowledge. Others are tips to improve performance or otherwise make life easier. Finally, there are the occasional cautions, which will help you avoid those "gotchas" that can trap an unwary user.

# Part 1

# The Entertainment PC

# Chapter 1

# Introduction: Why Games?

## Who Do You Want to Frag Today?

**The flight stick is slippery in your hands as you line up your sights on the enemy plane. After some serious aerobatics, you've finally lined up on the FW-190's six, but the plane in front is still jinking left and right. Just as your finger begins to tighten on the trigger, your wingman's voice screams frantically in your headset. "You've got one on your tail! Break right! Break right!"**

---

**Running frantically down the main corridor of the castle, you round the corner just in time. The rocket that had been closing in on you slammed into the end of the corridor and exploded. You took a little splash damage, but survived. You spin on your feet just as your opponent careens around the corner. Your rail gun bucks in your hand, and your enemy has now just become your former enemy.**

---

**The message pops up: There's a fire in the northwest corner of the city. Luckily, you'd had the foresight to build fire stations in most of the areas of the city, but you check the local firehouse and make sure it dispatches engines to the scene. Then you notice that property values have been falling in one of the neighborhoods on the East side. At first, it's a mystery, but then you notice that a nearby landfill has been getting pretty large. But you don't have much more free space for a new landfill. Just then, a neighboring city mayor contacts you and suggests that you pay them to take some of the garbage off your hands. The tax coffers are in good shape, so you gratefully accept the offer.**

# Why Games?

Games have been with us since the dawn of recorded history. Games like Chess, Go, and Backgammon have proven extremely popular over centuries. Even sports like basketball or soccer are games that simply require a high degree of physical skill.

Games are very emotionally affecting. You can be on the edge of your seat during a close Monopoly™ game, or feel certain exhilaration when you checkmate a tough opponent. Games can develop problem-solving and analytical-reasoning skills, and multiplayer games like Bridge enhance your social life. More sophisticated games, such as *Diplomacy* or *Squad Leader*, can stimulate an interest in history or the arts.

The PC games of today are sophisticated applications that have code bases that rival some operating systems and stunning graphics and audio capabilities. Whether the game is a fast and furious 3D shooter or a simulation of an historical battle, computer games have captured the fancy of much of the American public.

A few years ago, during an industry event, an Intel marketing executive spoke about the impact of computer games on home PC sales. Back then, the Pentium II was the hottest CPU around, and over 50% of all Pentium II systems were being purchased by home users. This had puzzled the Intel exec, as Intel's market research had indicated that most users were balancing checkbooks, writing letters, and doing a little Web surfing. Certainly, a fast Pentium II wasn't essential for those functions. So, Intel went back and surveyed users *after* they had bought a system.

Surveys taken before a computer was purchased showed around 15% of buyers cited "playing games" as a main use for the computer. But the post-purchase survey revealed that 85% of the buyers were playing games on a regular basis.

## Note

As we begin the new millenium, games are still pushing the limits of available PC technology—and beyond. The purpose of this book is to help you understand the underlying technology driving modern PC games, and to make intelligent choices when you upgrade your existing system or buy a new system. Along the way, we'll pop the hood open on the modern PC and show you how you can upgrade it yourself. Knowing how to incrementally upgrade your gaming rig in a planned and intelligent manner goes a long way toward delaying the inevitable time when you'll have to replace an aging system. Understanding how it all comes together can make the games more fun, too. After all, it's about *entertainment*, not frustration.

# It's About Performance

One of the fastest growing areas of computer hardware is for graphics cards that can accelerate sophisticated, real-time 3D graphics. In the business world, the need for high performance 3D graphics is minimal. However, a huge array of games is emerging that make demanding use of 3D graphics. It used to be that only a handful of games would benefit from 3D acceleration, and the majority of those were first-person shooter games like *Quake II*. Now, all the major game genres are incorporating 3D graphics. Whether it's a strategy game like *Panzer General III*, a role-playing game like *Might and Magic VII*, or a flight simulator like *Jane's WW2 Fighters*, 3D graphics has become increasingly pervasive in modern computer games.

It's not just about eye candy, either. Despite complaints to the contrary, the artificial opponent (called the "AI" by most gamers) is getting more sophisticated, requiring more CPU cycles. As more strategy games use 3D graphics, pathfinding—the art of making a unit in a game move where you want it to, through or around a lot of terrain—becomes more sophisticated. Games are also incorporating more realism, such as better physical modeling, which also requires a lot of CPU horsepower.

## Note

AI, or "artificial intelligence" is programming that enables computer characters and units to interact with each other or with you. The obvious use for AI is to create computer opponents that can be challenging in a single player game. But there's also "friendly AI." For example, if you're playing a real-time strategy game like *Tiberian Sun*, there are too many units on your side to manually control. So the friendly AI handles combat, pathfinding, and so on.

Then there's audio. Sound effects in games have progressed greatly since the days of four-tone beeps coming out of your PC speakers. Sophisticated math is now used to calculate exactly where a particular sound should be located. In a driving game, for example, you may "hear" an opponent's car come up on your left rear, and then fade into the distance as it passes you. In a game like Looking Glass' *Thief*, audio effects are such an integral part of the game that it's nearly impossible to play without sound turned on.

Some games simulate incredibly complex worlds. Hasbro's flight simulator *Falcon 4.0* simulates an entire ground and air campaign set on the Korean Peninsula. At any given moment, hundreds of vehicles and aircraft are moving and fighting. In fact, Falcon 4.0 is so demanding that it supports dual CPUs under Windows NT if they are available.

# The Edge of the Envelope

Other games are pushing the performance envelope in other ways. *Quake III: Arena*, from id Software, is making full use of advanced features of modern 3D graphics cards, including textures created in full 32-bit color, higher resolution texture sets, and OpenGL support. *Battlezone II* from Activision makes full use of SSE (streaming SIMD extensions) built into Intel's Pentium III CPUs. The Babylon 5 space combat game, *Into the Fire*, uses the DirectX 7.0 transform and lighting engine, allowing the game to immediately take advantage of 3D accelerators with transform and lighting hardware.

If you want to know more about 3D terms "transform and lighting", see page 68.

OpenGL is covered in more detail on pages 185 and 19.

Complex strategy games, such as *Braveheart* and *Shogun*, mix real-time 3D combat with sophisticated AI and resource management. As more strategy games use 3D graphics, *pathfinding*—programming that allows units to travel from one location to another—becomes more complex, requiring more CPU horsepower.

Faster CPUs also enable better physical modeling. Take flight simulators, for example. Flight sims use "flight models," which simulate how an aircraft should behave at different speeds, altitudes, and angles of attack. In the past, programmers would use large tables of data to create the flight model. But there were always situations where the table-driven flight model would break down—either "outside the envelope" (that is, when you tried to fly outside of the design specs for the aircraft) or between two table entries. With faster processors and more memory, programmers can now use fluid dynamic equations to actually calculate the behavior of airflow over various aircraft surfaces. This enables a more robust and realistic flight model.

# Technology Advances

For me, it all began with *Falcon 3.0*.

*Falcon 3.0* came out in 1991. The graphics by today's standards were extremely crude, but the game had a fairly sophisticated flight model and a flexible, dynamic campaign. However, if you wanted to use the highest-quality flight model, you needed a floating-point coprocessor. The top-of-the line at that time was the 33MHz 386, and most systems didn't have the optional 387 floating point coprocessor. So, I went out and bought one for my system. It was the first time I upgraded a system myself. A lot of *Falcon 3.0* fans upgraded their systems that year.

Then came *Strike Commander*.

Gamers who have been around for awhile will point to seminal games that have advanced the state of the art of computer games, like *Wolfenstein3D*, *M.U.L.E.*, *Civilization*, and others. But when Origin (now a part of computer game giant Electronic Arts) shipped *Strike Commander* in 1993, the PC game world changed (some might say for the worse). *Strike Commander* was a flight simulator that used a fully Gouraud-shaded, texture-mapped graphics engine for all the aircraft graphics. At the time, the fastest PC you could buy had a 66MHz 486 CPU; such systems cost $3,500 or more. Out of the box, *Strike Commander* could bring the fastest system available to its knees. It was one of the first major games to push the performance envelope so hard; state-of-the-art CPUs of the day couldn't run them if the user maxed out the game detail settings. In other words, it didn't matter how much money you spent; you could not run *Strike Commander* with all the detail turned on.

**Note**

*Gouraud shading* is a technique used in 3D rendering to blend the colors between two polygons. The result is that you can't see the "seam" between the polygons. For more information, see Chapter 4, "Graphics."

That's almost commonplace these days. You can find any of a number of games that allow you to turn the detail, resolution, and other features up high enough so that they run too slowly to be playable. On the one hand, they allow the user to scale the game to fit their system, while at the same time allowing users who upgrade frequently to get a little more out of their games.

## Processors: Faster, More Efficient

*Strike Commander* was merely the first example. Since then, there has been a steady stream of games that push the limits of performance of whatever generation of PCs was current at the time. The net result is the ongoing need to continually upgrade your system if you want to play the leading edge titles with the best possible performance.

The hardware companies sat up and took notice of the increasingly steep technology curve of modern computer games. The sales of computer games is a two billion dollar business—about one quarter of the total electronic games business. Most of the rest is console games, but that other six billion dollars also includes the cost of the consoles themselves. The PC game business only includes the software—hardware sales haven't been factored into the equation. Yet high-end PC games often drive hardware sales. Unlike console gamers, PC game players tend to be older, with some disposable income. Core game players, when confronted with a leading edge game that doesn't play well on their system, will often spend hundreds or even thousands of dollars to bring their system up to snuff.

The CPU companies are keenly aware of how games are driving users to upgrade existing systems or buy new ones. Both of the major CPU companies (Intel and AMD) now have technical staff dedicated to working with game developers to use new features in upcoming titles. It's not out of altruism—games using new features means that users will want to buy new CPUs. Optimists point out that these new games enable a richer, more immersive game experience, while cynics like to note that it traps users in an ever-upward spiral of upgrades.

More recent advances in CPU technology from Intel and AMD are targeted squarely at the homebuyer. Features like MMX, SSE (streaming SIMD extensions), and 3DNOW! can help in certain types of business applications, such as digital video editing and paint-like applications like Adobe PhotoShop. But the real impetus behind MMX, SSE, and 3DNOW! has been the game environment. Both the CPU companies and the makers of 3D graphics chips have been searching for a holy grail known as the "killer 3D app for business," but meanwhile, games are benefiting from the advanced features of these new CPUs.

New computer systems also use faster types of memory, and also have a faster system memory bus. The first Pentium II CPUs accessed memory at a clock rate of 66MHz. Later, the bus speed jumped to 100MHz, and we're now seeing memory buses at 133MHz and greater. Although this can certainly improve any applications performance, faster memory speeds mean quicker movement of complex 3D data (vertices and textures) across the system bus to the AGP card. In fact, AGP graphics itself was created to enable faster 3D graphics—mostly for better gameplay.

# 3D Graphics: Eye Candy for Gamers

In 1989, Apollo Computer shipped the DN10000. It was the first workstation offering hardware-accelerated, texture-mapped graphics. It's no coincidence that one of the architects of the graphics technology in the DN10000 is David Kirk, now one of the main 3D hardware architects at Nvidia. That DN10000 came with a whopping 16MB of RAM and 1GB of disc space. Although each DN10000 could support up to four CPUs, each CPU ran at all of 18.8MHz. By contrast, a 600MHz Pentium III clocks 32 times faster. The DN10000 could cost upwards of $200,000 for a fully loaded workstation, and probably wouldn't be able to run Quake II adequately. Today, you can get a 600MHz Pentium III with 128MB of RAM and a 64MB graphics card for 1/100th the cost of that DN10000, and it would run rings around the older system.

3D graphics acceleration is even more obviously targeted at games. As recently as three years ago, most computer game graphics were generated by the CPU; the graphics card only acted as a dumb display device. Now, there are graphics accelerators emerging in the $250 range that rival the performance of workstation graphics of a year ago. Features like rendering, 3D transforms, lighting, and triangle setup are all being offloaded from the CPU.

The technology inside the 3D graphics chips is advancing at an astonishing rate. As Nvidia, one of the leading graphics chips companies puts it, "Moore's Law is for wimps." Moore's Law, invented by Intel co-founder Gordon Moore, states that transistor counts will double every 18 months.

But the performance of graphics cards has been increasing 8-fold every 18 months. The Nvidia NV10 weighs in at a hefty 22 million transistors—more than a Pentium III or Athlon CPU. Nvidia's previous TNT2 chip only had seven million transistors. That's a three-fold increase in less than a year. The NV10 accelerates transforms, lighting, and rendering, something only the most expensive workstations could adequately do a year ago. Yet, you can buy an NV10-based card with 64MB of RAM for less than $300.

The response of game developers has been nothing short of phenomenal. There are a number of games now entering the market that *require* 3D acceleration. This means that 3D acceleration is no longer an optional feature if you're interested in games.

Interest in 3D graphics acceleration has migrated to other applications. One of the prettiest game "engines" around is the one developed by Epic for its game *Unreal Tournament*. Digitalo Design is taking the *Unreal* graphics engine and using it to create a virtual reality model of the Notre Dame cathedral. But the primary use for fast, real-time 3D graphics is games.

The array of jargon that surrounds both CPUs and 3D graphics technology is bewildering. It's easy to get confused by the sheer volume of arcane terms. If you're sitting there scratching your head, hang in there. Later in the book, we'll really dig into the heart of how 3D graphics hardware works, and how to get the best performance out of your 3D accelerator.

# Positional Audio

The current generation of 3D graphics cards can still be used for standard business applications, but positional 3D audio is all about games. You don't need real-time occlusion of sound waves to surf the Web or run a spreadsheet. Industry veteran Creative Labs, which essentially created the 3D sound card market, has invested heavily in EAX, a 3D audio technology that uses highly tuned reverb algorithms. (Creative licensed EAX to Microsoft for inclusion in DirectX 8.0, Microsoft's game-oriented API).

Another high-profile contender is Aureal Semiconductor. Aureal's A3D has garnered a lot of mindshare among game developers. Although not part of DirectSound3D, adding A3D support is fairly easy. A3D attempts to model the actual 3D environment, then calculate the movement of sound waves, much the way that 3D graphics attempts to model the visual environment.

The third major contender in the positional audio sweepstakes is Sensaura. Sensaura was formerly the central research laboratory for EMI records, and has a distinguished history in the audio arena (it invented stereo back in the 1930s). Now an independent company, Sensaura has layered positional 3D audio algorithms as extensions to Direct3D, which means that a Sensaura-equipped card works with any game that uses DirectSound3D.

3D audio technology takes advantage of the way your ear works. Using mathematical algorithms known as HRTFs *(head related transfer functions)*, the 3D chip companies actually shape the audio signal to fool the ear. They know what the ear expects when a sound comes from your left, so they apply the math to the audio waveform to fool your ear into thinking the sound did, indeed, come from your left. It can be quite an eerie feeling. Unlike 3D graphics, which ultimately has to be displayed on your flat PC monitor, well done 3D audio can really immerse you in a sound field that seems like it's all around you.

# DirectX

All this nifty technology would simply make life more difficult for game developers if there wasn't a standard API (applications programming interface) for writing games.

In the past, game developers had to develop every element of the game themselves. Even very low-level hardware, like writing files to the hard drive or accessing graphics memory, had to be hand-coded by the programmer. As more sophisticated graphics and sound hardware emerged, each different piece of hardware forced game programmers to write different pieces of code just to use them.

An API consists of software "building blocks" that take care of many of these low-level details so that programmers can focus more on the design of the game. They can use these building blocks in a standard way in any game, and not have to worry as much about the low-level hardware as in the past.

The hardware makers have to write drivers that then "plug into" the API. Think of it as a layer of LEGO™ building blocks, with the drivers at the bottom layer, the API in the middle, and the application (game) on top. The idea is that it all plugs together neatly—or as neatly as you can in software.

In the old days of MS-DOS, the hardware companies would fight for mindshare among game developers. A small industry emerged as companies wrote libraries of drivers that would work with all the disparate standards. Sound cards were a great example. The Creative Labs Sound Blaster emerged as the dominant sound card standard among game developers. Improvements in audio chips stalled because no one wanted to buck the standard. Companies like Miles Audio made a good living by supplying sound drivers that would work across a variety of sound cards in a consistent manner.

Similar things were happening across the board. Graphics were locked into the VGA/SVGA standard. No one wanted to try to build in 2D or 3D acceleration into games because every graphics chip vendor would require different, low-level software to be written.

When Microsoft was readying Windows 95, it took a look at the burgeoning home market, and the balkanized state of game development. Games had never really taken hold on Windows 3.x, but because Windows 3.x and DOS were completely separate, it wasn't a major issue. But Windows 95 would more closely integrate DOS and Windows. Plus, Microsoft really wanted to steer all applications development to Windows—and that meant Windows games.

The problem was that the standard Windows APIs were too clumsy and too slow for game development. Game programmers loved to write code that would wring out every ounce of performance from the hardware, something known as "writing to the metal." This entailed access to the most intimate internal workings of hardware such as sound cards and, especially, graphics.

Windows, on the other hand, used something known as GDI (Graphics Device Interface). *GDI* is the standard API for the graphics you see when you first start up Windows, and when you're in applications like a word processor or spreadsheet. GDI is great for doing things like drawing windows, title bars, and menus. It's even pretty good at moving them around when you drag them with a mouse. But as soon as a programmer tried to do something more sophisticated—even if it was simple 2D animation—GDI proved far too slow and cumbersome. And there is no way of handling 3D graphics in GDI.

Microsoft had taken a tentative step forward with a low-level API called WinG, but it was limited to 2D graphics. It did achieve some limited success, but game developers wanted more. They wanted all the speed of direct hardware access, but wanted to be free from the requirement to write radically different code for each new piece of hardware. So, Microsoft developed DirectX.

# Multiplayer and the Wave of the Future

It used to be that computer gaming was a somewhat solitary endeavor. People who like games would play computer games because finding real human opponents wasn't always easy or possible.

Even so, there's a fairly rich history of multiplayer games. Early PC multiplayer games would use a "hot seat." When it was your turn, you'd sit in front of the computer, then let the next player in when you were done. Some early Macintosh games took advantage of the presence of AppleTalk—the Macintosh's built-in peer-to-peer networking—to create networked multiplayer games. The traditional online services—CompuServe, America Online, and Genie—hosted a few popular games, like Air Warrior or Multiplayer Battletech.

Then along came the Internet, and that changed everything. Now, it's almost *de riguer* for a new game to have some multiplayer support. Games and tools developed for gamers have made it ever-easier to find opponents. New game-oriented services revolving around Web sites have emerged, such as Microsoft's Zone, Sega's HEAT.NET, and MPlayer. There's also been a recent trend towards massive multiplayer games, such as *Everquest* and Electronic Arts upcoming *USAF* flight sim. These games exist only on the Internet, and generally require monthly fees to continue playing.

There are other multiplayer-only games that don't require paying a monthly fee. Good examples include *Tribes, Quake III: Arena*, and *Unreal Tournament*. These have a lot in common with single player games in that they can have a standalone element—even if it's just a training mode—and generally smaller pools of players. Servers for these games are spread out over the Internet, sometimes hosted by individuals with a passion for these games.

That's not to say single player is dead. Single player games often make for a better story-telling environment. Also, online games tend to reward people who spend a lot of time online, so occasional gamers may find more reward beating the computer. Finally, Internet gaming is still somewhat impersonal—if the person on the other end is simply a substitute for the game AI, it's not exactly a social activity.

Now, the concept of a LAN party has emerged, in which a like-minded group of gamers will converge on a location with their PCs, assemble a local area network, and play against each other for a few hours or a weekend. Having hosted a few of these, I can tell you that these are very much social activities. When you can see and talk to your opponents or teammates, it adds a whole new level to gameplay.

# A Recent History of PC Games and Hardware

Let's take a look at the recent history of computer games as it pertains to hardware. This isn't meant to be a detailed history of games, but rather, how games have historically affected hardware or vice versa.

In the past few years, computers based on the Intel series of microprocessors and operating systems from Microsoft have captured as much as 90 percent of the PC market. Naturally, game publishers have taken notice of the 100 million plus PCs sold each year, and have responded. Although computer games don't sell in the same volume as home console games (such as Nintendo64 and Sony PlayStation), they are often more profitable due to the low cost of goods and the absence of stiff licensing fees.

With all this 3D-accelerated, positional-audio, mouse-driven goodness, it's easy to forget that PC games were second fiddle to other home computer titles. In fact, the IBM PC was originally conceived as a business computer, although IBM had the foresight to have a game port adapter as an option, something Apple forgot when it developed the Macintosh.

## The Prehistory of Computer Games

There have long been games that run on computers. *Space War*, one of the first computer games ever, ran on the PDP-1 minicomputer as far back as 1962. The text-based game *Adventure* captured the hearts and minds of users in the late '60s, followed by the more puckish and sophisticated *Zork: The Underground Empire*.

There have also been games on personal computers since the early days of the PC. Quite a few games were written for the Apple II. Games were written for other home computers, including the seminal Commodore Amiga. Some, like *M.U.L.E.* and *Empire* are considered classics to this day.

# Gaming: The Early Years

The modern era of IBM PC games began around 1988, when the first inexpensive sound cards appeared for the PC. Until then, the only audio you could get out of the PC were the impersonal beeps of the lowly PC speaker. Other home computers—particularly Commodore's Amiga—had much better sound. Then, the Adlib sound card, followed in 1989 by the original SoundBlaster, changed everything. The Adlib was really just an FM tone generator, which could do sound effects and MIDI music. The SoundBlaster offered sound at least on par with the Amiga and sometimes even better. It was fairly inexpensive—a little more than a hundred bucks. It was relatively easy to program, and offloaded the CPU by using the PC's DMA architecture. Most importantly, the Sound Blaster could handle digital audio—which meant more realistic sound effects and voices. The Sound Blaster also had an external MIDI port that did double-duty as a joystick adapter. Game developers wasted no time in adopting the Sound Blaster.

In 1987, IBM had introduced the PS/2 line of personal computers, trying to separate itself from the vast array of clones that were cutting into its market share. But IBM had actually been beaten to the punch by Compaq, which had shipped the first 386-based PC a few months before. For gamers, though, the most important announcement of 1987 was the VGA graphics adapter. The VGA adapter could display 16 colors at 640×480 or 256 colors at 320×200.

The combination of 256 colors and good audio, plus the increasing market share of the PC, made the PC platform increasingly attractive to game developers. Most games were originally designed for the Commodore or Apple platforms, and then ported to the PC, but that began to change. Eventually, even Electronic Arts, which had declared the Amiga to be the platform of the future, relented and began releasing games for the PC.

The 386 era that began with the PS/2 also meant that PC processors were finally rivaling the powerful Motorola 68000 that was in the Amiga. Game developers still had to contend with the arcane limitations of Intel CPU memory management and Microsoft's MS-DOS, which was much cruder than the Amiga's operating system. Truly seminal games began to appear on the PC: *Wolfenstein 3D*, *Civilization*, *Doom*, *Secret Weapons of the Luftwaffe*, *Falcon 3.0,* and others. 1989 also saw the shipment of the first CD-ROM–based game, *Manhole*, which ran on the Apple Macintosh.

When the first 486-based systems began shipping in 1990, the first systems with integrated floating-point coprocessors arrived. Intel also began shipping the 486SX, a 486 CPU *without* the integrated coprocessor, targeted towards low-end and home computers. At that time, games really weren't on the radar of the large PC companies.

## Sound Shapes the Nineties

As 1991 rolled around, Origin established itself as a technology leader by shipping *Wing Commander*. *Wing Commander* offered a branching story line, but more importantly from a technology basis, it had *speech*. The characters actually talked—but only if you had a Sound Blaster card, and only if you bought the speech pack add-on to the game. Also arriving in 1991 was *Falcon 3.0*, mentioned earlier. *Falcon 3.0* also had speech, but it was bundled into the game. *Falcon 3.0* also offered multiplayer campaigning on a local area network, one of the first popular PC games to have multiplayer capability. *Falcon's* graphics, however, were fairly crude, flat-shaded polygons.

In 1992, id Software shipped *Castle Wolfenstein*. The game initially shipped as a shareware title, but achieved a huge following. It was one of the first PC games to use texture-mapped 3D graphics. The boys at id followed up in 1993 with *Doom*, which sent a shock-wave through the entire game industry. While there had been other first-person shooters, *Doom's* stunning graphics, which had a very realistic 3D look, its creepy atmosphere, and network playability revolutionized gaming. *Strike Commander*, Origin's highly demanding flight simulator, had shipped earlier that year, setting a new performance benchmark for games.

## Games Distributed on CD-ROM

CD-ROM drives achieved more common acceptance in 1992 and 1993. *The 7th Guest*, a game making heavy use of video and 3D rendered sets, shipped to much acclaim. In 1994, Origin once again pushed the technology envelope, shipping *Wing Commander III* on four CD-ROMs. *Wing Commander III* also made extensive use of video cut scenes to propel the story line forward. The video was integrated into the game, but the actual combat was in SVGA resolution PC graphics running at 640×480.

Also shipping in 1994 was the first 3D accelerated game for the PC, a 3D fighting game called *Sento*. Developed by 47Tek, it was strictly a demonstration of the capability of a high-priced, Matrox graphics card. The MGA chip was capable of Gouraud-shaded 3D in 16-bit color, and *Sento* exploited the full capabilities. But most games were DOS-based, and the Matrox card was not only expensive, but abysmally slow in DOS, so *Sento* was seen by only a handful of people who failed to appreciate the technological leap. By 1995, all games were shipping on CD-ROM.

## ActiveX Changes the Gaming World

In 1995, Windows 95 shipped, and Microsoft announced the intention to ship a new API targeted towards fast game performance under Windows. It was called DirectX. DirectX shipped in 1996, but the 3D API wasn't part of the package. Redmond had acquired UK software developer RenderMorphics. Rendormorphics Reality Lab was a full-featured API with an impressively fast software renderer. Everyone in the industry was aware that 3D graphics accelerators were on the horizon. Rendition, now a part of Micron, had shown early simulations of 3D accelerated games running at the 1995 Game Developer's Conference. It was also the first graphics company to show id's *Quake* running with hardware acceleration. What everyone feared was a 3D API war, where each graphics chipmaker would seek to drive its own standard in hopes of capturing more of the market, and forcing game developers to use each chip's proprietary API.

Diamond shipped the Diamond Edge multimedia card. The Edge used the Nvidia NV1 media processor, which handled 2D and 3D graphics, audio, and game controller functions. Unfortunately, it didn't do any of them well.

With the Rendermorphics acquisition, Microsoft announced Direct3D. Everyone breathed a sigh of relief. Then, Direct3D slipped several months. The chip companies knew they couldn't wait, and several of them—Rendition, 3dfx, and Videologic most notably—developed "thin" APIs of their own; the most enduring of these has been 3dfx's Glide API. By the end of 1996, most of the major graphics chip companies were shipping or were on the verge of shipping 3D accelerator chips. Most offered extremely limited performance, with the Rendition Verité and the 3dfx Voodoo being notable exceptions.

# OpenGL Makes Its Mark

In 1997, John Carmack became disgusted with Direct3D, deeming it a "horribly broken API," and began writing an OpenGL renderer for Quake. 3dfx responded by shipping a "mini-GL" driver for Voodoo-based accelerators that translated the 57 or so OpenGL commands used by GLQuake directly into Glide. No other consumer graphics chip company shipped a working GL driver until 1998, so 3dfx became the accelerator of choice for hard-core action gamers.

# Intel Aims MMX at Gamers

Meanwhile, on the CPU front, Intel shipped the Pentium MMX CPU. The MMX instruction set consisted of 57 new instructions tuned for SIMD (single instruction, multiple data) operations. It was targeted squarely at the consumer market, and marked the first time Intel actually *added* features for consumers, rather than removing them. Unfortunately, MMX only worked on integer data, which was fine for some video and audio applications, but did little for 3D graphics or other operations requiring floating-point math. The first game using MMX-enhanced graphics, *Rebel Moon Rising*, shipped as a demo on CDs bundled with early retail MMX CPUs. Epic Megagames (later, simply, Epic Games) announced that its 3D action game, *Unreal*, would use MMX.

After a near-death experience, Nvidia returned with a vengeance, shipping the RIVA 128 graphics chip. Touted as a "Voodoo killer" by some, it wasn't as fast as the Voodoo, but was the first chip to give 3dfx heartburn. Rendition's V2200 proved to be a disappointment—it was faster than the original Verité—but not fast enough.

# The Recent Past

In 1998, Aureal and ESS shipped 3D audio chips. Rising from the ashes of the defunct Media Vision, Aureal's Vortex chip uses sophisticated algorithms to create an immersive sound field. The ESS Maestro uses straight DirectSound3D. The Pentium II arrived, combining the MMX instruction set with the much faster floating point of the Pentium Pro line. 3dfx shipped the Voodoo2 accelerator, maintaining 3dfx's position as the fastest consumer-level 3D card available, but a few months later, Nvidia shipped the RIVA TNT. The TNT fell short of Voodoo2 performance, but only by a relatively small margin, and could actually outpace Voodoo2 in some Direct3D games. AMD delivered the K6-2 to the market, with its take on floating point SIMD, called 3DNow! A few game developers support 3DNow!, but it failed to take the industry by storm. We'll cover floating-point SIMD in Chapter 2, "Engines of Entertainment: The Processor."

*Quake II*, id's successor to *Quake*, also shipped. It's not quite as bleeding-edge as *Quake* was, but is a better overall game. Epic finally shipped *Unreal* after a three-year effort and many delays. *Unreal* used a four-pass renderer (two-pass when using 3dfx's GLIDE API on Voodoo2), and grabbed the title of most demanding computer game for a brief time. The Pentium III processor arrived on the scene, complete with a robust, floating-point SIMD engine.

# Today: The Edge of the Envelope

A host of games are shipping that push even 550MHz CPUs and fast graphics cards to the limit. PC game developers seem hungrier for hardware resources than ever before. *Quake III: Arena*, id's multiplayer-focused 3D accelerated action game, uses 32-bit color throughout and large textures, pushing the bandwidth limits of high performance 3D graphics cards. The first graphics cards with transform and lighting acceleration shipped in 1999, too—most notably, the NV10.

# Part 2

# Technology Issues

# Chapter 2

# Engines of Entertainment: The Processor

## The Importance of the CPU

As we noted in Chapter 1, "Introduction: Why Games?" modern computer games are extremely demanding. Although 3D graphics accelerators and audio cards can offload some of the processing from the central processor, the CPU is the lynchpin of the gaming experience. You can put a fast 3D accelerator in a system with a slow CPU, and all you'll get is prettier renderings of a slideshow. An inadequate CPU just can't deliver the experience craved by hard-core game players.

Next to 3D graphics cards, gamers love to argue about which CPU is better. Whether it's AMD's K6-3, Intel's Pentium III, or the new AMD Athlon, the arguments are passionate—passionate beyond reason, sometimes. We'll try to cut through some of the jargon and emotion surrounding these engines of entertainment so you can better choose the right CPU for the type of game you prefer.

# Mathematical Functions of the CPU

Modern PC's revolve around the CPU (Central Processing Unit). In fact, PCs are very processor-centric. Not all computers are this way. Some high-end workstations, for example, consider the system bus to be the real soul of the machine, and the CPUs (or multiple CPUs) are just equals on the bus with graphics processors, networking hardware, and other subsystems.

Intel, of course, wants the PC to be CPU-centric because that's its chief reason for existence (although Intel is the world's leading motherboard manufacturer, too). And because today's personal computers treat the CPU as the center of attention, we'll begin our technology exploration there. We'll look at currently shipping processors, and their technical merits and warts and what kind of performance you might expect.

All CPUs for the PC have common features, though they may be implemented differently. This is true whether they are AMD or Intel CPUs. Let's take a look at these common pieces.

## Integer Execution

The majority of calculations that take place inside the CPU are integer-based. Integers are whole numbers, such as 5, –255, or 0. None of these numbers have any decimal or fractional component.

Integer calculations are used for everything from manipulating text to handling AI for computer opponents. It's the most common type of calculation performed on a PC, and is used in a wide variety of functions inside games. Computer games hide a lot of complexity under the surface, and integer math takes care of a lot of the details.

For example, *pathfinding* is the ability of a computer-controlled unit to find its way from one location on a map to another, around obstacles, without getting stuck or taking ridiculously long routes. Faster integer math means better pathfinding.

Artificial opponents—the "AI" or artificial intelligence—makes heavy use of integer math. The more calculations that can happen each second of game time, the deeper the AI. This means the opposing artificial opponents can be tougher or that friendly AI can react more realistically.

Wargame players are familiar with combat results tables—when two sets of combatants attack each other, combat results tables and die rolls synthesize the results of the combat. In a PC processor, random (integer) numbers can be generated with much more granularity than a simple six-sided die, and combat results can be much more complex.

Note that internally, integers are represented as binary data (strings of 1s and 0s). For example, the number 12 is represented in binary by 1100. Programmers use a shorthand called *hexadecimal* or *hex*. Our normal decimal arithmetic system is base10; binary is base2. Hexadecimal is base16. Base16 is handy because each digit represents four binary bits. Our number 12, above, would be the number C in hexadecimal. Table 2.1 compares decimal, hexadecimal, and binary numbers.

**Table 2.1—Contrasting decimal, binary, and hexadecimal numbers**

| *Decimal* | *Hexadecimal* | *Binary* |
|---|---|---|
| 0 | 0 | 0 |
| 1 | 1 | 1 |
| 2 | 10 | 2 |
| 3 | 11 | 3 |
| 4 | 100 | 4 |
| 5 | 101 | 5 |
| 6 | 110 | 6 |
| 7 | 111 | 7 |
| 8 | 1000 | 8 |
| 9 | 1001 | 9 |
| 10 | 1010 | 10 |
| 11 | 1011 | A |
| 12 | 1100 | B |
| 13 | 1101 | C |
| 14 | 1110 | D |
| 15 | 1111 | E |
| 16 | 10000 | F |
| 32 | 100000 | 20 |
| 64 | 1000000 | 40 |
| 125 | 1111101 | 70 |

Normally, you'd never need to worry about binary or hexadecimal, but you may see error messages report numbers in hex notation—now, at least, you know that those strange strings of letters and numbers have a meaning.

# Floating-Point Unit (FPU)

A few years ago, a floating-point unit was an optional add-on chip you had to buy separately. They were called "math coprocessors." (You still see that term used on occasion when referring to the FPU now built into all CPUs). It was generally used only for people who did a lot of spreadsheet crunching, or users of CAD (computer-aided design) applications. Starting with the 486DX, Intel began building the FPU directly into the CPU chip itself.

Floating-point performance is critical in 3D games. The calculations used in various stages of 3D graphics make heavy use of floating-point numbers. If you take a game like *Quake II* and run it on two systems—one with fast floating point, and one with a slow FPU, the one with the fast FPU will run substantially better.

If you mostly play turn-based strategy games, or games that are mostly 2D in nature, floating-point performance isn't as critical. A game like *Civilization II* probably uses integer calculations exclusively. However, with the increasing penetration of 3D graphics into a wide array of game genres, the importance of floating-point performance shouldn't be underestimated.

Floating-point numbers are numbers with a fractional component—numbers such as 3.14159, 2.78 or –5.44. Even 0, represented as 0.00, can be a floating-point number. Floating-point numbers are heavily used in the calculations for 3D graphics and for physics, such as calculating the fluid dynamics of airflow over the wing of a virtual aircraft.

Floating-point numbers are handled differently inside the CPU, usually in a dedicated part of the processor called a *floating-point unit*, or FPU for short. In the past, FPUs on personal computers were often separate chips that were optional. Starting with the Intel 486 line, the FPU was integrated into the main CPU chip itself. Fast floating-point performance is critical for most 3D games, even those that make heavy use of 3D graphics accelerators. Lately, new technologies such as AMD's 3DNow! and Intel's SSE (Streaming SIMD Extensions) stand to replace standard floating-point calculations with faster technologies—but even those faster technologies use floating-point numbers.

For more information on SSE, see page 32.

For more information on 3DNow!, see page 36.

# Connecting to the System: How CPUs Communicate

Even the fastest CPU would be a lump of useless silicon and plastic if there were no way to interface with the world outside the CPU. So a good chunk of the CPU is devoted to connections to the outside. If you look at diagrams of CPUs, you'll note that there is a lot of circuitry dedicated to moving data either into the processor or out to memory. The Pentium II moves data in 64-bit wide chunks. By contrast, the 8088 CPU used in the first IBM-PC moved data from the CPU to memory and back in 8-bit chunks.

Another facet of communication is memory management. When the processor wants a particular piece of data, it has to know where to get it. Memory management—the efficient location, retrieval, and movement of data to and from memory—is a critical component to CPU performance.

# All Aboard the Bus

CPUs communicate with the external world—memory, expansion cards, and so on—over *buses*. A bus is simply a collection of wires that move data around the system. The term is really a holdover from electrical engineering, and has nothing to do with the bus you ride through town. In fact, a bus inside the computer is more like the roadways a wheeled bus drives on.

In fact, the road analogy is a good one because different buses inside a computer can move data at different speeds. Take memory, for example. In Pentium and early K6 systems, the memory bus operated at 66MHz. Data could move on the 66MHz memory bus at a maximum speed of 512MB per second. Later, the memory bus speed on Pentium II and K6-2 systems was boosted to 100MHz, or about 800MB per second max.

Another important bus is the one from the CPU to cache memory. (Cache memory is covered in more detail in the next section.) The bus speed from the CPU to cache in Pentium II and Pentium III systems is 1/2 the CPU speed. For example, if you have a 400MHz Pentium II, the cache memory clocks at 200MHz. However, the speed of the *bus* is still 100MHz. Athlon, by contrast, runs the bus speed to cache memory at a full 200MHz.

Now, MHz (megahertz) is a measure of the clock rate of the bus. You can calculate the maximum speed that data will move pretty easily. For example, if the bus to memory is 64 bits wide (as it is with a Pentium II or Pentium III), and the memory bus runs at 100MHz, then you can move 100MHz*64 bits, or 64 million bits. Dividing that by 8 gives you 800 million bytes, or 800 megabytes per second.

Memory bus speed is important because games—especially 3D games—move data in and out of memory at prodigious rates. The faster your system bus, the faster the game will run, all other things being equal.

# The Cache: Turbochargers for Processors

One of the issues that is constantly wrestled with is the speed difference between the inner workings of modern CPUs and the much slower speed of memory. I noted earlier in the chapter that efficient memory management is another facet of CPU performance. But if the processor is having to constantly wait on slower memory to deliver or accept data, that would be a huge waste.

To that end, CPUs use cache memory—small pools of very fast memory—to buffer writes and reads. Think of the CPU cache as a kind of turbocharger for the CPU. Turbochargers gather up a lot of air quickly and force it into the engine of a car to facilitate better performance—so does the cache. A lot of work has gone into characterizing cache performance, to the point where small amounts of cache can be very efficient.

### Note

The cache concept was developed way back in the 1940s by Hungarian mathematician and game theorist John Von Neuman. He figured out that when a processor used a piece of data or an instruction, it was highly probable that the processor would need that data or instruction again. Having a small piece of fast (and quickly accessed) memory could deliver a substantial performance bounce.

There are typically two cache pools inside your PC. One is the level 1 cache (called *L1 cache*), and is typically embedded in the CPU chip itself. Some processors divide the L1 into two different caches, one specifically for caching instructions, the other for caching data. The Pentium III has 32KB of L1 cache, divided up into a 16KB instruction cache and a 16KB data cache. The AMD Athlon (K7) has a whopping 128KB of L1 cache, also split in half into data and instruction caches.

The L1 cache runs at the speed of the processor itself, so it acts as high-speed temporary storage. Typically, the cache will have the correct instruction or piece of data up to 95% of the time. Some applications go so far as to put key pieces of code directly into the cache.

Level 2 (a.k.a. L2) cache was historically a bigger pool of somewhat slower cache memory. For example, the Pentium III SECC2 cartridge contains 512KB of L2 cache that runs at half the clock rate of the processor. Cache memory on motherboards, such as those using the AMD K6-2, run even slower—typically at 100MHz.

Other chips, like Intel's Celeron and AMD's K6-3, have the L2 cache built directly onto the chip. This has a couple of benefits. First, the CPU can be mounted into a more compact package, reducing the overall cost. Second, the L2 cache will run at the full speed of the CPU, rather than half speed. Current Celerons have 128KB of L2 cache built in, whereas the K6-3 has 256KB of L2 cache on the chip. The Celeron has 20 million transistors. Contrast that with the Pentium II, with seven million transistors. The Celeron and the Pentium II share the same CPU core, but the difference in transistor count is the L2 cache.

The same is true for the Xeon and Pentium Pro line of CPUs from Intel. In the case of the Xeon, the cache isn't actually built on the chip itself, but does run at the full speed of the CPU.

### Note

The early, 266MHz Celerons and some 300MHz Celerons had *no* L2 cache. This severely degraded performance on business applications. Surprisingly, the lack of cache didn't adversely affect games as much, though it did have some impact. Games, as it turns out, aren't as cache-dependent as business applications. By a similar token, getting a Xeon isn't worth the additional cost because the full speed cache doesn't seem to benefit game performance much.

Both L1 and L2 cache add to the performance of the system, but note that most games seem to be less dependent on the existence of an L2 cache. Game benchmarking done on Xeon CPUs, which have a much faster cache than the equivalent Pentium II or Pentium III desktop CPU, show little change in performance. Although most of the industry criticized the early, cacheless Celerons, many gamers discovered that the Celeron with no cache actually performed quite well in games.

Just to throw in another wrinkle, the K6-3 often is on motherboards that still have 512KB of cache memory. But it's now used as a *level 3* or L3 cache. As you might imagine, it doesn't contribute much to performance.

# The Intel Processor Line

Intel has long captured the hearts and minds of gamers because of performance. Until recently, Intel CPUs were the fastest PC processors you could get for gaming—particularly 3D gaming. This was mainly due to the fact that the FPU in Intel processors was substantially faster than the competition. This has changed with the recent release of AMD's Athlon.

Because of Intel's dominance, Intel processors have not been cheap. The Celeron changed that a bit, but Intel's flagship Pentium III is still pretty pricey. That may slowly change now that AMD's new baby, the Athlon, has really raised the performance bar. Intel can no longer say it has the fastest CPU for gaming.

There are many Intel CPUs, past, present, and future. The following table delineates the Intel processor line into 2000.

### Table 2.2—Intel processor product line

| *CPU* | *Supported Clock Speeds* | *L1 Cache Size* | *L2 Cache Size* | *System Bus Clock* | *Other Features* |
|---|---|---|---|---|---|
| Pentium | 75-200MHz | 16KB | 0–512KB (depends on mother board) | 66MHz | NA |
| Pentium with MMX | 166–233MHz (some overdrive chips ran at other speeds) | 32KB | 0–512KB (depends on motherboard) | 66MHz | MMX |
| Pentium II | 233–450MHz | 32KB | 512KB | 66MHz (233–333MHz, 100MHz (350–450MHz) | MMX, Slot One |

*continues*

**Table 2.2—Intel processor product line** Continued

| *CPU* | *Supported Clock Speeds* | *L1 Cache Size* | *L2 Cache Size* | *System Bus Clock* | *Other Features* |
|---|---|---|---|---|---|
| Pentium III | 450–600MHz | 32KB | 512KB | 100MHz 133MHz | SSE, Slot One |
| Celeron | 266–500MHz | 32KB | 128KB (266MHz and early 300s had no L2 cache) | 66MHz | MMX only; some Celerons use socket 370 |
| Xeon | 4004–50MHz (Pentium II Xeon); 450–550MHz (Pentium III Xeon) | 32KB | 512KB–2MB running at full CPU clock speed | 100MHz | Slot 2 |
| Copper-mine | 600MHz + | 32KB | 256KB L2 cache on the chip at full clock speed | 100MHz | Socketed |

## The Pentium and Pentium MMX Processors

If you have anything slower than a 166MHz Pentium, then it's probably time to either replace your system or upgrade the CPU. Still, the old Pentium and Pentium MMX processors have some life left in them.

The Pentium is the successor to the 486. The original Pentium had 16KB of Level 1 cache. Intel doubled the L1 cache with the MMX version to 32KB. The original Pentium maxed out at 200MHz, whereas the Pentium MMX CPU topped out at 233MHz. (Note that some Pentium MMX chips designed for laptop computers topped out at 266MHz.)

As games become more demanding—particularly 3D titles—the Pentium really can't push polygons fast enough to meet the demands of games. However, a 166MHz or faster system may be fine for non-3D accelerated strategy games or puzzle titles.

## Pentium Pro Processors

The P6, a.k.a. the Pentium Pro, was the first Intel CPU with a 64-bit data bus. Also included was a much faster floating-point unit. But much of what was new in the P6 revolved around two concepts: predicting the future and moving data more quickly.

Many of the advances in modern CPU architecture have related to trying to either predict the future or create the future "ahead of time." Think about it: if the CPU can know what instruction will need to be executed next—or even several steps later—it can bring those instructions up "on deck," so they can be ready to go when the time is right. Technologies such as branch prediction, out-of-order execution, and deep instruction pipelines all serve to keep the instruction flow moving and minimize "stalls" (portions of the CPU sitting idle, waiting for something else to finish).

The P6 also introduced the concept of write combining, which essentially allowed the CPU to batch data and fire it off in large bursts, rather than letting it dribble out. This was particularly effective in moving data to graphics card memory quickly. Because graphics is such a big part of games, write combining can significantly speed up graphics performance in games.

**Note**

The word "superscalar" is often tossed around when referring to current CPUs. Superscalar refers to a variety of technical achievements, such as pipelining and branch prediction, so that the processor can actually crank out more than one instruction per clock cycle. Although the term is rarely used, a "scalar" processor refers to a CPU that takes one or more clock cycles (on average) to perform an instruction.

The Pentium Pro also introduced a much faster FPU than the original Pentium line. In fact, the good old Pentium Pro can still deliver a good punch in 3D games because of the faster FPU, though it's not in the same league as the Pentium II or Pentium III.

The Pentium Pro has some deficiencies, however. First, it is expensive. Most of the expense is due to the huge package, which consists of the CPU and level two (L2) cache memory in a single chip package—known as Single Edge Contact Connector (SECC), all running at the same clock rate.

# The Pentium II: Something Old, Something New

At first blush, the Pentium II package looks even bigger, but it is cheaper to make than the P6 package. Most of the cost savings is due to using slower cache memory—the L2 cache on the PII runs at half the processor clock speed.

Another key problem with the Pentium Pro was the poor performance in 16-bit code execution. Intel had hoped that the world would move to Windows NT, which was a fully 32-bit operating system. The Pentium Pro was heavily optimized to run 32-bit code well. But the huge installed base of Windows 3.1 and the equally huge success of Windows 95 took Intel by surprise. There was still a huge amount of 16-bit code running in applications and Windows 3.1. And although Windows 95 was a step along the path to 32-bit nirvana, a good chunk of the operating system was still 16-bit code. The net result was that the P6 actually performed slower in some cases than a Pentium 166 when running 16-bit code.

The Pentium II fixed all that, by reintroducing some of the 16-bit efficiencies that existed in the Pentium processor line. It also incorporated the MMX instruction set originally offered in the Pentium with the MMX CPU line.

When the 350 and 400MHz Pentium IIs were introduced, Intel finally increased the speed of the system bus. Pentium II systems under 350MHz accessed system memory at 66MHz, whereas newer P-II and P-III CPUs talk to system memory at 100MHz. Faster memory clocks by themselves resulted in better performance. It also increased memory bandwidth to the AGP port (see Chapter 13 for more on AGP).

The Pentium II's real contribution to gaming was higher clock rates and the addition of MMX to the Pentium Pro core. A 200MHz Pentium Pro would actually be a little faster than a 200MHz Pentium II because of the faster cache on the Pentium Pro. But the slowest Pentium II shipped at 233MHz, and you can't get one slower than 400MHz these days.

# The Intel Pentium III

The "III" in the Pentium III isn't quite accurate because the Pentium III is really derived more from the Pentium Pro, not the original Pentium. That makes the Pentium III the third processor in the P6 family. The Pentium III is a 32-bit processor with a 64-bit data bus. This means that all the math takes place in 32-bit chunks, but communication to the outside world can occur in 64-bit-wide chunks. The Pentium III is very much an evolutionary, not revolutionary architecture.

The key improvement of the Pentium III over the Pentium II was the introduction of SSE (streaming SIMD instructions).

## Single Instruction, Multiple Data

SIMD stands for *Single Instruction, Multiple Data*. To understand the importance of SIMD, we'll have to take a brief look at how CPUs worked historically.

Classically, when an operation takes place inside of a computer, a piece of data is fetched from memory and placed in a *register*. Think of the register as the LCD display on a pocket calculator. Before you can do anything, you first have to enter a number into the calculator. It appears in the LCD display. Then, you select an operation (multiplication, say), and enter another number. Finally, you have a result.

Similarly, inside the computer, the data is placed in a register. An instruction is loaded and then operates on the data. If two pieces of data are needed, they're fetched and placed into two different registers, then operated on. This kind of incremental approach is fine for many applications, but inefficient for others. If you look at audio processing, 3D graphics, or video streams, you'll see repetitive execution of the same instruction on lots of data in succession. CPU architects looked at this and thought that there might be a different way. These types of operations can benefit greatly from what chip architects call "parallelism." Imagine if you could load two, four, or more pieces of data into one big register. Then, you take your instruction and apply it to all the data at once. That's the idea behind SIMD. SIMD made its debut in the Pentium with MMX because MMX is just SIMD for integers.

However, MMX was fairly limiting. As stated previously, it only works on integers. Secondly, it only works on 16-bit integers. Although this is fine for some types of audio or 2D image processing applications, it is useless for 3D graphics or other applications that use a lot of floating-point data.

Also, MMX uses the floating-point registers as its temporary scratch space. This means that you can either have MMX working or floating-point, not both. Switching between the two takes a short period of time—but if you do it often enough, it is a performance hit.

So, Intel went back to the drawing board and developed SSE. SSE originally went by the code name Katmai New Instructions, or KNI for short. SSE has several major improvements over MMX. First, it includes a set of dedicated registers in the Pentium III to handle the new instructions, removing the switching delays when sharing the floating-point registers. Secondly, SSE operates on single precision (32-bit-wide) floating-point data when necessary. This can significantly improve the performance of calculating 3D graphics transforms. SSE also brings to the table higher performance memory transfers, expanding on the write combining feature that originally appeared in the Pentium Pro.

It's SSE that makes the Pentium III a compelling story for gamers. The floating-point SIMD can substantially improve performance in the kind of math used in 3D games. In fact, anything that makes use of matrix mathematics can easily benefit from floating-point SIMD, such as certain types of physics modeling used in games.

The "streaming" part also has a beneficial impact. It's an extension of the write combining technology developed for the Pentium Pro, and can speed up transfers of graphics data to and from memory.

One other feature that comes with the Pentium III is the processor ID (PID). A sort of serial number, the Processor ID created a small firestorm of controversy. Privacy advocates see the dark side of being able to ID individual PCs. That capability has existed in various forms anyway, but Intel's clout caused a lot of people to wring their hands. It was probably a tempest in a teapot, but if you're worried about it, you might consider alternatives to the Pentium III.

# Celeron Processors

Not long before the first Pentium III processors shipped, Intel delivered its first stab at a low-cost CPU, the Celeron. The first Celerons were essentially the same CPU cores as a Pentium II, but lacked any L2 cache, which hobbled their performance in many business applications. However, these CPUs proved surprisingly able with games. Later, with the Celeron 300A, Intel added 128KB of L2 cache directly on the CPU chip itself. Although it's only one-quarter the amount of cache on a Pentium II or Pentium III desktop CPU, it runs at the full speed of the processor.

The Celeron has a couple of other disadvantages relative to the Pentium III. First, it's based on the Pentium II core, so there are no SSE instructions. Secondly, like early Pentium IIs, the Celerons access the system bus at 66MHz. Even the 500MHz Celeron only talks to memory at 66MHz. This effectively cuts into memory bandwidth.

On the other hand, the Celerons are cheap, and have the floating-point performance of a Pentium II. They are generally quite good at games. A 500MHz Celeron is slower than a 500MHz Pentium III in games, but not by a lot (except for SSE-enabled titles, of course). Overall, the Celeron is quite a bargain for the gamer on a budget.

## Pentium II and III Xeon Processors

At the time of the Celeron's release, Intel faced a quandary. The Pentium II was selling well in midrange and high-end systems, but Intel was rapidly losing market share in the low end to AMD's K6 line of CPUs. On the other hand, Intel didn't want to cannibalize the sale of its flagship CPUs, either. The Santa Clara company had enjoyed some of the fattest profit margins of any chip company for a long time, and it's tough to give up that profitability. Shareholders tend to frown on it, too.

So, it embarked on a two-pronged plan. The Celeron was introduced to regain share in the low end of the market. But Intel realized it needed something to shore up those fat margins. At the same time, there was still a healthy demand for Pentium Pro CPUs for the server market—particularly the Pentium Pro with larger L2 cache. So Intel created the Xeon, which is now available in both Pentium II and Pentium III variants, and has anywhere from 512KB to 2MB of L2 cache running at the full speed of the CPU. Because the Pentium III Xeon with 2MB of L2 cache sells for close to $4,000, there's a fair amount of margin there. The Xeons come as huge cartridges that plug into a different slot (called Slot 2) than the Pentium II or Pentium III, and require a different motherboard.

But what about using the Xeon for gaming? All that L2 cache goodness must help.

Well, it does, a little, when the cache size exceeds 512KB. I had a chance to do some extensive testing on both a 450MHz Pentium II and a 450MHz Pentium II Xeon. Some raw CPU synthetic benchmarks ran somewhat faster on the Xeon. But there was *no* boost in performance in game testing. A fatter L2 cache helps, but not very much—and you have to ask yourself if the extraordinarily high price is worth it. I'd say not. Figure 2.1 shows the two major Intel CPUs—Celeron and Pentium III.

## Coppermine

The CPU codenamed Coppermine is an evolutionary step forward in the Pentium III line. Coppermine will have two key improvements over the Pentium III. First, it will be able to run at much higher clock speeds. Intel will be manufacturing Coppermine with a 0.18 micron manufacturing process. This makes for smaller chips that run cooler and can clock much faster. The other improvement is that the L2 cache will finally be moved onto the CPU itself. Coppermine will have 256KB of onboard L2 cache. Although this is half the amount in the Pentium III, it will run at the full speed of the CPU. Also, 256KB is kind of a magic number for processor cache sizes. At 256KB, the cache hit ratio rises above 90%, so Coppermine will be significantly faster than, say, Celeron, even discounting clock rate differences.

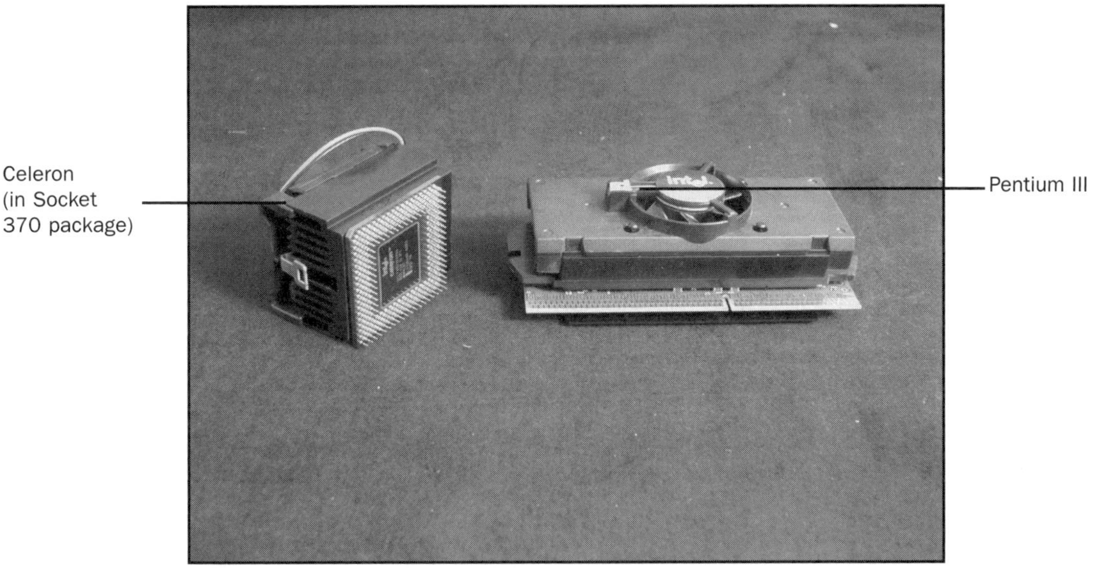


### Figure 2.1

The Pentium III is Intel's flagship processor, although the Celeron (shown here in socket 370 form) represents Intel's budget CPU line.

One major issue facing the adoption of Coppermine is infrastructure. Intel is trying to push the entire computer industry to adopt a new type of system memory called RDRAM (RAMBUS DRAM). RDRAM is likely to be very expensive initially, and first reports on performance haven't been very encouraging. In addition, Coppermine will return to a socketed format because the cost savings of embedding half-speed L2 cache in the cartridge format (for use in Slot 1 or Slot 2) disappears with Coppermine. The combination of the socketed format, plus the RDRAM requirement, means that upgrading to Coppermine may well be an expensive proposition.

## Note

Intel's new socket-based processors will utilize a new socket design called Socket 370, which is discussed in more detail in Chapter 3, "Motherboards and Memory."

Coppermine will start out life at 600 and 700MHz clock rates and go up from there.

For gamers, Coppermine has several advantages. First, it will run faster. By mid-year 2000, we may see Coppermine CPUs running at 1GHz (gigahertz). Secondly, it will usher in the RAMBUS era, which promises much faster data transfers to and from memory using the new RDRAM technology. There are no real architectural improvements to the core CPU itself.

For more discussion about RAMBUS and RDRAM, see page 54.

## Willamette

Not a lot is known about the processor code-named Willamette (a.k.a. the P7). Willamette is a completely new CPU, although it will no doubt build upon the roots of the Pentium III line. The internals are completely re-architectured, including a faster floating-point unit. Willamette is supposed to arrive in the second half of 2000.

If Intel can deliver the promised improvement in floating point, plus a much faster 32-bit core, it stands to perform much faster in games, especially games that use a lot of floating point, like 3D games and flight simulators.

## Merced

Merced represents a completely different tack for CPUs. Merced is a 64-bit CPU that will be initially quite expensive and targeted only for servers. Although it will execute code from IA-32 processors (that is, the Pentium III line), it will do so slowly. Applications will have to be recompiled to take advantage of Merced. It's not likely that Merced will be of interest to gamers until a couple of CPU generations have passed.

# The AMD Processor Line

AMD has consistently nipped at the heels of Intel over the years. Early on, Intel actually invited AMD to the x86 party, needing a second source for the 8086 and 80286 CPUs to satisfy skittish OEMs about product availability. As Intel grew, however, those fears subsided and Intel decided it wanted the whole pie to itself. During the early '90s, there was a set of legal skirmishes between Intel and AMD. Finally, in 1997, AMD shipped the K6 CPU. The K6 was a breakthrough for AMD. Although maintaining compatibility with Intel, including MMX support, the K6 was a better integer performer than the Pentium, and approached the Pentium Pro in integer performance. We'll focus here on the three primary members of the AMD processor line, the K6-2, K6-3, and Athlon.

## K6-2 and K6-3

The K6-2 was first introduced in 1998. AMD intended the K6-2 to compete directly with the Intel Pentium II, but found itself relegated to the budget PC market, fighting against the much cheaper Celeron. The K6-2 has 64KB of onboard L1 cache, MMX compatibility, and introduced AMD's 3DNow! instruction set. The K6-3 arrived in 1999. It's essentially an enhanced K6-2 with 256KB of integrated L2 cache.

3DNow! is a set of floating-point SIMD instructions specifically designed to speed up 3D transform and lighting operations. Unfortunately, it took some time for game developers to support 3DNow!. Programmers could get 3DNow! support directly by using the Direct3D transform and lighting pipeline, but most game developers shunned the D3D

T&L engine until recently. In the past, it was difficult to write code for the D3D T&L engine, and worse, in the eyes of game programmers used to wringing out every CPU cycle, it was inefficient and slow. By the time 3DNow! support became more prevalent, Intel shipped the Pentium III. SSE was more flexible and sophisticated than the first iteration of 3DNow!.

Although the K6-2 and K6-3 actually offered integer performance superior to the Pentium II at the same clock rate, it was substantially slower in floating-point processor calculations. Without support for 3DNow!, the K6-2 and 3 were no match for the Pentium II and III in 3D gaming performance. On top of that, there were numerous teething problems with the Super Socket 7 motherboards, including problems with USB and AGP 2x support. All these issues conspired to keep AMD from approaching Intel CPUs in performance or market share.

Despite these seeming deficiencies, the K6-2 and 3 are good choices for gamers on a budget. Systems using these CPUs are generally very cheap. Also, their solid integer performance makes them every bit the equal of the Pentium II and III in strategy games. It's only with 3D accelerated titles that Intel has the real edge over the K6 line.

# K7—the Athlon

You have to give AMD credit for sheer tenacity. After losing a lot of money over the K6 line, AMD kept plugging away at its next generation CPU. The result is the AMD Athlon (a.k.a. the K7). The Athlon has the potential to reshape the CPU market (see Figure 2.2). The Athlon is AMD's seventh-generation CPU, and is a completely new architecture. Unlike the K6 series, Athlon is capable of high-end applications, such as multiprocessing. Athlon also sports a host of new features:

- Super-pipelined, superscalar architecture designed for high clock speeds
- Superscalar execution (able to work on more than one instruction at once)
- A 200MHz interface to the system bus
- A staggering, 128KB of L1 cache
- A superscalar floating-point unit faster than the FPU on any Intel CPU
- L2 cache support up to 8MB (the initial Athlons will ship with 512KB)

Athlon has some key performance benefits over Intel. First, it has three floating-point units, two of which can handle 3DNow! instructions. Second, Athlon is shipping at higher clock rates than Intel. Third, the huge L1 cache also yields a substantial performance boost. Finally, the faster access to L2 cache via the 200MHz bus to the North Bridge helps in moving data. In games, this translates to faster frame rates and better game performance in general.

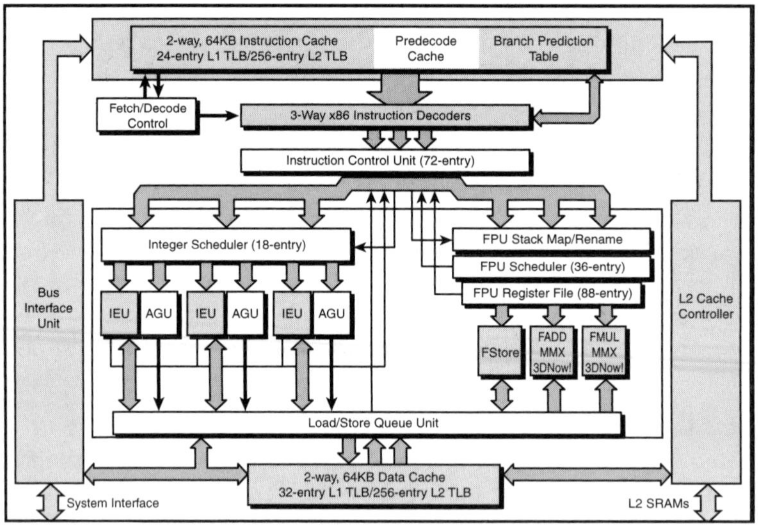


**Figure 2.2**

Athlon is the first seventh-generation, x86-compatible CPU.

Although Athlon's performance is superior to Intel, it does have an uphill battle. First, AMD needs to make enough of them to satisfy demand. Second, the issue of motherboard support looms. As with the Super Socket 7 motherboards (socket 7 motherboards with AGP and USB support), the Athlon requires a different motherboard. The Athlon looks much like a Pentium III cartridge. The L2 cache resides on separate chips inside the cartridge, just like the Pentium III. Despite appearances, however, the Athlon cannot operate in a Slot One motherboard.

Because of patents held by Intel, AMD couldn't design a slot-one–compatible CPU. Instead, AMD licensed the system bus technology used by the DEC Alpha processor. (DEC is now part of Compaq.) Because of the Alpha connection, AMD has dubbed Athlon's slot "Slot A."

This means Athlon will require a motherboard with a new chipset. After all the early problems with K6 motherboards, AMD designed its own high-performance core logic chipset. The company sees this as a stopgap until 3rd-party chipset suppliers like ALi and VIA put out their products. Systems with the AMD chipset seem quite speedy and very stable, however.

Initial testing with both synthetic benchmarks and games demonstrates Athlon's superiority to the Pentium III at the same clock rate. Table 2.3 shows some sample benchmarks comparing the performance of a 600MHz Athlon to a 600MHz Intel Pentium III. Except for the motherboard, all other components were identical.

**Table 2.3—Athlon versus PIII game tests (units in frames per second)**

| *CPU* | *Quake II Crusher* | *Expendable* | *Half-Life* | *Powerslide* |
|---|---|---|---|---|
| Athlon 600 | 68.1 | 74.3 | 47.3 | 187.3 |
| Pentium III 600 | 57.3 | 53.0 | 39.4 | 154 |

It's clear that Athlon is substantially faster than the equivalent Pentium III. If AMD can manufacture enough of them, users may have the first really viable alternative to Intel for a broad range of gaming.

## Other CPUs

There are several other alternatives to Intel which are compatible with the Intel CPU line. They include Cyrix and IDT's Centaur processor lines, both now owned by Via. Another little-known contender is Rise, although it hasn't yet shipped a part.

If you have a Cyrix CPU, it's probably residing in a socket 7 or Super 7 motherboard. The best thing you can do is upgrade it to a K6-2 or K6-3 if your motherboard can handle it. The same is true if you have a Centaur C6 CPU. If you can possibly afford it, upgrading the motherboard (or entire system) to even a Celeron-based system will improve your gaming performance substantially.

### Tip

If you have a socket 7 motherboard, but it can't handle a newer CPU like an AMD K6-3, consider a CPU upgrade kit. Companies like Powerleap (`www.powerleap.com`) wrap some circuitry around a K6-3 that allows it to work in most socket 7 systems. Check with the company to be sure about compatibility.

# Game Performance Considerations

Different games and game genres often have different performance needs. A first-person shooter, like *Quake III: Arena*, has a far different performance profile than a 2D strategy game like *Imperialism II*. Even genres that may seem to have similar performance needs can vary. At first blush, a 3D accelerated game like *Unreal* may appear no different in its performance curve than a high-end flight simulator like *Falcon 4.0*. In fact, they're quite different—*Unreal's* graphics engine is much more demanding, but *Falcon 4.0* is much more CPU-intensive.

In the past, you could make some easy generalizations. Flight sims and 3D action games required heavy CPU and graphics horsepower. Turn-based strategy gamers could get by with far less. That's no longer true, however. First, there's been a trend towards real-time strategy games—even among game genres that had been classically turn-based, such as wargames. In fact, some real-time strategy games can bog down a system faster than a first-person shooter. But even the turn-based games that are out can be pretty CPU-intensive due to deeper AI and the larger scope of many such games.

So, my advice is to get the best CPU you can afford, then consider the graphics card. Even though the newest 3D accelerators will offload transform and lighting acceleration, those free CPU cycles will be rapidly consumed by newer titles with more demanding physics and AI.

Also, buy a CPU with an eye towards upgrading. For example, let's assume that you can afford either the fastest Celeron system or the slowest Athlon-based system. I'd strongly suggest going for the Athlon-based system, even if it benchmarks slower. The Athlon system will give you much greater headroom for future growth by simply replacing the CPU.

On the other hand, if you can afford the fastest possible system, by all means, go for it—even if all you do is play turn-based wargames. I guarantee you that next year, some game in your genre will come out that will completely consume all the performance of that former hotrod. Buying the fastest system you can afford does extend the life of the system somewhat. But as long as PC game developers continue to push the performance envelope by creating more realistic, immersive games with deep AI and accurate physics modeling, faster CPUs will be needed. And just when I get tired of the upgrade treadmill, some title comes along that knocks my socks off, but needs some new hardware.

It's a price I'm willing to pay for a more entertaining time.

# Chapter 3

# Motherboards and Memory

## The Soul of Your PC

Buying a computer these days is an exercise in cutting through jargon. Reading an ad from a systems company touting "Intel 820 system with UDMA 66 and AGP4x" is almost like deciphering the Rosetta Stone. We'll try to translate some of the arcane jargon so you can make a better buying decision.

Underneath every large city is an invisible infrastructure. Electrical wiring, sewers, and the city's communications grid all either lie under the ground or are carried by poles we hardly notice. Supporting this infrastructure are elements such as power stations, microwave relays, and water treatment plants.

Similar to a city, the personal computer has an underlying infrastructure that ties together all the disparate elements. The core of this infrastructure is the *motherboard*. The motherboard contains the all-important core logic, expansion slots, power regulation, and other speeds and feeds necessary to keep the PC humming along.

Just as cities contain highways designed to flow traffic in and out of the metropolis, the computer contains a "highway" better known as the CPU, which does just the same thing. Your concern should be whether this highway is an eight-lane marvel or a two-lane dirt road. The most powerful 3D accelerator on the planet will not perform up to its potential if it can't get the data from the CPU fast enough. If the 3D accelerator can't perform up to snuff, that translates directly to slower game performance.

In this chapter, we'll focus mostly on current generation and future motherboard technologies, so you can plan efficient upgrade strategies.

# Motherboard Components

Here's a laundry list of the key sections of the motherboard (see Figure 3.1):

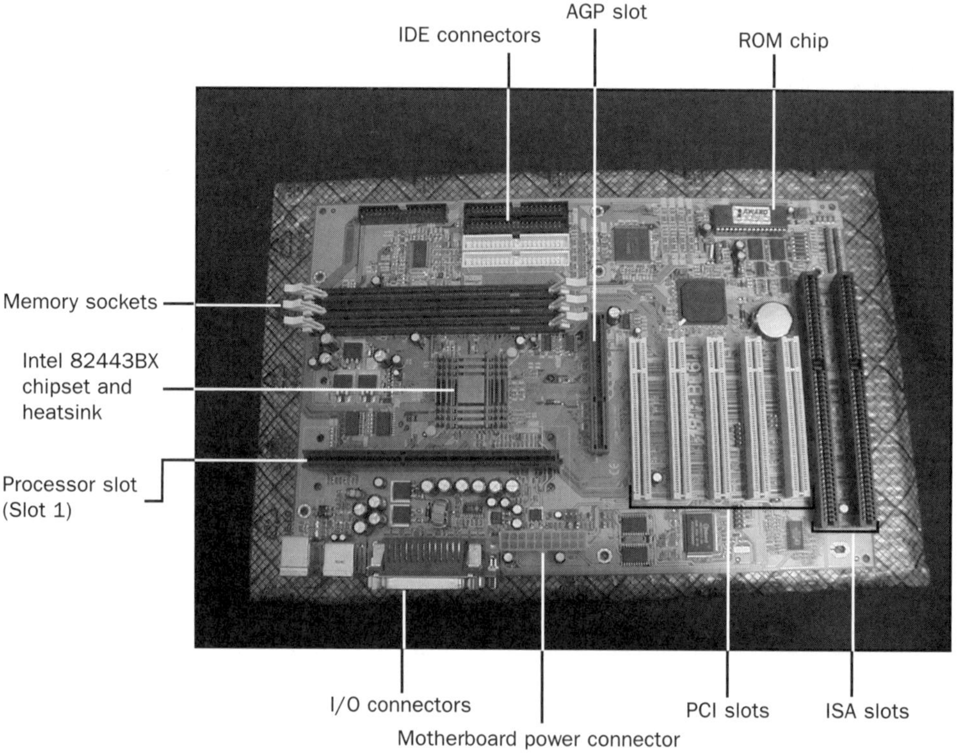


**Figure 3.1**
A typical motherboard layout is shown here (ABIT BE-6).

The key motherboard components are:

- **Core Logic (chipset).** These are the chips on the motherboard that determine the actual features of the system. It's the chipset that determines how much memory you can use, how your disc will perform, and the type of graphics card you can use.
- **Expansion slots.** One key ability determined by the chipset is the number and type of expansion slots. A straightforward gaming system may only need three PCI slots plus an AGP slot. A more elaborate system may need more slots. Knowing the number of available slots is critical for future planning.
- **I/O (input/output).** The various input/output connectors are here, including hard drive and floppy drive interfacing; serial, parallel, and USB ports; and keyboard and mouse connectors.
- **Power regulation.** Modern motherboards often have to support CPUs with different power requirements, as well as deliver adequate power to the expansion slots. For example, some AGP graphics cards require the full 6A current at 3.3v power that the AGP standard specifies. Some motherboards cannot deliver the rated current. The end result is numerous system crashes and poor game performance.
- **Cache memory.** This is more important in K6-2 systems. Most CPUs now have the cache integrated into either the CPU chip itself or the CPU cartridge.
- **Memory sockets.** Some motherboards have only two sockets for memory, severely limiting expansion.
- **The BIOS.** The BIOS resides in a ROM chip on the motherboard, and is a kind of "mini-OS." It contains all the code necessary to first boot up the system, assign IRQs, scan for hard drives, and so on.

Now that we've covered some of the key components on the motherboard, let's delve into the complexities of choosing a board.

# The Motherboard

Choosing the right *motherboard* (also called *main board* or *system board*) determines the ultimate capabilities of your gaming system.

First, understand what chipset is on the motherboard. As we noted previously, the chipset is the real determiner of what your motherboard can and can't do. Table 3.1 shows some of the more common chipsets used today and the key capabilities of each.

### Table 3.1—Chipset features

| *Chipset* | *Typical CPU* | *System Memory* | *AGP Support* | *USB Support Bus* | *UltraATA Support* |
|---|---|---|---|---|---|
| Intel 440LX | Celeron | 66MHz | Y | Y | Y, 33MHz |
| Intel 440BX | Pentium II/III | 100MHz | Y | Y | Y, 33MHz |
| Intel 440EX | Celeron | 66MHz | Y | Y | Y, 33MHz |
| Intel 440GX | PIII/Xeon | 100MHz | Y | Y | Y, 33MHz |
| Intel 440ZX | Celeron, Pentium II | 100MHz | Y | Y | Y, 66MHz |
| Intel 810 | Celeron | 66MHz (100MHz to North Bridge) | Y (built-in only) | Y | Y, 66MHz |
| Intel 820 | Pentium III/ Coppermine | 100MHz; SDRAM 133MHz RDRAM | Y, AGP 2.0 (4x) | Y | Y, 66MHz |
| Via MVP3 | K6-2/K6-3 | 100MHz | Y | Y | Y, 33MHz |
| Via MVP4 | K6-2/K6-3 | 100MHz | Y, built-in only | Y | Y, 33MHz |
| Via Apollo Pro Plus | Pentium II/ III/ Celeron | 100MHz | Y | Y | Y, 33MHz |
| Via Apollo Pro133 | Pentium II/ III/ Celeron | 100MHz, 133MHz | Y | Y | Y, 66MHz |
| Via Apollo KX133 | Athlon | 100MHz, 133MHz | Y, AGP 2.0 (4x) | Y | Y, 66MHz |
| ALi Aladdin V | K6-2/K6-3 | 100MHz | Y | Y | Y, 33MHz |
| AMD 752 | Athlon | 100MHz | Y | Y | Y, 66MHz |

# System Memory Speed

The system memory speed affects performance in two ways. First, it very simply determines how fast data is moved in and out of memory. This is important for performance in a general sense. The system memory speed can also determine the maximum capability of AGP performance—which can, in turn, directly affect performance in graphically rich games.

You will see this highway from the CPU to main memory called the *frontside bus*. This is directly contrasted with the backside bus, which is the path to the CPU cache, if the cache isn't actually embedded on the chip itself.

There are three system memory bus speeds that are common: 66MHz, 100MHz, and 133MHz. Let's look at 66MHz, first. Most systems that use Intel's Celeron CPU are limited to the 66MHz-frontside bus. This can have a direct impact on your game performance. Let's examine why.

Every new motherboard has a way of connecting a graphics card called *AGP* (*accelerated graphics port*). The AGP port is a direct connection between the graphics card and the CPU, unlike the PCI bus, which has to go through some intermediate circuitry. The AGP 1.0 specification sets the clock rate of the AGP port at 66MHz, and is 32 bits wide. If we do the math, the AGP port at 66MHz can move (66*32/8), or 256MB of data between the graphics card and the system each second. AGP also has a faster mode, known as AGP 2x, which runs twice as fast. That means it can move 512MB of data per second.

Now, let's look at the frontside bus. The speed of the frontside bus determines the overall memory throughput of a system. On a Celeron system, it also runs at 66MHz. However, because the memory bus of a Celeron is 64 bits wide, the memory bandwidth is (66MHz*64/8) or also 512MB per second peak throughput. So, what happens when both the CPU and AGP graphics want access to memory at the same time? Graphics and the CPU contend for memory, and your game performance suffers accordingly.

Now, consider the 100MHz frontside bus. The overall memory throughput (100MHz*64 bits/8) is 800MB per second. That gives both graphics and CPU more memory bandwidth to play with, allowing for faster gameplay, all other things being equal.

Does that mean that a Celeron-based system is a poor choice for gaming? The answer is: not necessarily. System memory bandwidth is only one part of the performance equation. But a system with a 100MHz frontside bus will perform *better* than one with a 66MHz bandwidth.

However, it's only going to get worse. Everyone wants some of your memory. As graphics cards become more advanced, the game developers will be pumping up the graphics detail of their titles—which means trying to pump even more data through the memory subsystem. PCI sound card makers are also storing MIDI samples in memory. There are two solutions that hope to alleviate this problem somewhat.

- One solution is to somehow make the memory go faster. We'll talk about this in the section on memory in "Thanks for the Memories," later in this chapter.
- The other tack is to streamline the memory transfers. Intel has done this with the 820 chipset. In the older, 440BX chipset, moving data to the graphics card would occasionally run into several different potential bottlenecks when trying to compete with the CPU for memory bandwidth. The 820 does a much better job of handling multiple memory transfers, which can smooth out transfers of graphics information to the local video memory on the graphics card.

The bottom line of this discussion is that you should care about how fast the memory runs on your system. That can have a direct impact on game performance due to the massive amounts of data that games can move to and from memory and the graphics card.

# Something for Nothing: Overclocking

One practice that's become prevalent among some users in the PC gaming community is overclocking. Overclocking is the practice of running a component at higher than the rated clock speed. For example, if you took a 300MHz Celeron and ran it at 450MHz, that would be overclocking the Celeron. Theoretically, you pay for a 300MHz CPU and get the performance of a 450MHz CPU. In the following discussion, we'll use the 300MHz Celeron as our example—it's a popular CPU for overclocking. But the discussion applies to any CPU.

Overclocking is accomplished by changing a setting in your motherboard. The clock rate setting may be in the BIOS, as it is with many newer motherboards, or handled by jumpers on the motherboard. However, it's not as simple as flipping a switch. There are a couple of concepts you need to know. The first is the idea of the CPU bus multiplier.

Earlier, we discussed the 100MHz system memory bus and the 66MHz memory bus. When you drop a 300MHz Celeron into a system running at a system memory speed of 66Mhz, the CPU is running at 4.5 times the memory bus speed. (Note that the *actual* memory bus speed is 66.67MHz.)

As it turns out, the Celeron CPUs are *multiplier locked*. That means that a 300MHz Celeron will *always* run at 4.5 times the system clock. If you do want to run it faster, you'll need to run it in a motherboard that supports higher system memory clocks. Quite a number of 440BX motherboards allow this. There is even at least one socket 370 motherboard using the 440BX chipset, but you can always use a socket 370-to-slot one adapter (known as a *slotket*). Not surprisingly, no Intel motherboard supports manual setting of the system memory clock.

If you run a Celeron 300 in a system at a 100MHz bus speed, it will try to run at 450MHz. Here's where the crapshoot starts. Many Celeron 300s will run fine at 450MHz—but some won't. You can lower the system bus clock. Most 440BX motherboards can run at 66, 75, 83, 100, 103, and 112MHz. A few will go as high as 133MHz—but remember, the 440BX chipset itself is rated only at a maximum clock speed of 100MHz.

Table 3.2 shows system memory clocks versus the Celeron 300.

### Table 3.2—System memory clocks versus the Celeron

| *System Memory Clock* | *Celeron 300 Clock Rate* |
|---|---|
| 66MHz | 300MHz |
| 75MHz | 337.5MHz |
| 83MHz | 373.5MHz |
| 100MHz | 450MHz |
| 103MHz | 463.5MHz |
| 112MHz | 504MHz |

There are three other issues you need to worry about:

- Core voltage setting
- AGP/PCI bus clock
- Cooling

The core voltage—that is, the voltage that the CPU runs at internally—of the Celeron is 2V. If you push it really hard (100MHz or more), you may need to tweak up the core voltage—but don't go any higher than 2.2V. Only a few motherboards allow you to vary the core voltage incrementally. This is tricky stuff, so proceed cautiously. Of course, a Celeron 300 is only about $75, so frying one isn't quite like frying a 700MHz Athlon.

Some motherboards lock the PCI bus multiplier to the system memory clock. At 66MHz and 100MHz, the PCI bus will run at 33MHz, but at 83MHz, it might try to run the PCI bus at 41.5MHz. Check the Web for reviews and try to get a board that keeps the PCI bus at 33MHz at all times. Be aware that something similar can happen with the AGP port. Abit motherboards allow you to manually specify the AGP/system clock multiplier. You can set it to 1:1 or 2:3. At a system memory clock of 100MHz, you'd want to run at 2:3, which clocks the AGP port at 66MHz. Note that if you push the clock rate even higher, the AGP port clock will also go up—and some AGP cards will not operate properly.

Finally, there's cooling. If you overclock, you *must* be concerned about cooling. An overclocked CPU will run hotter. Get a better CPU fan, and add extra cooling fans to the case. Consider also getting a temperature sensor that can be mounted on the inside of the case.

# Just Say No

I don't overclock my systems, and unless you really know what you're doing, I don't recommend you do it either. I may just be conservative, but I've run into many problems with overclocking, including

- AGP graphics cards not working properly
- UltraATA/66 and SCSI host adapters failing intermittently
- Games crashing mysteriously
- Corruption of data on the hard drive

I've never burned up a CPU, but it will fail over time. There's a phenomenon known as *elecromigration*. The circuitry inside the CPU consists of traces that are less than a micron (one millionth of a meter) wide. Run a processor too hot, and those traces can actually grow together, resulting in an inoperative CPU. This takes some time, of course, and you could argue that replacing a $75 CPU once a year is no big deal.

I've personally run into too many headaches overclocking. So if you are interested, approach the topic with a little care and caution. If you're lucky, you may indeed get something for nothing.

**Note**

Overclocking a graphics card is something else altogether. For more on this topic, see Chapter 4.

# Expansion Slots

Here are Case's Laws of System Expansion for Gamers:

1. The more PCI slots, the better (up to a point).
2. If you have any ISA cards, lose them.
3. A graphics card should *always* plug into a slot.

If you follow these simple rules, you'll maximize the life of your system. Let's touch on these points, one at a time.

## PCI Slots

You can never have enough PCI slots—at least, not until you run out of system resources (such as IRQs) to support them. Some of you may be scratching your heads at this. After all, if you have a system with a PCI sound card and AGP graphics, what else do you need?

You might be wondering why I recommend having a lot of PCI slots. For starters, your hardware needs may change. Today, that AGP graphics card and PCI sound card may be just fine. But let's just say that 3dfx comes out with an amazing new graphics technology that allows you to pop in another PCI card or two to significantly improve your graphics performance. Then, a newer, faster hard drive technology comes out—do you swap motherboards, or just drop in a PCI expansion card to handle the new drives? You decide you want to interface to your new home theater system with your PCI, so now you need a firewire expansion card.

Oops, you bought a system with only three PCI slots.

In my main system, I have a motherboard with five PCI slots. They are all filled. The system has a PCI SCSI host adapter, PCI network interface card, PCI audio card, a Voodoo2 card, and a PCI TV tuner card. I'm scratching my head, trying to figure out where to put the DVD decoder card.

However, there are some gotchas with lots of PCI slots. First, you may easily run out of IRQs or other resources.

### Note

System resources include IRQs (hardware interrupt requests), DMA channels (Direct Memory Access), and I/O addresses (memory addresses that correspond to I/O devices). The PC architecture has 15 hardware IRQs available. (An IRQ lets the device interrupt the system to get attention.) While Windows 98 is very good at allowing devices to share the same IRQ, it's not perfect. Some hardware simply refuses to share its IRQ. If you have too many of these IRQ hogging devices, you won't be able to expand your system any further no matter how many slots your system may have.

Some very expensive motherboards pile on the slots, and manage them using an additional chip called a *PCI-to-PCI bridge*. You should avoid them, as they can have compatibility problems with some PCI cards.

Even with the potential problems, having a healthy supply of PCI slots will allow you future growth—and anything you can do to put off dropping a bundle of cash on a new system can only be a good thing.

## Lose Any ISA Cards

ISA stands for *Industry Standard Architecture*. The current ISA slots in today's PCs are holdovers from the days of the IBM PC-AT. In other words, ISA slots are seven-year-old technology.

They're also slow, clocking at a maximum of 8.33MHz. That's fine for something like a dedicated game port card or modem, but pretty poor for anything else. Today's games can make tremendous demands on audio cards, so ISA sound cards are out.

Really, though, you should get rid of any ISA cards. Most good PCI sound cards now have at least a decent game port. You should get an external modem (preferably USB). So there's no reason to have an ISA card.

The final reason is system performance. If you have ISA cards hitting the bus, they can actually slow down PCI cards because their data transfers take so much longer than PCI cards. Eliminating ISA cards can maximize the throughput of PCI cards.

### Tip

If you can eliminate all the ISA cards in your system, you can improve your PCI card performance a little more, if you have the right system BIOS. Some BIOS setup programs allow you to specify a parameter called *PCI latency*. PCI latency defines the amount of time a PCI card can hold the PCI bus before having to release access to another card. In most systems, it defaults to 32 clock cycles. This is because many ISA cards will hang if they wait too long to get access to the system, so the low setting forces PCI cards to get off more quickly so ISA cards don't wait so long. Set it to something high, like 255 cycles (the maximum setting). That will give each PCI card a little more time to do its thing.

# AGP Graphics Slot

If you want to maximize the life of your system, always buy a motherboard with an AGP slot. I can't stress this enough. If you buy a system or motherboard with an AGP chip soldered to the motherboard, you will *never* be able to upgrade your graphics capabilities because there can only be a single AGP controller in a system (and yours is soldered to the motherboard).

## Caution

There is a trend among chipset makers to ship core logic chipsets with the graphics actually embedded in the chipset. The most visible of these is the Intel 810 chipset. For the most part, the game graphics performance of the embedded chipsets is *abysmal*. It's not merely bad, it's truly awful. Never get a motherboard with the graphics chip built into the core logic chipset if you plan on using it for computer games.

AGP stands for *accelerated graphics port*, and is a single slot just for graphics cards. The word "port" is key: AGP is *not* a bus. It is a dedicated interface between the graphics controller and the CPU. No other peripheral device shares the connection with the graphics card.

AGP can be confusing because there are several terms bandied about that sound similar, yet are different. Let's break down some of the terms to clear up confusion.

- **AGP 1.0.** This is the original specification for AGP, as defined by Intel.
- **AGP 1x.** This defines the standard clock speed of the AGP port, 66MHz. People often confuse AGP 1x with AGP 1.0. Remember, 1.0 is the *specification*, whereas 1x represents the standard speed of the AGP connection. Because of the way data is transferred, AGP 1x can move data at a maximum rate of 256MB per second.
- **AGP 2x.** AGP 2x defines the ability of the graphics card to move data to or from memory at 2 times the normal AGP clock rate. Because AGP clocks at 66MHz, this means that AGP 2x defines a 133MHz interface to memory. Note that AGP 2x is part of the AGP 1.0 standard. This distinction between AGP 2x and AGP 1x is probably the single most confusing issue about AGP. AGP 2x can move data at 512MB per second.
- **Sideband addressing.** This is the ability of a graphics card to demultiplex addresses from data. This means that data can be moved faster across the AGP interface, because memory address information is handled separately.
- **AGP Texturing** (often called "direct execute mode"). Texture map data for 3D graphics can be stored in main memory. This chunk of memory will appear to be part of the graphics card memory. The key point here is that *only the part of the texture actually needed is pulled into the graphics card local memory*. This can be more efficient than pulling in the entire texture. (There's a lot more on texture mapping in the graphics chapter.)

- **AGP 2.0.** This is the latest specification for AGP, and defines some additional elements, such as AGP 4x (4x66MHz, or 256MHz), which can move data at up to 1 gigabyte per second. This is *not* the same as AGP 2x.

You may have seen some graphics chip vendors pooh-poohing AGP—usually in relation to AGP texturing. After all, they say, even 512MB per second isn't nearly as fast as the local video memory bandwidth, which can exceed 3GB per second. They often forget that only the immediate data needed is moved via AGP when using AGP texturing, not the entire texture.

More importantly, AGP is completely independent of the PCI bus. An AGP graphics card now doesn't have to wait for an Ethernet or sound card to finish up what it's doing. If the PCI bus is the milk run, then AGP is the express train from the graphics card to the CPU.

Finally, AGP transfers can occur at 2x speeds. Even a Voodoo3 graphics chip, which cannot do AGP texturing, benefits from the ability to move texture map or vertex data across the AGP interface at 512MB per second. That can minimize the pauses that occur during heavy texture loads in many 3D games.

# Other Connections

As discussed at the beginning of this chapter, there are a number of connectors built into current motherboards in addition to PCI, ISA, and AGP slots. Refer back to Figure 3.1 to see these connections.

- **IDE controllers.** Today's motherboards have a minimum of two ports to connect to IDE hard drives (known as Primary and Secondary IDE). All motherboards currently shipping support a minimum of 33MHz per second to the hard drive, a standard known as ATA/33. Many of the newest ones support ATA/66, though you see little real speed gain over ATA/33. All motherboards today still have a connector for a floppy disc drive.
- **Power connection.** There's a single power connector that connects to a cable from the power supply.
- **Memory sockets.** Typically, there are three or four memory slots for SDRAM DIMMs (or RDRAM RIMMs in the case of 820 motherboards).
- **External connectors.** On the back of the motherboard are connectors for parallel, serial, keyboard, mouse, and USB ports (see Figure 3.2). USB will be critical for the new generation of game controllers coming out. See "Universal Serial Bus" in Chapter 9 and "USB and Multiple Controllers" in Chapter 11 for more on USB.

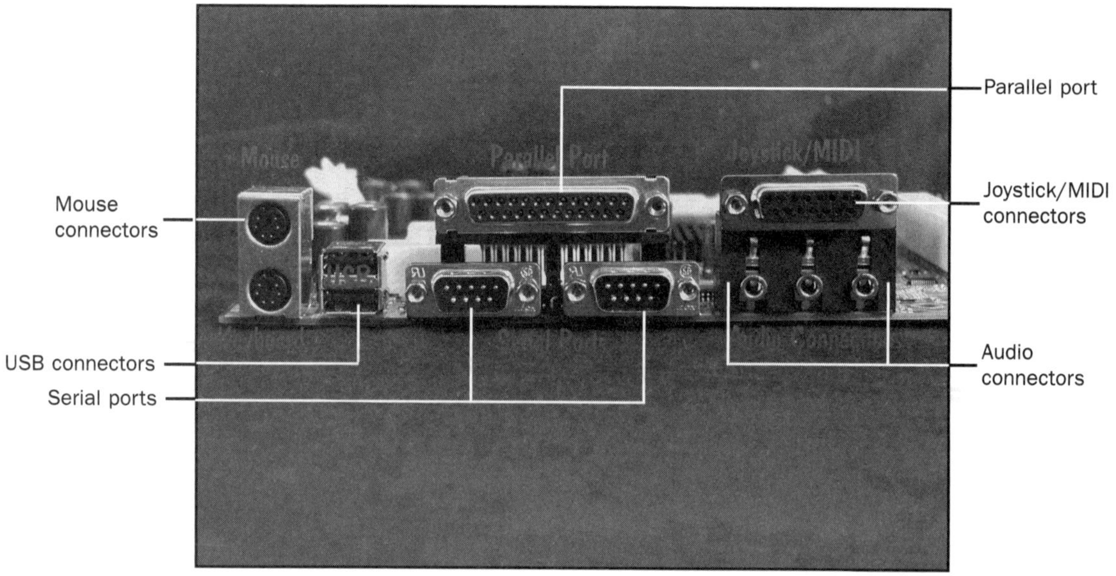


**Figure 3.2**
The external connectors on a motherboard. Note that this particular motherboard has a built-in sound chip.

As you shop for motherboards, check the layout. Is there enough room for all the cards you want to put in? Is the power supply connector in an awkward location? Is the board physically too large for your case? A bit of attention paid to these little details will spare you major heartburn later.

# What to Look for in a Motherboard

Upgrading or building your own gaming system can be a very satisfying endeavor. When shopping for a good motherboard (assuming you're building your own system, or upgrading an existing one), there are a number of key features to look for:

- **Stability.** The fastest system in the known universe is a hunk of junk if it spends more time crashing than it does running. Look for a motherboard manufacturer with a reputation for stability as well as features. Also, stick with core logic chipsets from the top tier: Intel, VIA, and ALi (though consider AMD for an Athlon system).
- **Features.** You won't build an ideal system if it has two PCI slots and one memory socket. Look for a board with good expansion capability—one AGP and four PCI slots is the minimum. Also look for adequate memory slots; don't accept less than three sockets for RAM expansion.

- **BIOS features.** A flexible, adaptable BIOS is a key asset. More and more BIOSes allow you to change CPU and core logic clock rates in the BIOS setup program (instead of using jumpers). This is a must if you want to experiment with overclocking. But it's something worth considering if you never overclock, but want to make life easier when you upgrade your CPU. Other BIOS features, such as being able to assign IRQs to individual PCI slots, can be lifesavers.
- **Ease of installation.** Look at the layout: Will that full size PCI card fit in the slot you want to put it in? Is the fan power connector blocked by power regulation capacitors? Study the layout and make sure it will meet your needs.
- **Check the layout.** Nothing is more frustrating than discovering that one of your slightly-larger-than-average expansion cards won't fit, or that the power supply connector is in an extremely awkward location.

Be sure also to check the manufacturer's Web site to see how well it supports its product. If you build your own system, you won't have the luxury of calling the company's tech support (most motherboard vendors don't have much in the way of end-user support), but you do want to be sure they upgrade the BIOS and supply answers to frequently asked questions.

Having a flaky motherboard is one of the most insidious time sinks you can run into when upgrading your own system. Motherboard problems can be masked as memory, graphics, or even CPU problems. Games will crash mysteriously, or refuse to run. There's often a tendency to blame the graphics card or the sound card when the problem lies in the motherboard. Don't skimp when choosing your motherboard. And make sure you buy it from someone with a good support and return policy.

# Thanks for the Memories

Hard-core gamers seem to be willing to spend any amount of money to wring out that last frame-per-second of performance from a beloved game. Even so, there's no point in simply throwing good money after bad. One area where you can maximize your investment is memory. Memory upgrades used to be fairly simple, but the landscape for memory has suddenly gotten complicated. Let's take a look at the various memory types and how to make the most of your DRAM dollar.

## Grading Memory

Memory comes in various speeds, like PC66, PC100, or PC133. The numbers refer to the clock rate at which the memory is guaranteed to run. The numbers refer to the system memory clock speed at which they're designed to operate. PC100 SDRAM, for example, will work in systems with a 100MHz frontside bus (FSB).

Not all PC100 SDRAM is created equal. There are two types of memory modules: branded and generic. Branded memory (also often called grade A memory) carries the name of the company that makes it (see Figure 3.3). It's usually warrantied for at least a year, sometimes much more. All the memory chips on the module are the same brand of memory, and rated at the same speed.

**Figure 3.3**
Branded PC100 SDRAM, such as these Corsair DIMMs, are always a better choice.

Generic modules, on the other hand, often don't carry a maker's name. The chips may be from one source, or from many. It's often warrantied for only 30 or 90 days. Almost all of the memory problems I've ever encountered have been with generic RAM. For that reason, I tend to recommend branded SDRAM from companies like Corsair, Crucial Technologies, Kingston, and other name-brand manufacturers who are willing to stand behind their products.

The other type of memory, already available on chipsets from Via, is 133MHz SDRAM. That's fairly easy to understand—the memory runs 33MHz faster, and can yield a potential memory throughput of about 1GB per second. There are also proponents of a new type of SDRAM called DDR SDRAM—the "DDR" stands for double data rate. DDR SDRAM can move data at twice the speed of standard SDRAM at the same clock rate. No current system supports DDR SDRAM, however.

## RAMBUS

Back in 1998, Intel announced that it wanted to move to a radically new type of memory called RAMBUS. RAMBUS will be used in the new 820 core logic chipset that accompanies Intel's new Coppermine CPU.

RAMBUS DRAM (RDRAM) has some interesting features, including a 1.6GB per second throughput at 400MHz. It uses a banked architecture that allows memory accesses to occur in parallel. Intel estimates that RDRAM maintains up to 95 percent efficiency during peak memory usage, as opposed to 70 percent for SDRAM. RDRAM will come in modules called RIMMs (RAMBUS inline memory modules). As of this writing, Intel hopes to ship systems using 600MHz and 800MHz RDRAM. Intel has lined up most of the major suppliers of memory to manufacture RAMBUS memory chips.

This can translate directly into faster game performance. The Coppermine and Pentium III CPUs can take advantage of RDRAM through their streaming memory technology. Toss in the added efficiencies of the 820 chipset, and you'll probably see higher frame rates in the most demanding game titles.

It looks like the supply of RDRAM may be tight—and therefore expensive—for some time. The good news is that it looks like many 820-based motherboards will also have SDRAM slots, and the 820 is capable of supporting PC100 SDRAM.

# Planning Your Memory Upgrades

With a little forethought, you can plan your memory upgrades so that they affect your wallet as little as possible.

First, if you are upgrading from a Pentium or older (sub-300MHz) K6 system, there's probably not much you can do to preserve your existing memory investment. At best, you may have PC66 SDRAM; at worst, EDO DRAM.

However, if you have something like a Pentium II/350 or K6-2 400, you almost certainly have PC100 SDRAM. That memory is perfectly sufficient if you plan on upgrading to a system using the Coppermine CPU. When you do upgrade, get a motherboard that has DIMM slots for SDRAM as well as RDRAM sockets. Use your PC100 SDRAM. While it's true you won't get maximum performance out of the system, it will let you wait until RDRAM prices drop to less heavenly levels. Even if you sell your existing system with the memory that's in it, just get plain PC100 SDRAM for the 820 motherboard—unless you enjoy paying excessive prices for the latest memory technology.

If you're planning on an Athlon upgrade, you can still use your PC100 SDRAM, but PC133 memory is only a small increment in price—so consider upgrading the memory. It isn't all that hard on your wallet, and you can recover some of it by selling your existing motherboard, CPU, and RAM.

# Chapter 4

# Graphics

## Religion and Graphics Cards

When you get a group of people together who are relative strangers, there are some rules of thumb you should follow. One of the primary ones is to never discuss politics or religion. If the group is a bunch of computer gamers, you should add graphics cards to that short list of forbidden topics. Nothing gets a gamer's blood boiling—particularly people who play a lot of 3D accelerated games—than arguing about graphics cards. It can get nasty enough that you wonder if they might be discussing a religion after all.

We'll try to cut through the morass of jargon, hype, and religious fervor to discuss graphics hardware dispassionately. After all, it is just a piece of hardware, right?

## Monitor Basics

Before tackling the intricacies of multiple pixel pipelines and blend modes, we need to cover some very basic stuff that still confuses a lot of people.

Computer games are viewed through a flat piece of glass—your monitor. Holographic projection isn't here yet, and although there have been attempts at 3D displays, such as LCD shutter glasses or VR helmets, they're still novelty items. The limitations of the 2D monitor are both obvious and subtle. It's obvious that you have a limited area for display, ranging from 14" diagonal to a maximum of about 22 inches for modern computer displays. If you use special multimedia displays, you can get more size, but not more resolution—one of the subtleties.

## Resolution

Your monitor is a *raster* device, meaning that it's made up of lines of dots. These dots are called *pixels*—picture elements. The pixel is the fundamental unit of modern computer graphics. Resolution is usually described as:

(Number of horizontal pixels) × (Number of vertical pixels)

For example, if you see 800×600, that means the display is 800 pixels wide by 600 pixels tall. Here's the key point: If the resolution is 800×600, *it doesn't matter how big your monitor is. The display is still 800×600 pixels in resolution*. Certainly, a bigger monitor might be easier to view, but that doesn't necessarily mean the resolution of the game is bigger.

## Color Depth

Inside the tube of a standard PC monitor is a coating of phosphors. Phosphors are chemically active sites on the glass that glow when the display's electron beam shines on them. (If it's a flat panel display, the display might consist of many LEDs that generate the individual colors.) Each phosphor generates a fixed frequency of light; there are red, green, and blue phosphors. A PC monitor creates the illusion of color by lighting up adjacent red, green, and blue phosphors at different intensities. Because the phosphors are small and very close together, your eye "blends" them into a single color.

The key point here is that blending different signals at different intensities creates color on a computer. The signals are generated by the graphics card and transmitted to the monitor electronics. A *true color* image might have 256 different signal levels for each of red, green, and blue. This creates a theoretical maximum of 256×256×256 colors, or 16.7 million total available colors. This also is called 24-bit color because 256 different intensities can be represented by 8 bits, and 8+8+8=24 bits.

So, what is 32-bit color? That's another term commonly bandied about. The additional 8 bits represent the *alpha channel*, which is used to transmit transparency data. Those extra 8 bits are used only in the graphics card; only 24 bits of signal are sent to the monitor itself.

The concept of 16-bit color is also confusing. You'll see 16-bit color variously as (5,5,6), (5,6,5), or (6,5,5). These numbers again refer to the number of levels of signals. With 5,6,5 color, there are 5 bits for red, 6 bits for green, and 5 bits for blue. That's (32×64×32) colors, or a total of 65,536 (64K) available colors.

At this point, you're probably digging out your calculator and noting that a 1024×768 pixel display only consists of 786,432 total dots—more, certainly, than 65,536, but far less than 16.7 million colors. It seems that 16-bit color isn't enough, but true color is overkill. Yet 16-bit color can look very good.

There's a couple of other things going on. First, no image consists of each pixel being a completely different color. A close-up of a leaf, for example, might consist mostly of shades of green. If so, that means that 65,535 colors should be enough, right?

Not necessarily. The human eye can discern far more than 65,535 colors. Let's look at our leaf example again. 65,535 might seem perfectly adequate to render a bunch of shades of green. But now let's pull back our virtual camera, and notice that the leaf is part of a larger scene consisting of many flowers of different colors. Now, 16-bit color might not be good enough, and you'll see artifacts such as color banding.

There's another reason for more colors, too, when multiple textures are blended to create certain effects. If the textures being blended are 16-bit color, blending many such textures can create image quality flaws called *quantization errors*. If the source art is 32-bit color, this doesn't occur. We'll talk about that more in "3D Graphics Demystified" (later in this chapter).

# Refresh Rate

A standard PC monitor is essentially a giant vacuum tube with phosphors coating the flat (display) side. An electron gun fires a beam of electrons at the phosphor-coated surface, which lights up the phosphors. The phosphors themselves stay lit for a relatively short period of time, then have to be "repainted" with the electron beam. The beam itself is relatively narrow, so it is constantly scanning each horizontal line of pixels, one at a time at a fairly high rate (see Figure 4.1).

The beam starts at the upper-left corner, then scans each line until it reaches the lower-right corner. Then, the beam turns off momentarily, the gun retargets on the original starting location, and the beam starts painting the phosphors again. The number of times this scan/repeat cycle occurs each second is the *refresh rate*.

## Note

Early computer displays and most current televisions would display an *interlaced* image. The scan gun was so slow, that it would paint every other line, then start again on the second line and paint every other line. This alternate painting of odd and even scan lines is interlacing. All modern computer monitors use *progressive scanning*, which is what we described above.

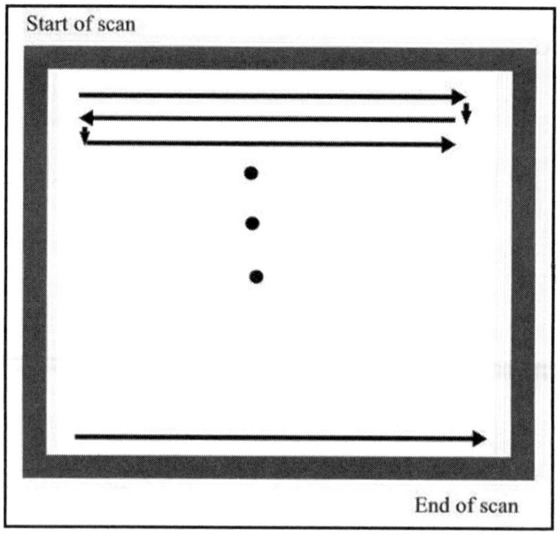


**Figure 4.1**
Electron beam scanning across the tube.

You've probably been told that the higher the refresh rate, the better it is for your eyes. Although this is certainly true for applications like word processing, too high a refresh rate can be a problem with 3D games, because too high a refresh rate cuts into the bandwidth of the graphics card. Also, there are issues with performance, which can actually be dependent on refresh rate. We'll talk about this in the section on the frame buffer, "Page Flipping and the Frame Buffer," later in this chapter.

## Frame Rate

Another key topic I want to touch on is *frame rate*.

With normal business applications, you generally see a static image. However, most computer games have some level of animation. Computer animation tricks the eye into thinking that movement is occurring when you're really looking at the static computer display. It's much like going to the movies. A movie is just a series of still pictures, projected at a relatively high rate of speed. The number of pictures displayed each second is the frame rate, in frames per second or *fps* for short. Films (movies) have a native frame rate of 24 fps. The frame rate of game animation can depend on a number of factors: the CPU, the graphics accelerator, the game itself (the more intense the action, the lower the frame rate), and the refresh rate of the monitor.

PC game players tend to think of frame rate as a 3D graphics issue, but it's actually applicable to 2D games. If you've ever seen the performance of a game like *Starcraft* start to drop, you've seen a slow frame rate in a 2D game.

# Page Flipping and the Frame Buffer

The *frame buffer* is the memory in the graphics card that holds the actual image being displayed. (You'll often see the term used to describe the entire amount of graphics memory, such as "16MB frame buffer," but that's not strictly accurate.) If there was only enough memory for a single frame buffer, and each succeeding animation frame had to be written into that one frame buffer, computer animation would look pretty ugly, even with a very fast graphics card. (If you want a graphic display of this effect, run Ziff-Davis' 3D WinBench 99 in front-buffer mode.) It takes a fixed amount of time for the graphics memory to accept data, convert it from digital data to analog signal, and send it to the monitor.

However, all graphics cards now have large amounts of video memory. Game programmers take advantage of this by using more of the memory to create *buffers*. The simplest type of buffering is double buffering. Here's what happens.

The first frame is created, and then displayed. This display memory is the *front buffer*. Although that first frame is displayed, the next frame is created in memory (*not* display memory). This is called the *back buffer*. When the frame in the back buffer has been fully created, the back buffer is *flipped* with the front buffer. This is called a *page flip*. During the flip, nothing has changed, except that the area of memory that *was* the back buffer is now the front buffer, and vice versa. The former front buffer is now the back buffer—and the game begins writing the next frame into what is now the back buffer. This process continues, resulting in smooth animation as perceived by the person watching the monitor.

Double buffering isn't perfect, however. But before we discuss why, we need to digress, and return to the idea of the refresh rate.

Most games are designed so that the page flip occurs right when the refresh cycle starts. If you recall, the refresh cycle starts when the electron gun returns to the start position and begins painting the phosphors (pixels) anew. This idea of performing the page flip at the start of the refresh cycle is known as *flip on v-sync*.

### Note

*V-sync*—short for vertical sync—is just another term for the refresh rate cycle.

Either the game or the graphics subsystem can be set to flip the back buffer *as soon as it's finished*. This might happen before the next refresh cycle. Flipping the back buffer to the front buffer before v-sync is at the start of its cycle is known as *v-sync off*.

Now, back to our double buffering problem. If the game is set to perform the buffer flip in time with a new v-sync cycle, the fastest frame rate for a double buffered animation is the same as the refresh rate of the monitor. But with slower graphics cards (or too high a refresh rate), a strange thing occurs. You begin to see frame rates that are 1/2 or 1/3 the refresh rate. This happens when the back buffer isn't quite filled, and the electron gun returns to the origin and starts painting the image again. Because the back buffer isn't ready, it won't flip until the *next* v-sync cycle.

There's an easy way to get out of this harmonic frame rate problem: triple buffering. Instead of having one back buffer, use two back buffers. That way, you'll always have a buffer ready to flip when the v-sync cycle begins again.

Why not just leave v-sync off? Some games allow you to do this, although many graphics cards have control panel or Registry settings that enable this. The problem is that you can see unpleasant image artifacts (called *screen tearing* or just *tearing*). So, you should leave flip-on-v-sync on for best image quality. If you run into the harmonic frame rate problem, just turn down the refresh rate. Although you'd never want to run at 60Hz for normal business applications, a 60Hz refresh rate is perfectly adequate for games, and doesn't seem to fatigue the eyes the way it would on a static desktop.

# 2D Games

With all the hoopla surrounding 3D graphics, you'd think the entire world would be 3D, but you'd be wrong. There are a large number of compelling titles that are 2D only, ranging from games like the *Civilization* series, *Age of Empires II*, any number of card and puzzle games, and more. It's true that there's been a tendency to use 3D when it's not needed—call this the "hammer syndrome," from the saying "If all I have is a hammer, then all my problems look like nails."

The good news is that 2D games aren't generally as performance-intensive as 3D titles. Even so, a few 2D games can push the performance envelope. *Baldur's Gate*, the role-playing game from Bioware, makes use of advanced DirectDraw modes, yielding stunning special effects in 32-bit color with nary a polygon or texture map in sight.

### Note

We talk about 3D graphics, including polygons and texture maps, in more detail in "3D Graphics Explained," later in this chapter, and in "Direct3D Features Explained" in Chapter 13.

In fact, there can be sophisticated animation and effects with 2D graphics, ranging from color cycling to sprite animation. *Mechcommander*, the realtime strategy game based on the *Battletech* board game, has up to 15,000 frames of animation per sprite. Nearly every building, tower, wall, and other objects can be blown up or otherwise altered. Both *Mechcommander* and *Baldur's Gate* show what can be done with 2D.

The good news is that almost all of today's graphics cards have good 2D performance, particularly with DirectDraw. It's not like the bad old days of DOS games, where VGA performance of a particular graphics chip made a huge difference.

Animation in 2D games can take a variety of forms. In some cases, it's done in a brute force way. An entire screen is drawn in the back buffer, and then flipped to the front buffer as fast as possible. However, there are more elegant methods. One way is to use *sprites*. These are small, discrete graphics (such as a single unit in a game like Starcraft). When the back buffer is being drawn, only the pixels that change in that frame are actually changed before the page flip occurs. Another slick technique is *color cycling*. This is often used for water or sky effects. A pattern of clouds moving across the sky can be generated just by rapidly changing the color of existing pixels on the front buffer—and no page flip is even needed.

# 3D Games

The 2D computer display is our window into the fast-paced, visually stunning virtual world of 3D games. When game developers speak of "true" 3D games, they are talking about graphics engines that account for the 3rd dimension in a realistic way. The key to all this is calculating depth. If you think of 2D graphics as being described by two axes—x and y, the third dimension would be that of *depth*. This is the z-axis (see Figure 4.2).

**Figure 4.2**
3D graphics means taking depth—the z-axis—into account and translating it to the 2D computer screen.

Adding the z-axis to the graphics engine entails a huge increase in complexity. The math needed for 3D graphics is well-known, and very computer-intensive. Until the advent of fast CPUs and 3D accelerators, 3D graphics were quite primitive. For example, *Falcon 3.0*, which shipped in 1990, rendered an entire F-16 jet fighter in roughly 20 flat-shaded polygons. There's a story that one of the *Falcon 3.0* programmers showed the flight simulator to his mother—who couldn't see the jet. All she could see was a random collection of triangles. The F-16 in *Falcon 4.0* now exceeds 300 polygons, all of which are texture mapped and Gouraud shaded. Consequently, it looks much more realistic.

3D graphics requires very fast floating point, fast transfer of large amounts of data, and good 3D-accelerator hardware.

Game developers can create 3D game graphics in one of several ways:

- Create the entire 3D graphics software "engines" themselves, including the application, the geometry, the lighting, and the rendering. This is how it was done in the days before 3D accelerators.
- Use an available 3D API as just a rendering engine. This makes sense in an era where the 3D graphics hardware only handles rendering chores. The programmers still worry about geometry and lighting.
- Use an available 3D API for geometry, lighting, and rendering. In fact, most OpenGL titles use the API for geometry, and *Quake III: Arena* uses some of the OpenGL lighting elements as well. In the past, most game developers have avoided this with Direct3D because Direct3D was slow and cumbersome to work with. That changed significantly with DirectX 6.0. In DirectX 7.0, the API supports hardware acceleration of geometry and lighting. The huge increase in performance and visual quality made possible by the new generation of 3D accelerators with geometry and lighting built into the hardware, and the improvements in Direct3D, mean that more game developers will be using Direct3D as their 3D engine.

# 3D Graphics Explained

Let's briefly cover what 3D graphics actually *is* before we talk about 3D hardware. At first blush, it seems like it should be easy. After all, we live in a 3-dimensional world, with depth, color, and freedom of movement in any direction. After all, if you've ever seen a movie like *A Bug's Life*, or *Star Wars: The Phantom Menace*, you've seen highly sophisticated 3D graphics at work.

It's not that easy. First of all, any 3D graphics in movies is *pre-rendered*. That means that large banks of computers (sometimes called a "rendering farm") calculate each frame of the animation and write it out to disk. That pre-created frame is then output to film or video. It's like the animated cut-scenes in many computer games, such as *Mechwarrior 3* or *Might and Magic VII*. The other key point about movies or video is that there's no freedom of action: What you see is what you get.

Now, imagine a 3D computer game—particularly simulations of the real world, such as *Panzer Elite* or *Falcon 4.0*, or 3D action games like *Oni* or *Unreal*. In those games, you can move freely through the virtual environment, picking your direction and even interacting with objects in the environment. All of this is happening in realtime, at 30 or more frames per second. Note also that other objects can also be moving, such as enemy aircraft or vehicles.

# A Window to the World

First, think of your computer monitor as a window into the virtual world. If you look out a real window, you can see part of a scene. As I write this, I can look out and see most of a tree from a second floor window. Part of the tree is obscured. Part of the window frame is obscured behind the computer monitor. Down below, several people are moving, but they are out of my view. Clouds are scudding across the sky.

Now, imagine trying to capture this as realtime 3D graphics animation. How do I represent the tree? Do I draw every single leaf as a separate object (a huge computational challenge), or do I "cheat" by creating a 2D, partially transparent image that looks okay from most viewpoints? How do I account for the people moving below? They're not immediately visible, after all. But let's say one moves partially into view. I can now see a head, shoulders, and arms. Do I draw the legs, even though I can't see them?

What about all the objects behind me? How do I account for them? If I want a virtual environment through which I can "move," I would want to be able to turn around and see the items behind me.

What about objects with volume? A basketball is thrown through the air. Do the polygons that make up the ball have both an inside and an outside? This sounds very odd, but 3D graphics allows you to render only one "side" of a surface. If you were to go around to the other side, nothing would be seen.

We begin to see that the number of details you need to track are enormous. The good news is that it simply comes down to a bit of math. The bad news is that math is hugely computational in nature. Let's explore how it comes together without having to cover too much math.

# Polygons

If you look at the world around you, you will see a multitude of shapes, ranging from flat surfaces (floors, windows, and tabletops) to curved objects like basketballs, cars, and coffee cups.

Trying to re-create a perfect sphere to model something like a basketball using computer-generated 3D graphics turns out to be incredibly difficult. Even if it could be done, it would require massive computing power—well beyond a 1GHz Pentium III. Instead, an object like a basketball is created out of many flat surfaces—polygons.

A polygon is simply a flat, enclosed geometric shape drawn with straight lines (see Figure 4.3). A square or a pentagon is a polygon. Most 3D objects are constructed with triangles as the base polygon type. The reason for this is that triangles—which consist of three points and three sides—are guaranteed to have a flat surface. A square or more complex polygon might actually generate a surface that's curved.

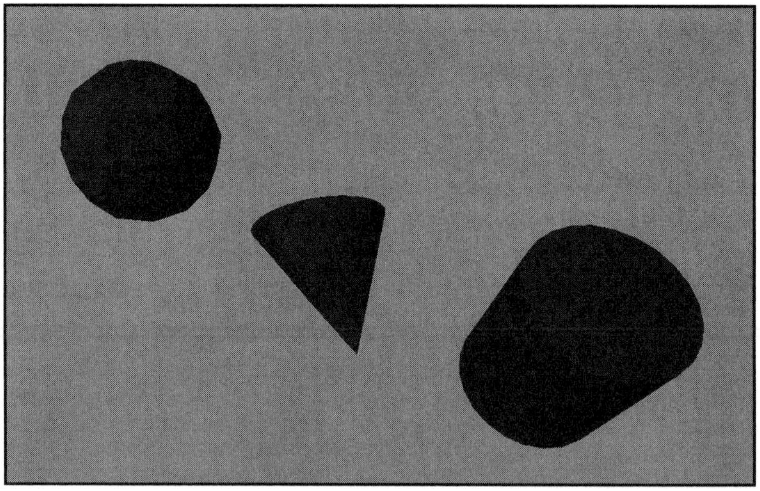

**Figure 4.3**
Curved objects in 3D games are constructed by combining triangles to approximate the shape of the object.

Why, then, do objects in games look much smoother than those in Figure 4.3? There are tricks that 3D games can do with shading (coloring) individual pixels, including texture mapping, Gouraud shading, filtering, and other techniques. We'll discuss this question in more detail.

# What's Visible?

In a 3D game, each frame is rendered, one after the other. Each frame consists of a single scene that might or might not change relative to the one before it. One of the challenges is to figure out what's visible and what's not. The first chore is to simply determine what's in the visible scene and what's not. After all, you don't want to render everything that's *behind* your view—that would be a major performance hit. Rendering just the viewable area is known as *viewport clipping* or just *clipping*.

The next thing that's needed is to determine what's partially visible. Let's say there's half of a car in view, to the left side of the screen. We now have to figure out what part of the car is in the scene and what part isn't. At a very basic level, we also have to figure out which polygon on the 3D car is in view and which isn't. Again, we don't want to render things that aren't in the scene.

The third step is to figure out what objects are behind other objects . If an object is completely hidden behind another one, there's no point in rendering it. This task is known as *z-sorting*. One method used for z-sorting is *z-buffering*; many 3D accelerators can perform z-buffering in hardware. There are other techniques used in 3D games as well, but only z-buffering is performed in hardware in modern 3D accelerator chips.

Finally, there's the issue of what *surface* is visible. We only want to render the visible sides of the polygons; there's no point in rendering the rear faces of a polygon (see Figures 4.4 and 4.5). This is *backface culling*. If the backfaces of all the polygons were calculated, that could actually double the amount of work done.

**Figure 4.4**
In this figure, we don't see the wooden cone at all; it's behind the cube and spheroid rock. Note also the ellipsoid that's partly embedded in the ground.

# Change over Time

As successive frames of animation are rendered, the next thing to do is figure out what's changed in each frame. There are several different types of changes, including movement, rotation, and scaling. The entirety of things that change over time is called *transforms*.

Simple movement, such as a car moving down the road a few hundred feet, is called *translation*. Turning or spinning an object is *rotation* and changing the size of an object is *scaling*.

But it's not as simple as moving an object like a car. Other things can move, too. One of the most important things that can move is the "camera." The camera is your viewpoint into the virtual world. In a first-person shooter, *you* are the camera. In a third-person game, like *Drakkan* or the *Tomb Raider* series, you manipulate the camera to some extent, but it usually follows a single subject. In a realtime strategy game like *Myth 2*, or SSI's *Fighting Steel* you can move the camera freely through the virtual world.

**Figure 4.5**

Moving the camera a bit reveals the wooden cone. Depth sorting ensures that the objects closest to the viewer are rendered correctly, and the ones completely obscured aren't shown.

Also, scaling doesn't just mean changing the size of the object relative to the virtual world. A 3D airplane might not change in actual size at all, but will change in visual size as it moves closer to you.

The type of math used in most of these kinds of operations is *matrix math*, and consists of arrays of numbers. We won't get into any detail about the math, but suffice it to say that 3D graphics generated in realtime is hugely computational in nature. That's why very fast CPUs and graphics chips are needed for today's 3D games.

# Lighting

A 3D world with no lights would be very dark indeed. A 3D world with only flat, ambient lighting would look very stark and uninteresting. Game environments with complex lighting effects, including spotlights, point light sources, and shadows, are much more interesting. Fox Interactive's *Alien vs. Predator* sets a very scary mood with its dim, ever-changing lighting and spooky shadows.

There are several ways of doing lighting in 3D graphics. The first is to attempt to calculate the actual, visible lights in the scene. That is, the physics of light are used as the basis for calculating the way light is generated, moves through a scene, is reflected, and casts shadows. This type of lighting calculation is mathematically complex and is used sparingly in most games. These are *geometric* lights.

The other way is through the use of light maps. The game does some rough calculation as to the lighting effects desired, but instead of calculating the actual beams of lights or the actual shadows, special texture maps called light maps are applied to key areas of the scene.

# Understanding 3D Graphics Hardware

Now, you have a basic understanding of the complexities of 3D graphics. Now, let's explore 3D graphics from the perspective of the hardware accelerators, and how they solve some of the problems. If the discussion on how 3D graphics works seems overwhelming, it should be. That's why chip designers break the problem down into discrete pieces that are easier to solve.

## The 3D Graphics Pipeline

Think of the 3D graphics pipeline as an assembly line. Certain tasks must be completed before others can be done. Before the actual graphics come into consideration, there's the application and the API. The application is the game, and takes care of issues like collision detection (solid objects should collide realistically, not merge together), physics, AI, and so on. The API—Direct3D or OpenGL—is the code that the application uses to handle the 3D graphics. Underlying any 3D API, whether it's one homegrown by the programmer or a standard API—is the 3D graphics pipeline.

Figure 4.6 shows the four basic steps graphically.

The four basic steps are

- **Transforms.** As noted earlier, transforms are the basic moving, scaling, or rotating of objects or the "camera" (your viewpoint).
- **Lighting.** The world consists of many disparate light sources, and the graphics pipeline needs to account for that. Here, we're talking about "geometric lights," as distinguished from lightmaps, which show up in the rendering part of the pipeline.
- **Setup.** This is where the 3D data gets translated to a format that the graphics accelerator needs in order to convert it to the 2D format of the computer screen.
- **Rendering.** This is the actual act of assigning colors and shades to individual pixels for display on your monitor.

Until quite recently, all 3D graphics accelerators handled only the setup and rendering steps of the pipeline. Game programmers think in terms of performance budgets—how much of the CPU is allocated to a certain task, for example. When the first 3D graphics cards emerged, as much as 80 percent of the CPU was allocated to rendering in some games. That didn't leave a lot for physics, AI, and a host of other functions. It also meant that a graphics chip that offloaded just the rendering chores yielded a huge payoff for the game. But the CPU still handles the geometry and lighting calculations.

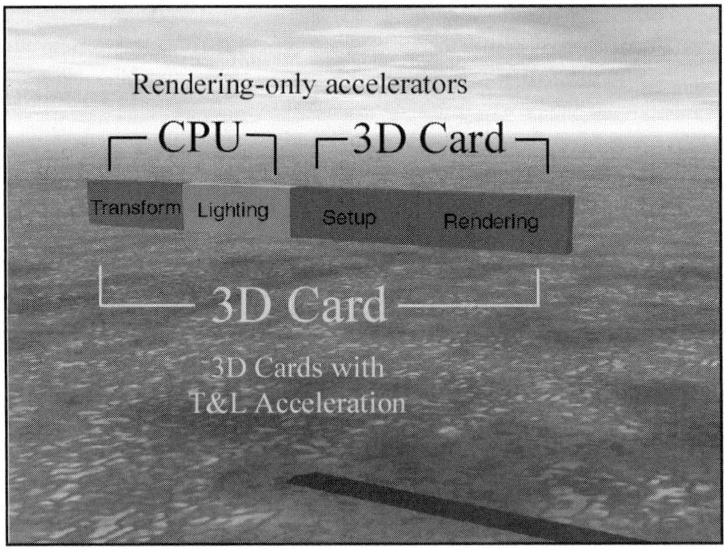


**Figure 4.6**

The 3D graphics pipeline. Note that the CPU handles the transform and lighting chores with many current 3D cards.

## Note

Despite the apparent focus on graphics and sound when you read the back of many computer game packages, there's a lot going on "underneath the hood" that has nothing to do with hardware. In single-player games, the "AI" is tremendously important. "AI" stands for *artificial intelligence*, and is generally used to describe the behavior of the computer-driven characters and opponents. Developing "smart" computer opponents is a difficult challenge, and the more CPU available for it, the better.

Physics modeling takes care of how the physical environment operates. It's responsible for the trajectory of a bullet, the flow of water in a virtual stream, the airflow over an aircraft wing, the friction of a sliding object, and much more.

Collision detection is another key issue inside a game. When two vehicles collide in a game like *Midtown Madness*, the computer has to determine exactly when the polygons that make up one vehicle collide or intersect with another.

Lately, the CPU budgets have shifted so that the front end of the 3D graphics pipeline—geometry and lighting—has as much as 50–70% of the CPU allocated. So it's logical that the next step would be to offload geometry and lighting to the graphics card (refer to Figure 4.6). Although this type of functionality has been available on very expensive, workstation class machines, we're now seeing graphics cards with this capability that cost less than $300.

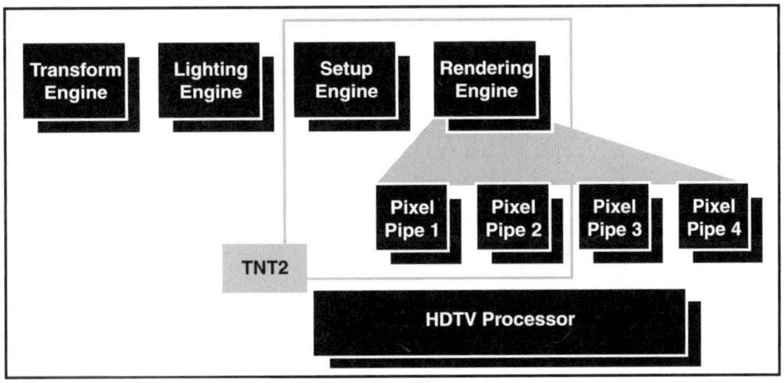


**Figure 4.7**
nVidia's GeForce 256 is the first consumer-level graphics chip to offload geometry and lighting calculations to the graphics card.

# Rendering

Because most of the 3D accelerators available still handle just rendering, it's helpful to understand a few terms.

## Shading

Shading is the act of applying the correct color to a pixel to achieve a certain visual effect. The simplest type of shading is *flat shading*, in which each polygon consists entirely of a single, discrete color. More complex is *Gouraud shading*. With Gouraud shading, colors close to where two polygons join are blended in such a way so that the transition between the two polygons appears smooth, rather than abrupt. There are other types of shading, such as *Phong shading* and *ray tracing*, but they aren't commonly used in PC games.

## Texture Mapping

A texture map is simply a picture, in computer format. Think of a long, narrow polygon—a rectangle, receding into the distance. We want to make the rectangle look like a brick wall. So we apply a picture of bricks to the wall. In order to make the brick texture also look correct as the wall recedes into the distance, *perspective correction* is applied to the texture.

There are various other tricks that apply to texture mapping to manage what's known as *level of detail*, or *LOD* for short. *MIP-mapping* uses copies of the same texture, but at different resolutions. An object in the distance will have a lower resolution version of the texture applied. These various, lower resolution copies (often as many as eight) are called MIP maps. This saves on memory and increases performance. As the object comes closer, a higher resolution version of the texture is applied, making it look more realistic.

## Filtering

Finally, *filtering* is applied to the texture. Until recently, there was a limit to the resolution of texture maps; the maximum was usually 256×256 pixels. The net result was that if you moved very close to an object, the texture detail would first max out, and then the individual pixels of the texture would be visible as huge squares. What's going on is that the texture pixel no longer corresponds to the pixels on your screen. Filtering blends the colors of several nearby pixels so that the texture might look a little blurry, but at least you don't get the huge, blocky effect.

There are various types of filtering. The simplest is no filtering at all, and this is called *point sampling*. *Bilinear filtering* blends a number of adjacent pixel colors. *Trilinear filtering*, also called *trilinear MIP-mapping*, blends colors between various MIP maps as well, so you don't notice the strange popping effect when a new MIP map is applied to an object. Finally, there's. *anisotropic filtering*, which blends pixel colors in various, specific directions, depending on the look the programmer wants to achieve. Anisotropic filtering can also substitute for trilinear filtering, though it's, more computer-intensive.

## Textures: The More the Merrier

One other key use of texture mapping is to blend (merge) different textures in multiple ways to achieve a certain look or generate a particular effect. Light maps, for example, are a kind of texture map used to create the appearance of a lighting effect. *Multitexturing* is the ability of many current graphics cards to blend two or more textures in one operation. Texture mapping, and the associated features that improve the image quality of texture maps, have revolutionized modern computer games. It's no longer just a matter of applying pictures of cobblestones to a street. Now, texture mapping, through the use of blending and multitexturing, can create realistic effects and striking imagery so far beyond the flat shaded polygons of *Falcon 3.0* that it's hard to believe that those were ever playable.

## Variations on Texture Mapping

Texture maps can be used for effects other than surface appearance. Light and dark (shadow) maps are frequently used to create moody or realistically lighted environments.

*Bump mapping* is a type of texture mapping that gives a surface a more three-dimensional look, even though it's still a flat texture. There are several types of bump mapping, but the most commonly used variants in games are *emboss* bump mapping and *environmental* bump mapping. Ideally, you'd rather have a surface with realistic depth to it, but that can be quite costly in terms of polygon counts in many cases, so bump mapping is a good "cheat" in the right circumstances.

*Reflection mapping* is a technique in which a texture is applied to a surface that should be reflective to make it appear like it's actually reflecting the surrounding environment. In fact, real reflections would be too computationally intensive, so reflection mapping is another "hack" that adds a touch of realism.

*Cubic environment mapping* is a variant of reflection mapping in which the surrounding environs are reduced to a texture map. It's more realistic than simple reflection mapping (because the map is drawn from the actual surroundings), but does take a little more horsepower than a precalculated reflection map.

# Fill Rate Versus Polygon Count

The 3D-accelerated computer games of recent years have consisted of scenes that have a relatively low polygon count. Scenes rarely had more than 3,000 polygons, and many had far fewer. When you have a relatively low number of polygons, that leaves more area to be filled with pixels. How fast those pixels could be blasted into a polygon was called the *fill rate*, and was perhaps the single most critical measurement of a 3D card's performance.

However, as games become more complex, and as geometry acceleration begins to make its presence felt, the triangle count of these games increases dramatically. Raw fill rate, although still important, isn't the critical measurement it used to be. As polygon counts get high, other issues start to become important: how fast triangle data is moved across the bus, how many polygons per second can be generated, and so on. In fact, with a graphics card that has geometry acceleration, you want to be sure that the triangle rate of the hardware geometry engine is much higher than anything that can be generated by the CPU.

Where fill rate is still important is in multitexturing and texture blending effects. To that end, all current and future 3D accelerator chips have multiple *pixel pipelines*—essentially, there are two or more rendering engines working in parallel.

# Underneath the Hood of a 3D Card

Now that you have a basic understanding of the features that go into a 3D accelerator, let's take a look at the hardware itself.

A 3D graphics card consists of the accelerator chip, memory, and perhaps some glue logic. If the card supports additional features, such as TV out, there's a TV encoder chip as well. The graphics chip will have a heat sink or fan attached to dissipate heat away from the surface of the part.

The majority of 3D graphics cards available only handle the 3D rendering chores. That means that the data sent from the PC, over the AGP bus, to the card consists of texture maps and transformed, lit triangles. Actually, it's the vertex data (the lines that make up joined triangles) that's sent over the AGP bus.

Lying between the application and the graphics card is the driver. The driver is a piece of software that enables the operating system and applications to recognize and use the hardware. The driver generally acts as a traffic cop, managing the data streams that pass back and forth between the system and the accelerator. Note that some drivers might do some fraction of the actual rendering work—which means that the CPU is doing some of the tasks you thought your 3D card was performing. This is less common than in the past, given the rich feature set in today's 3D hardware.

After the graphics data is in card memory, the 3D chip takes over. The graphics chip handles much more than just 3D rendering. It has to manage the memory on the card and handle the 2D graphics chores, for example.

### Note

Many graphics cards now allow users to set the clock speed of the graphics chip and graphics memory. This is akin to overclocking the CPU, as we discussed in Chapter 3, "Motherboards and Memory." You can also alter the clock rate using tools like Powerstrip from Entech (`www.entechtaiwan.com`). Although you can realize some performance gains out of overclocking the graphics card, the same caveats apply here as they do to CPUs: You could see heat problems, intermittent failures and even cause permanent damage to the card.

# 3D Hardware Features Versus Reality

The hype surrounding various 3D graphics chips is exceeded only by the hype surrounding presidential candidates. No 3D card or chip is perfect, yet if you read the ads or product packages, you'd think that the cure for world hunger resides inside the box.

So be wary of promises made by the 3D hardware companies. Here are just a few items to chew on:

- 3dfx likes to talk a lot about its multiple TMUs (texture mapping units) with Voodoo2 and Voodoo3. But in Direct3D games that don't support multitexturing, the second TMU goes unused. This explains why a Voodoo3 doesn't run as fast in some Direct3D games as their competition.
- The feature list on boxes of products using the Nvidia TNT2 chip includes trilinear filtering. In fact, the TNT and TNT2 synthesize trilinear filtering through the use of anisotropic filtering. (Note that chip spec sheets don't list trilinear filtering.) This can create visual differences when compared to true trilinear filtering.
- Cards using ATI's Rage 128 chip talk about "DVD support." In fact, the chip handles a key math function that assists in MPEG-2 decoding for DVD, but the chip itself can't handle full DVD functionality, including regionalization and copy protection. This means that you need an additional software DVD player simply to view DVD movies. If you want a game that uses DVD video to operate properly, you still need a hardware DVD decoder.
- Matrox touts the G400 chip as having support for 32-bit z-buffer. But if you run in 32-bit color mode, the Matrox only uses a 16-bit z-buffer unless the game requests a 32-bit z-buffer, or unless the user checks a special box in the Matrox control panel. In some games, this could result in visual issues like objects "popping" into existence as you move towards a distant object.

All these 3D chips are actually quite capable rendering parts, so the presence of unneeded hype doesn't mean you'll get a bad product. In fact, even the slowest of current generation cards do a credible job in most games at 800×600 resolution or lower. Of course, the faster cards tout their higher resolution superiority, but they usually cost more. Recently, there were some cards using S3's Savage4 chip with 32MB of onboard RAM for *less than $100*. It's a trade-off between price and performance. Go ahead and read the boxes and ads, but be aware that the playing field is much more level than it was a few years ago.

On the other hand, the game developers continue to ratchet up the requirements, creating games that look much more realistic and beautiful. In the process, though, the CPU and graphics requirements keep climbing.

# 3D Chipsets

With these cautions in mind, let's survey the 3D card universe as it exists today. Table 4.1 provides a quick and dirty list of popular 3D chipsets and the key settings.

**Table 4.1—3D chipsets**

| *3D Chip* | *Key Features* | *Maximum Possible Memory* | *Estimated Fill Rate (megapixels per second)* | *Additional Features/ Specs* |
|---|---|---|---|---|
| Voodoo3 | Glide support; high clock rates | 16MB | 286–366 | NA |
| "Voodoo4" | Glide support; high clock rates; T-buffer | 32–64MB | 600–800 | Unknown |
| TNT2 | Dual rendering pipelines; 32-bit rendering; robust OpenGL support | 32MB | 250–350 | NA |
| GeForce 256 | Transform and Lighting acceleration; four rendering pipelines; cubic | 128MB | 480 | 12–18 million polygons/sustained transform performance; 8 hardware lights; DXTC texture compression |

ues

**Table 4.1—3D chipsets** Continued

| *3D Chip* | *Key Features* | *Maximum Possible Memory* | *Estimated Fill Rate (megapixels per second)* | *Additional Features/ Specs* |
|---|---|---|---|---|
| | environment mapping; 32-bit rendering | | | |
| Savage4 | S3TC texture compression; 32-bit rendering | 32MB | 140 | NA |
| Savage 2000 | S3TC texture compression; Transform and Lighting Acceleration; 32-bit rendering | 64MB | 700 | 8–12 million polygons per second sustained transform performance; 8 hardware lights; 2 multitextured pixels/clock cycle |
| Rage 128 Pro | DXTC texture compression; 16-tap anisotropic filtering; 32-bit rendering | 32MB | 300 (est) | Hardware assist for MPEG-2 decompression |
| Matrox G400 Max | Environmental Bump mapping; dual monitor support; 32-bit rendering | 32MB | 250–330 | NA |

## 3dfx Voodoo2, Voodoo3, and "Voodoo4"

The Voodoo2 will someday take its place alongside the Apple II as one of the classic pieces of PC hardware. It's a 3D-only card, and works alongside any 2D-capable primary card. The Voodoo2 was one of the first 3D cards to put two rendering engines on a single card, but the flaw in its architecture is that one TMU (texture mapping unit) is idle in non-multitexture Direct3D games.

If you take Voodoo2, reduce it to a single chip, add solid 2D functionality and jack up the clockrate, you'll have Voodoo3. There are other enhancements, but that's still a reasonably accurate way to think of Voodoo3.

3dfx likes to tout its own proprietary API, Glide, as being an advantage, but the age of proprietary APIs is drawing to a close. Although you can get a performance advantage using Glide, no game developer will exclude Direct3D or OpenGL support today. The company was tardy getting out an OpenGL ICD, and it's still a work in progress. The Voodoo3/3500 has a TV tuner and supports MPEG-2 video capture.

The Voodoo3 has been criticized for its lack of leading edge features, but the fact remains that, until recently, only a handful of games used features like large textures, 32-bit rendering, and bump mapping. The Voodoo3 architecture is extremely efficient when it comes to texture downloads (at least in Glide mode), but the Direct3D drivers haven't been so robust. Due to the 16-bit rendering limitation, there's no need for a large memory footprint, and Voodoo3 maxes out at 16MB.

### Tip

Not much was known about the "Voodoo4" at the time of this writing. It is likely that it will incorporate a new technology developed by 3dfx called the *T-buffer*. The T-buffer renders into multiple frame buffers at the same time, then can blend the frames so that certain types of special effects can be created. One effect that will be "free" (meaning that all games will instantly use it) is full screen antialiasing. Antialiasing minimizes the "jaggies," which is the odd stairstep effect you often notice with computer graphics. Other effects, such as motion blur and depth-of-field focus, will require developer support.

## 3dlabs Permedia 3

3dlabs focuses on the users who use 3D in professional applications, including computer aided design (CAD) and 3D modeling. The Permedia 3 was originally meant to be a chip targeted at consumers, but it failed to meet performance expectations. It's still a decent chip, with dual pixel pipelines and all the texture blending modes for today's games. 3dlabs has always had excellent OpenGL support, so this chip might be ideal for the CAD user or 3D modeler who occasionally boots up a 3D game. I wouldn't recommend this chip for the hard-core game player, though.

## ATI Technologies' Rage 128 and Rage 128 Pro

The Rage 128 is a reasonably capable 3D accelerator with some additional features that help MPEG-2 decoding. It has two rendering engines. It's actually quite efficient, although benchmarks place it fairly low on the raw performance spectrum. Its clock rate is also fairly low. True color performance is also fairly decent, relative to its 16-bit performance. Cards using the Rage 128 include the Rage Fury and All-in-Wonder 128. The All-in-Wonder is an interesting card, in that it has an embedded TV tuner and can capture video in MPEG-2 format. You can also find ATI Rage 128 chips in a variety of computer systems, like those from Sony and Apple. Rage 128 cards can be quite inexpensive.

ATI's real problem has been its inconsistent driver support. Early Rage 128 drivers yielded poor image quality in 16-bit color. It's gotten better, but there are still problems with some 3D games. ATI's OpenGL ICD (installable client driver) steadily gets better, however. The Rage 128 supports up to 32MB of video memory.

The Rage 128 Pro is the latest incarnation in the Rage 128 product line. The Rage 128 Pro runs at a much higher clock rate than the original Rage 128. ATI has added 16-tap, anisotropic filtering to the chip and hardware texture compression, but that's the only significant new feature that's been added. Given the higher clock rate, the fill rate of this card should be much better.

# Matrox G400 and G400Max

The G400 is another chip with dual pixel pipelines and support for most major 3D features. In addition, the G400 adds support for environmental bump-mapping and multiple monitor support in a single card. The G400Max is simply a higher-clock-rate version of the G400.

The performance of the G400 is quite good for a chip at its clock rate (estimated to be 125MHz; Matrox doesn't release clock rate figures). The G400Max runs at a probable clock rate of 166MHz. Yields on the G400Max have been very low, however, so this board is still fairly scarce.

Matrox's 2D performance has always been topnotch and the color saturation of the G400 series results in a rich looking image in both 2D and 3D. Matrox supports large textures, non-square textures, and 32-bit rendering throughout the 3D pipeline.

Recently, Matrox has released the Marvel G400, combining a TV tuner and strong video in-and-out features for the video hobbyist. All the G400 cards are available with up to 32MB of RAM.

# Nvidia TNT2 and GeForce 256

The TNT2 is a solid, third-generation part. It builds on the original TNT with a streamlined 3D pipeline and AGP 4x support, and it supports up to 32MB of RAM. It has dual pixel pipelines that can be combined to double the throughput in non-multitexture games. Nvidia was one of the first consumer-level 3D chip companies to ship a robust OpenGL ICD.

The TNT2 is available in a standard and high-clock-rate version (called the TNT2 Ultra). Although Nvidia specs the Ultra at a core clock rate of 150MHz and a memory clock of 183MHz, it has left the door open for board vendors to clock the chip higher. Several companies have shipped boards at 175MHz core clock. The TNT2 supports advanced 3D features like large texture support and 32-bit rendering throughout the pipeline. TNT2 boards offer very good performance and a solid set of features.

The GeForce 256 promises to revolutionize the 3D graphics industry. It's the first consumer-level part to have onboard transform (geometry) acceleration and also has support for up to eight hardware light sources. In addition, there are four pixel pipelines with a 256-bit-wide data path to the frame buffer. The video features of the GeForce are unique, too, with hardware scaling and color space conversion at HDTV resolutions (1080i and 720p). Hardware scaling and color space conversion of video data improve both the speed of TV/HDTV/DVD video and its image quality. Nvidia rates the geometry processor as capable of a sustained, 12–18 million polygons per second, roughly three to five times a Pentium III/600. The sustained fill rate at the initial, 120MHz clock speed is 480 megapixels per second. The chip can support up to 128MB of RAM, though initial boards will probably max out at 64MB.

With the ability to offload geometry and some lighting from the CPU, game programmers will be free to create more detailed models. Equally important, users with lower speed systems might be able to get a significant performance boost with just a graphics card upgrade. Note, though, that the game itself must support the hardware transform and lighting engine. There are two ways to do this: either Direct3D or OpenGL. OpenGL titles should gain some benefit immediately, but few Direct3D games in the past supported the D3D transform and lighting engine. Given the performance of the GeForce, that is already beginning to change. However, the quad pixel engines will certainly help in other games, and the GeForce 256 also supports S3 texture compression through Microsoft's DXTC implementation.

## S3 Savage4 and Savage 2000

The Savage4 is a relatively low-cost chip that actually offers decent performance for the price. I've seen name brand boards with 32MB of RAM for less than $100. The Savage4 has all the usual features: dual pixel pipelines, 32MB support, 32-bit color, and so on. In addition, it has two key features that distinguish it from the pack. First, it does trilinear filtering with almost no performance penalty. Secondly, it supports S3TC (S3 texture compression). Even a 32MB board might not have enough memory to properly support a rich set of large textures. S3TC allows game developers to compress textures up to six times smaller. The textures are only decompressed when the game actually needs them. Games with high resolution textures and S3 texture compression look much more detailed than others. The look is quite remarkable, and there's no performance penalty.

Note that the Savage4 doesn't clock as high as the TNT2 or Voodoo3, so you wouldn't want to run it any higher than 800×600. However, performance with large textures in a game like *Unreal Tournament* is quite good at 800×600×32.

Like the Nvidia GeForce 256, the Savage 2000 supports hardware acceleration for transform and lighting. It's likely that the Savage 2000's T&L performance will trail the GeForce a bit, but should still be considerably faster than even a 1GHz Pentium III. S3 has taken a slightly different approach than Nvidia, opting to push fill rate rather than T&L performance. The Savage 2000 is built on a 0.18 micron semiconductor process, which should support very high clock rates. A 200MHz Savage 2000 will be capable of up to 800 megapixels per second of sustained fill rate—a far cry from the Savage 3.

# Performance Issues

There are subtle issues with 3D game performance that can come into play unexpectedly. Sometimes, the hottest 3D accelerator can seem slug-like in performance. Here are a few things to look for:

- Games that were originally written for 3dfx's Glide and ported to Direct3D and OpenGL might have performance issues on non-3dfx hardware. That's slowly changing. Epic's *Unreal* and Sierra's *Tribes* have gone through several versions, and now the Direct3D version of Unreal and the OpenGL version of Tribes run very well on non-3dfx hardware. But it's still something to watch for on older games.

- Some games run well on all hardware. For example, most driving games don't seem to be dragged down by either the graphics card or, within reason, the CPU.
- Some games are more CPU-dependent than graphics card–bound. Flight simulators, for example, are much more demanding on the CPU, and any individual 3D card might not run all that much faster than others.
- All OpenGL ICDs are not created equal. Matrox lagged for quite some time, though it's finally getting better. S3's Savage4, whose Direct3D performance seems relatively poor, has a very decent ICD.
- Some motherboards might not adequately support the high-clock-rate graphics cards due to the inability to deliver adequate electrical current to the AGP port.

Play around with the AGP aperture size. Depending on the card, it might make a difference. Most BIOS setup programs allow you to alter the aperture size.

Turn OFF BIOS features such as video shadowing, ROM caching, and so on. But if your BIOS setup has a setting for write combining, try setting it to USWC (uncached, speculative write combining).

Check for newer graphics drivers—they often fix significant performance and image quality problems.

# Choosing the Right 3D Card

Most current-generation 3D cards have strengths and weaknesses. Some offer higher performance, but at a cost. Some lack features, but cost less and can handle 16-bit rendering quite speedily. Others cost more, but offer features and performance ahead of the rest.

The thing to do is to take a look at the games you play. If you're seriously into competitive deathmatch play with *Quake III*, you'll want to get the best, fastest graphics card possible—money might be no object. But it's no longer a matter of finding the card with the highest fill rate. For example, the Savage4's raw performance isn't all that great compared to the competition, but throw in S3TC and a willingness to run at 800×600 or less, and some games can look amazingly realistic.

On the other hand, flight simulators are more CPU-bound than graphics-limited. If you're a flight sim buff, trading off a slightly slower 3D card for a faster CPU makes a lot of sense. The flip side of this coin is that many racing games are fill rate–bound, barely taxing the CPU. If you're a real racing buff, look for a card with a very high fill rate. You should also take a look at your CPU. It would make little sense to get a 175MHz TNT2 Ultra card if you have a K6-2 running at 300MHz—the card would be idle much of the time as the CPU struggled to pump out polygons.

Another issue to think about is API support. If you need to use professional 3D CAD or modeling tools, a robust OpenGL ICD is critical. On the other hand, if you have a library of old, 3dfx-only games that you dearly love, you'd definitely want a card that can support 3dfx's Glide API.

Then there's the issue of graphics on the motherboard. Many systems these days ship with the main AGP graphics chip soldered to the motherboard. *You cannot upgrade the graphics on these systems*. You can, however, add a Voodoo2 3D-only card to complement the chip on the motherboard, if that chip isn't a good 3D accelerator.

Two chips that might break a lot of the old rules are the GeForce and Savage 2000. But boards with the GeForce aren't cheap, and not enough games support hardware lighting and transform acceleration yet. But one of these boards is certainly cheaper than an upgrade to a top-of-the line CPU, and that's where it might be revolutionary. Only time—and the games—will tell. Although the Savage 2000 might not have the T&L punch of the GeForce, it has a very high sustained fill rate and costs less—so it might be in the sweet spot for many users.

# Chapter 5

# Displays

## Display Technologies

You may have the fastest CPU on earth and a killer 3D graphics card, but you really view all your games using a 2D display device: your computer monitor. If your display isn't up to snuff, all the money spent on CPU and graphics can be wasted. If you spend any significant amount of time in front of a PC monitor, you owe your eyes the sharpest, most ergonomic display you can afford. Let's look at some key issues when monitor shopping.

There are two primary types of monitors: cathode ray tube (CRT) and flat panel (LCD). The traditional, bulky PC monitor uses technology that predates the PC by over 100 years: the vacuum tube. The glass bottle that makes up most of the bulk and weight is about as old tech as you can get. Flat panel monitors, on the other hand, are leading edge—but may not always be well suited for gaming.

# Cathode Ray Technology (CRT)

The glass bottle technology used in most monitors actually has a couple of key variants. Which you choose depends partly on your personal preference and partly on your budget. Although there are dozens of monitor manufacturers, there are really only a few companies that make the actual CRT "guts."

All tube displays have several things in common. First, there are a series of electron guns inside the monitor that fire a stream of electrons at the face of the tube. The inside of the face is coated with chemicals known as *phosphors*. These phosphors light up briefly when the electron beam touches them. The phosphors are arranged so that red, green, and blue phosphors are close to each other. There is an electron beam dedicated to each of the primary colors, so that only one beam will light up a red phosphor.

When the beam is fired, the intensity of the beam is determined by the color value that the graphics card has set. Think back on our discussion about graphics cards. When a true color image is displayed, each of red, green, and blue can have 256 discrete values. If the values for red, green, and blue are all set to 0, you get black. If they're all set to 255, you get white. Any time all the settings are identical, you get some variation of gray. This is why you usually only get 255 shades of gray.

It's when the values of R, G, and B differ from each other that you start to get some interesting colors—16.7 million of them, with true color images. But if there are just three discrete red, green, and blue phosphors, how is it that we see multiple colors?

First, let's dispense with that 16.7 million number. No monitor is capable of displaying all 16.7 million colors. There are limits due to the makeup of the phosphors themselves, which simply can't reproduce that wide a color range. Still, the number of colors possible range in the millions, so the limitations don't affect computer games themselves.

The phosphor dots are arranged so that there are trios of red, green, and blue phosphors arranged very closely to each other. When the electron beams light up these close-spaced phosphors, the light "blooms," and blends to create a single color. It's a little like a color newspaper photo. If you've ever looked at a color newspaper picture up close, you'll notice that it's really made up of tiny, variously colored dots. At a distance, though, it fools the eye because all of those various colored dots blend to form an illusion of a solid color.

There are two primary technologies used today to layer phosphors and build electron guns inside the vacuum tube. Let's briefly touch on these.

# Invar Shadow Mask

In Chapter 4, "Graphics," I talked about the electron gun scanning the front of the tube, which has a coating of phosphors. The gun actually fires through a sheet placed in front of the large end of the tube, full of miniscule holes. Invar shadow mask monitors use sheets of plastic that don't expand when heated (monitors can get quite warm). The Invar mask uses tiny, round holes through which the electron beam passes.

In modern color tubes, there are actually *three* electron guns, one for red, one for green, and one for blue. There are also three phosphor types, one for each of the primary colors. These are arranged in tiny triangles, and which one lights up depends on which gun fires through the hole in the shadow mask at a particular angle.

## Aperture Grill Monitors

The other main type of tube monitor is the aperture grill monitor, popularized by Sony's Trinitron line. Other brands include Sonictron (Viewsonic) and Diamondtron (Mitsubishi). The aperture grill is really just another type of mask, but instead of a sheet, it consists of a series of closely spaced wires. The electron guns are arranged side-by-side rather than in a triangle. To keep the array of wires taut, two tension wires are used, and these can show up as faint, horizontal gray lines on a white background. Aperture grill monitors generally offer a brighter and crisper image than shadow mask tubes. Aperture grill tubes can be constructed so that one axis (usually the vertical axis) is relatively flat, as opposed to the more spherical curve of the shadow mask tube.

There's a new twist in aperture grill monitors that has appeared in the past year: the flat screen. When you first see one, it almost looks like there's a sense of depth. The vacuum tube is still the same—curved in one direction—but two additional layers of glass are placed over it. The first one is a kind of lens that refocuses the image onto the next layer of glass, which is completely flat. It's visually stunning, and looks better than most flat panel displays, though it's slightly bulkier and heavier than traditional monitors.

# Choosing a Monitor: The Specs Game

When shopping for a monitor, there are some things you should look for. Like any high-tech commodity, though, the monitor companies tend to play the "specsmanship" game. The only real way to shop for a monitor is to go somewhere where they carry a selection of displays and look at them critically. Still, it's worth knowing about some of the more important specs.

## General Guidelines

Monitor prices have dropped drastically in the last several years, so it's a good time to upgrade an older monitor. The first buying hint, though, is to *never* buy a monitor unless you can see it in action first. If the dealer allows, bring a couple of your favorite games and run them on the monitors you're considering. Don't worry about performance (frame rate), just see how the picture looks. Monitors are probably the one item I prefer buying locally, rather than mail order. The shipping costs of a large monitor can be quite high, and tube displays are fragile enough that a little jarring can result in permanent convergence problems. It's very handy to be able to just haul a defective tube back to the dealer.

Should you choose an invar shadow mask or an aperture grill monitor? It really comes down to personal preference and budget. Aperture grill tubes are still more expensive than shadow mask displays, though the price difference has narrowed as the overall prices have dropped. My personal preference is for the brighter, crisper picture of aperture grill monitors. But some people prefer the more muted tones of shadow mask tubes, or find the slightly visible, gray lines of the aperture grill tension wires to be annoying. Note that both types of displays can offer great specs and look good to the eye.

## Dot or Stripe Pitch

Many people believe that monitors have infinitely fine resolution, but that's not quite true. Remember, the phosphor coating is really a large array of phosphor dots arranged in threes, representing the three primary colors. There are only so many of these dots that can be coated on the inside of the glass tube.

Secondly, the electron beams are not infinitesimally small spots—they have a finite focus. If you've ever shone a flashlight on a wall, then slowly backed up, you noticed that the beam can spread out and get more diffuse. The same is true of an electron beam. At the initial firing point, the beam is tightly focused, but as it travels through the length of the tube, it spreads out a bit. If it spreads out too much, or is slightly off center, you can see convergence errors, which appear as discrete, colored highlights near text.

The other piece of the puzzle is the aperture grill or shadow mask itself—the dot or stripe density of the mask comes into play when determining the native resolution of the monitor. A very fine grill or dot pitch allows the electron beam to create a smaller spot.

So, the phosphor density and the quality of the mask itself are the key parameters to determining dot or stripe pitch.

If you've ever seen a 320×200 image displayed on a 21-inch tube, you've probably noticed a certain graininess because the image pixels are made up of multiple monitor pixels. By the same token, there are limits to the maximum resolution of a tube, which is set by the number of holes in the shadow mask or stripes in the aperture grill. For the most part, all good-quality tubes can handle resolutions that most game players use.

The dot or stripe pitch refers to how fine-grain the resolution can be. Dot pitch applies to shadow mask tubes, while stripe pitch is an aperture grill spec. Ideally, you want the finest pitch available. However, a pitch of 0.26 for dot pitch or 0.28 for stripe pitch or better is usually "good enough." When the dot or stripe pitch is that fine, it's time to start looking at other specs.

### Tip

Bear in mind that when looking at dot or stripe pitch, the *lower* the pitch, the better. So, a monitor with 0.26 dot pitch will likely have a better picture than one with a dot pitch of 0.30.

Because every monitor has a native resolution that's determined by the dot or stripe pitch, what happens when the picture image doesn't match the monitor resolution? If the mismatch is toward the low end (as in the 320×200 example), you may see some of the granularity of the image. On the other hand, if the resolution of the image is higher than the display's native resolution, you may see a little blurriness. See Table 5.1 for a list of suggested maximum resolutions displayable on different monitor sizes.

Note that some monitors may quote different dot pitches for the center of the screen and the corners. This is perfectly acceptable, as long as the picture itself looks sharp. Because the gun beam can focus more tightly at the center of the tube than the periphery, *all* monitors have slightly different dot pitches at the corners than the center—the ones that quote the differences are just being honest.

# Megahertz (Bandwidth, Bandwidth, Bandwidth)

The bandwidth of a monitor, usually measured in megahertz (MHz), gives you an idea of how resolution and refresh rate play together. Ideally, you want the highest bandwidth possible. For example, the current bandwidth champ as of this writing is the Viewsonic P817, which sports a 360MHz bandwidth. It can run at 1800×1440 at a refresh rate of 85Hz.

You probably don't need something like the P817, though. Anything above 200MHz is adequate. If the bandwidth spec isn't stated, look for the maximum refresh rate at the highest supported resolution. You want to be able to run at a minimum of 75Hz at the highest *usable* resolution. Although it depends on how good your eyes are, see Table 5.1 for a list of maximum usable resolutions.

### Table 5.1—Maximum usable resolutions[1]

| *Monitor size (diagonal)* | *Maximum Usable Resolution* |
|---|---|
| 14" | 800×600 |
| 15" | 1024×768 |
| 17" | 1152×864 |
| 19" | 1280×1024 |
| 21" | 1600×1200 |

*1 Monitors with a 75MHz refresh rate*

If you recall our discussion on 3D graphics, I had noted that 60Hz refresh rate was perfectly acceptable for 3D games, and in fact might yield higher frame rates than a higher refresh rate in some cases. However, not all games are 3D, and you don't spend all your time playing games. Ideally, you want a minimum of 75Hz refresh rate at the resolution you use most of the time. I prefer 85Hz. You can go higher than that with the right monitor and graphics card combination, but you're just eating into the graphics memory bandwidth with no real benefit.

# The Onscreen Display Controls

In the past, most monitor controls were either on the front of the bezel, or buried somewhere in the rear of the housing. Most monitors today, though, use digital *onscreen displays* or *OSD* for short to manage most of the settings. Some of these OSDs can be quite functional, but almost all of them are a little awkward because they're trying to perform multiple functions with only a handful of physical controls. You end up spending a lot of your time pressing buttons and turning wheels to achieve a desired effect.

There is a minimum set of features that any onscreen display should handle:

- Horizontal and vertical size and position.
- Pincushion control. Pincushioning occurs when the screen looks like it's bowed at the sides or top.
- Screen tilt adjustments. Trapezoid adjustments alter the slant of the two sides, whereas screen tile (sometimes called screen rotation) rotates the entire image. You want the top, bottom, and sides to be parallel with the bezel.
- Moiré controls. At the least, you want basic moiré controls. Moiré looks like regular, small, geometric patterns that can appear when the electron guns don't quite focus correctly.
- Brightness and Contrast—obviously.
- Color temperatures. More monitors these days ship with color temperature controls. This is something used more by graphics artists. They'll also tell you to set the color control to something lower (such as 5500 degrees Kelvin). Most monitors ship with this setting at the highest level (usually 9300 degrees Kelvin) because the picture appears brighter—and people buy monitors that look brighter in the stores.
- An information display that will show you the actual horizontal and vertical sync rate. The manual that came with your display will usually have a table of resolutions and horizontal sync rates.

One trend in monitor controls is software control of monitor settings. Onscreen displays are often very cumbersome to use because the monitor makers are constrained to a few buttons or controls. Some monitors have a USB or serial port that can be used by a PC to communicate with the monitor. The manufacturer supplies software that's much easier to use than the typical OSD for changing monitor settings (see Figure 5.1).

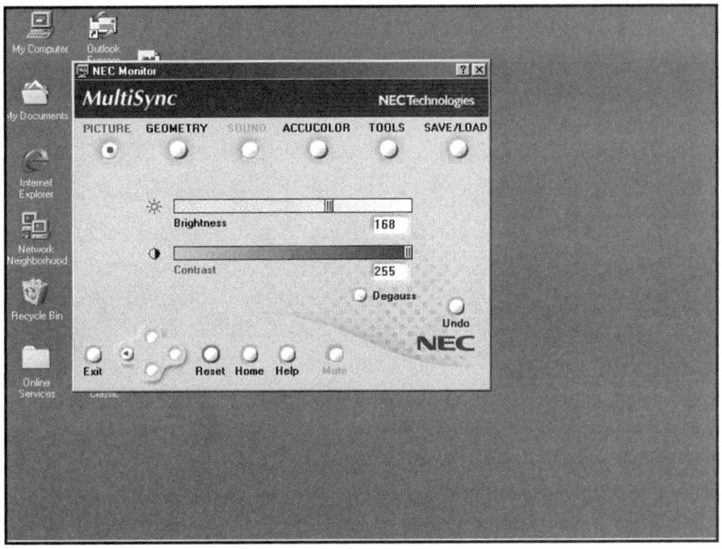


**Figure 5.1**

This is the Windows-based control for the NEC FP950 monitor. It's vastly easier to use than the front panel OSD.

# The Digital Monitor Conundrum

Most modern computer monitors have digital controls these days, coupled to onscreen displays. This is where you adjust parameters like the horizontal and vertical picture size, fix visual problems like *pincushioning* (in which the sides of the picture appear bowed) and other settings. Some very expensive monitors have some arcane settings, such as "color purity." It's easy to get lost in the morass of settings, but it's better to have greater flexibility than less. It's worth spending some time playing with your monitor's controls to get the right picture at different resolutions.

Some digital monitors simply don't work properly with some games. For example, I once had a Nokia 21" monitor that simply would not run at 512×384—yet a few games default to this resolution. So, simply because a monitor is expensive and has nifty-sounding features doesn't mean it's an ideal monitor for computer games.

On the other hand, good digital monitors can switch resolutions more quickly and with less stress on the tube than the old electromechanical relays in older monitors. If the monitor you're contemplating buying makes a huge clicking noise, and a very distorted picture is temporarily visible during a res switch, you might consider a different display.

## Other Useful Features—and Things to Avoid

There are additional monitor features you should look for, if you can afford them. With the increasing availability of hardware that uses the universal serial bus (USB), a monitor with built-in USB ports can save you the cost of a $40–$70 dedicated USB hub.

Software controls can be handy, too, and many monitors equipped with USB hubs also have software controls. A software control is simply the onscreen display control panel replicated as a piece of Windows software. Why would you want to have the same functionality in software? I've found that the software versions are usually easier to use because they'll accept mouse and keyboard input, rather than having to futz around with two or three buttons on the front of the monitor.

There are some "features" you should definitely avoid, however.

- If you're serious about games, never, never, *never* get a monitor with built-in speakers. The speakers themselves are almost always compromises when it comes to audio reproduction fidelity. On top of that, what happens if the speakers fail? You can either replace them—and hence have a useless feature permanently attached to the monitor—or replace the display. Either alternative is unappetizing.
- Another "feature" to avoid is the permanently attached monitor cable. This seems like a handy convenience feature, at first. But if you've ever munged a VGA cable when you've upgraded a graphics card or moved a display to a new system, or broken a VGA connector pin, this supposed convenience suddenly becomes very inconvenient indeed.

# Flat Panel Displays

Flat panel displays are simply a sexy, cool idea for computers. Unfortunately, they're not always perfect for gaming. But if you're tight on desk space, some flat panel displays are worth considering. We'll take a look at the different technologies as they apply to desktop displays—notebook displays are slightly different, and have inherent compromises due to the low power requirements of portability.

There are two primary types of flat panel displays: expensive, and *really* expensive. Okay, that's a bit of an oversimplification, but it comes close. Let's dispense with the *really* expensive displays first: plasma displays.

## Plasma Displays

If you've ever seen a 42" flat panel display, it seems drop-dead gorgeous at first. There are several problems, though. The most significant problem for mere mortals is the cost; some plasma displays cost in excess of $10,000. Assuming you have infinitely deep pockets (dream on), then the next problem is resolution. Many of these displays max out at around 800×600 or a little better. Most also seem to be 16:9 aspect ratio, meaning that they are wider than standard computer displays. Since most games use a more standard 4:3 aspect ratio, you get either a weirdly distorted wide image or a "sideways" letter box, with large black gaps on the left and right of the image. So, for anything except some 2D strategy games, plasma displays are more of a nuisance than a solution.

# LCD Displays

The more common type of desktop flat panel is the active matrix liquid crystal display (LCD). Liquid crystals change how much light they allow to pass through depending on how much signal current is applied. Active matrix displays mean that each native display pixel is driven by a discrete transistor. This can make for a vibrant, more responsive display. Active matrix displays also retain their color when viewed "off-axis," or from a side angle. Because desktop displays don't have to worry about battery life, they can also be brighter than your average laptop panel.

LCD monitors are not cheap, though. Expect to pay in excess of $900 for a 15" display; an 18" display can easily run over $2,500. On the other hand, a 15-inch flat panel is more akin in size to a 17" tube because of the way tube display sizes are quoted. A 15-inch flat panel is actually measured 15" diagonally, whereas most 17" tube displays are 15.8–16" diagonally.

There are two types of LCD displays: analog and digital. Analog LCD panels plug into standard VGA connections, and look to the graphic card like any analog tube monitor. Unless carefully made, though, analog panels can be noisy—that is, you'll see a lot of visual jitter around individual pixels, and color registration will look off. It's wise to avoid cheaper analog flat panels. A good analog flat panel can look quite beautiful, though.

Digital flat panels require graphics cards with specialized digital panel connectors. There are a couple of standards for connecting digital panels, though, so make sure they match up. In fact, digital flat panels are probably not a good idea currently because of the standards confusion. Most digital panels come bundled with graphics cards that will work with them—and the 3D performance of most of these cards is usually pretty limited.

## LCD Displays and Resolution

Like tube-based displays, LCD panels have a native resolution. However, there can be visual problems when running outside the native resolution that are more apparent than with standard monitor. For example, most 18" LCD panels have a native resolution of 1280×1024. If you run a game at 640×480, the graininess of the image is far more apparent. Some flat panels simply shrink the image so that the panel pixels correspond to the image pixels, though this seems more common on laptops than desktop displays. Smaller, 15" displays usually have a native resolution of 1024×768, and some of them can look quite sharp at most game resolutions.

# Using a TV as a Monitor

Many current generation graphics cards ship with the capability to connect to a television. It sounds really cool—after all, a 31" TV can cost less than a decent 21" monitor. But as with most things, you get what you pay for. The best TVs can support a resolution of up to 800×600, but the image quality at anything less than sofa distances can look terrible. The interlacing of standard TV displays just doesn't make for good image quality. So, I generally recommend that you avoid using a TV as a monitor. On the other hand, attaching the TV out connector to a VCR can be fun—just make sure the graphics card supports simultaneous TV and computer displays. That way, you can record your successful victories and gloat over your friends. Be advised that too much of this, though, may result in fewer friends....

# Chapter 6

# The Sound and the Fury

## The Evolution of PC Sound

In the early years of computer games, a number of people tried to hook me on various types of games, but I never found them particularly compelling. One day, though, I picked up an original Adlib sound card and a copy of the combat flight simulator *Their Finest Hour* by LucasArts. The game was a combination flight simulator and strategy game based on the Battle of Britain. It was one of the first games on the PC to support audio beyond the monotones of the PC speaker. (The Apple II and Amiga had better audio support at that time.)

All of a sudden, it all seemed much more real. The drone of the aircraft engines, the *whap-whap* of enemy bullets drilling your fuselage and the audible explosions as enemy aircraft blew up drew me in. As a recovering audiophile, I've always been tuned to the aural side of things. The admittedly modest realism of the audio in *Their Finest Hour* opened up a whole new dimension for me. Since then, I've used my modest bully pulpit to push the audio side of things as much as the graphics. Most recently, *Thief,* a fantasy 3D action game from Looking Glass Studios creates a virtual environment in which positional audio cues are absolutely essential to getting through the game.

The past three years have seen a revolution in PC audio. We've moved from the low-fidelity, 8-bit digital audio of the original Sound Blaster to the multistream, 3D positional audio prevalent in today's PCI sound cards. However, audio is nearly as confusing as 3D graphics, so let's take some time to explore the aural side of computer games.

# Human Hearing

The human ear is a marvel of bioengineering. The ear, coupled with the auditory part of the human brain, evolved over the millennia so that we can accurately determine the directionality and movement of a sound source. Audio engineers have studied the ear for decades. In fact, the first patent for stereo was filed in December of 1931 by the Central Research Lab of EMI records. CRL, as it was known, eventually evolved into what is now Sensaura, one of several companies pushing audio technology forward.

One of the big advances in game audio in the last several years has been positional audio—true "3D" audio. The term "3D audio" has been terribly misused over the years. Everything from simple, stage-widening technologies like spatializer, to sophisticated technologies like Dolby Digital, have laid claim to "3D Audio." So, I generally prefer the term positional audio. Positional audio fools your ear into thinking a sound comes from a particular direction.

During the '60s and '70s, NASA conducted fundamental research into how the human ear senses the directionality of sound. This area of study is called psychoacoustics. The research revolved around how the sound waves interacted with the pinna, the actual physical shape of the ear. Researchers were able to build mathematical models of how the sound waves would wash over the human head and impinge slightly differently over the left ear versus the right ear. These models are called *head-related transfer functions (HRTFs)*, and are the basis for much of positional audio today. As it turns out, we can "see" more with our ears than we can with our eyes.

Also important is how the ear distinguishes between low and high frequencies. Your ears can tell, with pretty good accuracy, the direction of a high-pitched sound, such as a flute playing. But deep bass is different—it's often difficult to pin down the direction of sound that's under 250Hz. That lack of directionality of low frequencies is how a three speaker setup can work. The speaker rig only needs a single bass unit, due to the lack of positional presence of low frequency sound. In fact, sophisticated Dolby Digital setups with front, rear, and center channel speakers can sound quite striking, even though they may only have a single subwoofer handling bass chores.

Before we go into details on positional audio, however, let's tackle some more basic concepts.

# Digital Audio

When the first audio CD players arrived in the early 1980s, it was the first mass-market exposure to truly digital sound. After some early teething problems, mostly with mastering hardware, CD audio can now sound like the best analog sound sources. But rendering audio from a standard CD player is relatively straightforward because a CD player is dedicated to that one function.

The PC is a different beast. The electronic environment inside a modern high-speed PC is awash with noise, and creating high fidelity audio is a real challenge. The chip and sound card makers have been up to the task, though, and we now have some remarkably high fidelity sound emanating from the PC.

But what *is* digital audio?

A sound wave is an analog signal, consisting of rapid variations in air pressure as the sound travels through the air. When a microphone captures sound, it can be stored as analog data—waveforms—on devices like tape recorders. However, it can also be *sampled* digitally and stored as sequences of 1's and 0's on a digital storage device like a hard drive or CD-ROM. CD-quality sound is sampled 44,100 times each second for each stereo channel, at a resolution of 16 bits. The 16-bit resolution means that each sound sample can have 65,535 different levels. But CD audio is no longer the epitome of audio quality. Recently, a standard for DVD audio has solidified, with resolutions of 24-bits and a sampling rate of 96KHz. (There's also DAT—digital audio tape—that samples audio at 48KHz, but still at 16-bit resolution.)

Game sound, though, isn't quite so robust. Sound can take up a lot of space. For example, CD stereo takes up roughly 176KB of disk space per second. It's an unfortunate truth that sound is considered secondary in many games, so the audio budget is given short shrift, both in terms of the performance budget and the storage space allocated for it. Because CD-ROMs store "only" 650MB of data, 176KB for one second of sound is often deemed excessive.

So, sound designers take shortcuts. They drop the resolution to 8 bits, or the sampling rate to 22Khz, or both. Sometimes, the audio is shipped as monophonic, rather than stereophonic. Of course, with the greater emphasis on positional sound these days, the sound guys have gotten a little more respect, but only a little.

# MIDI

MIDI stands for Musical Instrument Device Interface. MIDI is a way of representing musical data in a kind of shorthand that's then decoded in a standard way. In a sense, it's a programming language, but mostly a data-driven one. Think of it as a digital "piano roll." It contains no actual sounds; it's just a list of instructions of which sounds/notes are to play when. MIDI data is sent to a MIDI device, which then decodes the MIDI stream and attempts to play back the musical representation. It's mostly used for music in games, and not as often as in the past.

In the early days of gaming, MIDI was a confusing topic for both game developers and game players. Different hardware companies pushed competing MIDI standards, and if a composition was created on one piece of hardware, it could sound totally different when played back on another synthesizer. So, the synthesizer manufacturers got together and developed General MIDI (GM). General MIDI defines 128 standard instruments, so that music created for General MIDI will sound correct on all synthesizers and sound cards.

The early Adlib and Sound Blaster sound cards had FM synthesizer chips on them. FM synthesis can sound good with some instruments, but it generally sounds pretty artificial. Later, sound card makers began using *wavetable* synthesis. A wavetable is nothing but a bunch of carefully recorded digital samples of real musical instruments or real sounds captured and stored on read-only memory (ROM) on the sound card. More recently, wavetable data is stored in system memory on current PCI sound cards. Wavetable MIDI generally sounds much better than FM, but a lot depends on the quality and resolution of the captured samples.

Because of all the variations, most game music is now recorded and played back digitally. But MIDI has recently gotten a shot in the arm because of two initiatives by Microsoft. The first is the incorporation of a standard, high-quality software wavetable synthesizer in Windows 98. This wavetable is licensed from Roland, a major synth manufacturer. Game developers can now be assured of a good-quality MIDI sound, although if the software wavetable is used, it can have an impact on overall performance because the CPU is rendering the MIDI music.

Microsoft has also developed the DirectMusic API, which is a dynamic music scoring technology. The composer still creates the basic themes, but DirectMusic varies the tempo and keys according to the action in the game. It's tough to do music that responds interactively to the game with digitally recorded music. It remains to be seen whether DirectMusic and DirectSound's standard software wavetable synth will make MIDI acceptable to game developers again, but there is hope.

If you're a dabbling musician, you should consider a sound card with a better wavetable synthesizer, like E-Mu's APS, or Guillemot's ISIS.

# Digital Audio Hardware

A typical sound card consists of a circuit board that plugs into either an ISA or PCI slot. There are connectors on the back: outputs for speakers and inputs for microphone and other audio devices. There's usually an IBM-compatible gameport that does double duty as a connector for MIDI breakout cables and game controllers.

There are usually connectors on the circuit board itself. One is reserved for CD audio, and connects to your CD-ROM or DVD drive. There may be additional connectors for voice modems, wavetable daughtercards and digital I/O boards (see Figure 6.1).

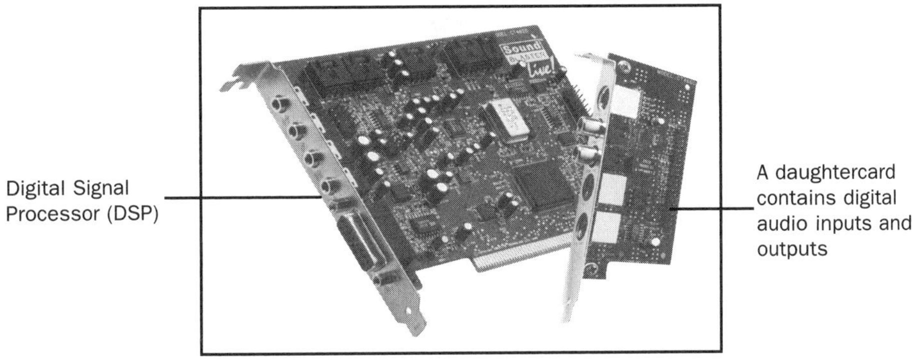


**Figure 6.1**
The Sound Blaster Live full version. Note the daughtercard, which contains digital audio inputs and outputs. Photo used by permission of Creative Labs, Inc.

The heart and brain of the audio card is usually a single chip called a DSP (digital signal processor). There is occasionally a separate chip for MIDI, but most modern PCI cards now use a single chip, with some minor supporting chips. It's the DSP chip that handles the task of converting digital audio to analog output, as well as generating all the various audio effects. These can range from simple reverb effects to more complex 3D audio imaging.

A typical sound card now supports 44.1KHz, 16-bit audio; some support 48KHz sound and all support the lesser resolutions needed for game sound. Most current generation cards also have two speaker outputs; the second output is typically used for rear channel speakers for 3D sound.

The signal-to-noise ratio has steadily gotten better over the years; the better cards have S/N ratios rivaling home stereo gear. And all of this aural goodness usually costs $100 or less. Some higher-end cards that support professional audio features may cost more—a lot more. For example, the Maxigamer Isis from French manufacturer Guillemot costs nearly $400, but ships with a breakout box that has 8 inputs and 4 outputs, as well as a near-studio quality digital mixer.

Although there are still some ISA sound cards available, most newer cards are now PCI cards. Most PCI sound cards have a very low parts count and no onboard memory. These days, MIDI wavetable data is actually stored in system memory. Don't sell these low-cost boards short, however. The onboard DSP is capable of 600–800 million instructions per second of computational horsepower—and it's needed, as audio can get quite complex.

One other key technology with most game audio is audio compression. All current generation sound cards, and many older ones, support sound compression in various formats. The latest standard for audio compression is AC97, as defined by Microsoft and Intel. The actual act of compressing or decompressing audio is handled by the *codec*, which is an abbreviation for *compressor/decompressor*. The codec may be a separate chip on the card, or built into the main audio chip.

Now that we've explored the basics of a sound card, let's cover 3D positional audio.

# 3D Positional Audio: The Basics

Unlike 3D graphics, which is all simulated on the 2D surface of your computer monitor, properly designed and rendered 3D audio can immerse you in a sound field that makes you really feel like things are happening around you. It's startling, and really adds to the effectiveness of a good game.

### Note

The 3D positional audio arena is a little confusing partly because it's still in its infancy. As DirectSound3D improves, and as game developers become more comfortable with designing in high quality, directional audio, we can expect future games to immerse us in a rich sound field. Now, if only 3D graphics would also surround us...the Holodeck, anyone?

Earlier, I covered the idea of HRTFs (head related transfer functions) as mathematical models for the way sound enters the human ear. But positional audio isn't as simple as plugging a bunch of math equations onto a hardware chip and letting it run. There's a lot for the sound designer in a game to worry about. It's all well and good to talk about 3D sound, but how accurate do you want the positional audio to be? How many audio streams does the game developer want to support? How many different effects will be generated? Often, the 3D environment has to be calculated, including all the obstacles between your virtual location and the sound's location.

Also, there's the issue of two speakers versus four speakers versus headphones. Some 3D audio technologies do a fair job of creating the illusion of directionality with two speakers. But they aren't perfect. For one thing, you have to be sitting in a "sweet spot," with the speakers carefully placed. Even then, there are limitations. For example, you get very few vertical sound cues with two speakers. Secondly, there's often a "dead zone" for most people, although it's somewhat dependent on the shape of your head (see Figure 6.2). The last variable is the toughest to plan for: Humans localize sound with varying abilities.

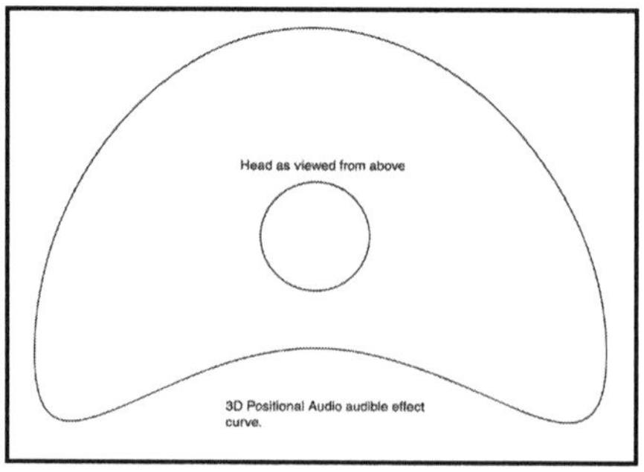


**Figure 6.2**
With two speakers, even the best positional audio technologies have limitations.

This means that if the game designer wanted to hear something that was directly behind you, you might actually hear it in front or off to one side.

If you've thought about this, you may spot a potential problem. What happens when sounds that come out of the left speaker, intended for the left ear, strike the right ear? Wouldn't that result in something truly awful? Yes, it would, but the audio engineers realized the problem and solved it through *crosstalk cancellation*. Although mathematically complex, all crosstalk cancellation does is cancel out right ear sounds from the sound stream intended for the left ear and vice versa.

If we expand to a four speaker setup, the rear speakers can fill in the dead zone, but there are still relatively poor vertical sound cues. Four speakers can give us some startling audio panning and Doppler effects, which occur when a sound source is moving rapidly towards you; you can hear the pitch of the sound change as the object gets closer. Think of when you hear a train coming, and as it passed by you, the pitch of the sound it's making drops.

With technologies like Aureal's A3D, the best positional audio actually comes from using a good set of headphones. It's probably worth investing in a decent set of headphones not only to get superior sound, but to save a little grief with roommates or neighbors. There's nothing more unsettling than a firefight going on in the room next door—if you're not a gamer.

# 3D Audio Technologies

Now that we can see some of the issues with positional audio in general, let's touch on the specifics of several competing technologies.

## DirectSound3D

When DirectSound3D first shipped as a part of DirectX 3.0, it was essentially a software-only solution because Microsoft actively tried to discourage alternative 3D APIs from using DS3D. That stance softened with DirectX 5, and now alternative APIs can work on top of DirectSound3D.

For more on DirectSound3D, see page 169.

With DirectX 7.0, DirectSound3D has gotten even better. There's now full support for HRTF functions through the use of vMax technology licensed from Harmon-Kardon. There's no hardware that accelerates vMax today, but it's a fallback for older sound cards that don't have HRTF built-in. However, if vMax kicks in, it will eat some CPU cycles.

More interestingly, other hardware-accelerated positional audio technologies like Sensaura and EAX can layer on top of DirectSound3D easily.

# Aureal A3D

Aureal Semiconductor rose from the ashes of former sound card maker Media Vision, which crashed in spectacular fashion a few years ago. The chip part of Media Vision reconstituted itself and focused only on audio semiconductors for the first few years of its existence. A3D, which is based on the original HRTF work done by NASA, burst onto the scene when Aureal shipped the 8820 (Vortex 1) sound chip in 1997. Since then, both Aureal's hardware and software have evolved. In late 1998, Aureal shipped the 8830 (Vortex 2) chip, which supports the company's A3D 2.0 audio API. A3D 1.0 was a fairly simple API that used HRTF to simulate straightforward audio directionality, with some reflection capability.

A3D 2.0 is a different animal entirely. The new API mimics, to some extent, 3D graphics APIs. First, Aureal moved to higher resolution HRTFs, which can be rendered at up to 48KHz. Up to 64 reflection sources are supported as well.

More significant is the incorporation of *wavetracing*. Wavetracing takes into account the actual 3D environment of the game. The 3D environment can get quite complex. Imagine you're standing in a room with irregular walls. There might be doorways or openings. When a sound source generates sound waves, those waves can both travel through walls (if they aren't too dense) and reflect off of walls and through the doorway. A3D 2.0 takes into account the actual path of the waves, and also calculates the effect of the sound traveling through solid objects.

All this sounds really cool, but A3D does have some limitations. For one thing, as of this writing, A3D only supports HRTFs through the front speakers. The rear speakers in a four-speaker setup are used for panning and filling in the sound field. Also, the A3D 2.0 API has strayed even further from DirectSound3D, although it can still work with it if need be. When falling back to straight DirectSound3D (not all games support A3D, after all), the Vortex 2 chip itself only supports 16 DirectSound3D streams.

A3D has gotten a lot of mindshare from developers, in much the same way that 3dfx did with it's Glide API for 3D graphics. However, with Creative's EAX becoming a part of DirectX on one side, and Sensaura's solid HRTFs that work on top of DirectSound3D without the need for a proprietary API, Aureal may now have an uphill battle. For now, though, it has good mindshare, the technology works well, and it does a credible job with DirectSound and DirectSound3D as well as its own API. Aureal has announced that it will support EAX in its hardware. Doing so will require extensive driver modification, but the company expects to have this in place soon.

# Creative Labs EAX

When Creative Labs announced EAX (which stands for *environmental audio extensions*), people thought Creative was trying to create yet another API. In fact, EAX, as the name implies, is an extension to DirectSound3D. EAX 1.0 mostly used panning and reverb to generate simple 3D effects, but it has evolved over time to incorporate HRTF algorithms. Using the additional new features does require additional API work on the part of game developers, but because Microsoft agreed to adopt EAX as an integral part of DirectSound, that effort may be mitigated somewhat.

Unlike A3D, EAX makes no pretension about working with two speakers. The best EAX effects are realized through four speakers. Creative is encouraging the push to four speakers by selling a line of speakers that have four satellites at a relatively low cost. Creative Labs has research that shows that two-speaker HRTF only works with about half the population's ears. The other half turn their heads when hearing directional sounds, and that tends to severely diminish the HRTF effect.

Although EAX effects may not go to the extent that A3D does in an attempt to create a realistic sound field, the fact is that the effects can sound pretty good through four speakers. With the inclusion of EAX in DirectX 8.0 next year, everyone will be able to hear it for themselves. Today, however, hardware support for EAX only exists in Creative's Sound Blaster Live line of sound cards, including the Sound Blaster Live, SB Live Value Edition, and SB 512.

## Sensaura and Sensaura Multidrive

Sensaura is a spin-off of U.K. recording company EMI. Formerly EMI's Central Research Lab, Sensaura is doing more original audio research than most other companies. The company uses carefully crafted digital models of the human ear and head to tune its HRTF algorithms. Unlike either EAX or A3D, Sensaura's technology simply works with DirectSound3D. Developers don't have to write to anything other than DirectSound3D to take advantage of Sensaura. Interestingly, Sensaura has "virtualized" EAX. In other words, some EAX effects can be realized through two speakers. This is typically done through the sound card driver, however, not through hardware acceleration.

Sensaura Multidrive is a four-speaker extension to Sensaura that makes full use of HRTF algorithms through all four speakers. The effect can be quite good if you're willing to invest in a four-speaker setup. Currently, ESS and Yamaha use Sensaura with their audio chips.

# Choosing a Sound Card

In many ways, making the right choice in sound cards is much like choosing a 3D graphics accelerator a few years ago. There are several competing, though similar, technologies. Underlying it all is Microsoft's DirectSound3D. Some of the difficulty will be removed when key parts of Creative Labs EAX moves into DirectSound, but that won't happen until late 2000.

In fact, the choices aren't that difficult because most aftermarket, brand name, retail sound cards are pretty good at 3D audio. If a game doesn't use the proprietary API that's native to your sound card, there's always DirectSound3D, which is getting better. I've used all of the competing sound card brands, and all work pretty well—and all have various problems, too. If you want the current darling of many gamers, get a card that uses Aureal's

Vortex 2 chip. On the other hand, Creative Labs has a very broad reach and very wide distribution, so depending on your location, it may be easier to find a Sound Blaster Live! card.

Both the Aureal Vortex2–based cards and Sound Blaster Live! Series sound very similar with four speaker audio setups. The Sound Blaster Live is a little less CPU-intensive, but Aureal has recently released the "B" revision of the Vortex 2 that closes the gap in performance up to 16 streams of 3D audio. If all you have is two front speakers, the Vortex2 boards have better positional audio through a single pair of speakers.

One interesting new contender in 3D audio chips is ESS' new Canyon3D chip. One of the problems with current sound cards is that if you want four-speaker 3D audio for games, you can't have 5.1 Dolby Prologic or Dolby Digital sound for DVD movies. The Canyon3D ship enables both types of audio to be played, with a little extra cabling effort. On top of that, because it uses Sensaura's Multidrive technology, all DirectSound3D games will benefit from better positional audio.

Table 6.1 provides specifications on some popular PCI Audio chips that will assist you in making a purchasing decision.

**Table 6.1—An overview of key audio chip features**

| *PCI Audio Chip* | *DirectSound Acceleration?* | *3D Audio Acceleration?* | *Four Speaker Support?* |
|---|---|---|---|
| Sound Blaster 64 | No | No | No |
| Sound Blaster 128 | No | No, EAX in software | No |
| Sound Blaster Live, 512 (EMU 10K1) | Yes, 32 streams | Yes, 32 streams, EAX, DS3D | |
| ESS Maestro 2 | Yes, 16 streams | Partial, Sensaura, DS3D | Yes |
| ESS Canyon 3D | Yes, 16 streams | Yes, Sensaura, Sensaura Multidrive, EAX, A3D 1.0, DS3D 16 streams | Yes |
| Aureal 8820 (Vortex 1) | Yes, 16 streams | Yes, 8 streams, A3D 1.0, DS3D | No |
| Aureal 8830 (Vortex 2) | Yes, 96 streams | Yes, 16 streams, Yes A3D 2.0, DS3D | |
| Aureal 8810 | Yes, 16 streams | Yes, 8 streams, A3D 1.0, DS3D | No |
| Yamaha XG | Yes, 32 streams | Partial, Sensaura DS3D | Yes |
| USB (digital) speakers | No | No | No |

# Don't Forget the Speakers

I've said it before, and I'll say it again: Hooking up cheap, $10 speakers to a good sound card is like attaching a garden hose to a fire hydrant. All that money you spent on a good sound card is wasted on cheap speakers.

Like a lot of other technology, speakers have advanced over time, and good speakers have come down in price. Companies like Yamaha, Boston Acoustics, and Creative Labs have shipped speakers in the sub-$100 range that sound very good.

A speaker consists of one or more devices that can vibrate to the response of an electrical signal, generating sound waves. Speakers come in a variety of shapes, including cones, flat panels, and dome shapes. There are three general types: woofers for low frequencies (mid-bass and bass); midrange speakers, which handle the widest variety of audio frequencies; and tweeters, which are designed to reproduce high frequency sound.

## Speaker Types

There are several types of speakers on the market: two piece, three piece, quad (five pieces, really), and 6.1.

A two-piece speaker is what most people think of when talking about speakers. Computer speakers usually take the form of two smallish units capable of sitting on a desktop. The problem with small pairs of speakers is that the drivers can't move enough air to generate any significant bass volume. There are a couple of exceptions, but they're usually large—usually too large for most desktops—and expensive.

Three-piece speakers consist of two satellite speakers that sit on your desk, plus a powered bass unit that can be placed in a variety of locations. The powered bass unit is usually called a "subwoofer," but that's a misnomer. (A subwoofer augments existing woofers; the powered bass unit in three-piece speaker rigs *is* the woofer.) In this kind of setup, the desktop satellites can be very compact because they don't reproduce bass at all.

Quad units, a.k.a. four-speaker setups, are also misnamed—they're usually *five* pieces. There are four satellites and a powered bass unit. They are designed specifically to reproduce 3D audio for computer games. Two satellites are for the front and two for the rear. The front and rear pairs actually plug into separate connectors on the sound card.

Dolby Prologic and Dolby digital-capable speakers also have a center channel speaker, known as a 6.1 setup. There are also 7.1 speaker setups, but these are mostly for home theater (there's a true powered subwoofer, a bass unit, four satellites, and a center channel speaker). Speakers designed to reproduce Dolby-encoded audio aren't really good gaming speakers because they usually plug into a single output on the sound card. Four-speaker rigs designed for positional audio plug into two-speaker outputs.

### Caution

There are now "USB digital audio speakers" on the market that can operate without a sound card. I *strongly* recommend that you don't pitch your sound card if you get one of these speaker setups. In fact, don't use the USB bus for audio at all. This is because USB speakers use the host CPU to handle the lion's share of the audio processing. This translates directly into poorer game performance.

Some of these speakers sound pretty good, and you can plug them into your sound card. Just remember that you really can't get something for nothing.

## Buying Speakers

Companies have noticed that hard-core gamers are willing to spend a little more for really good audio. Although a pair of sub-$100 speakers today do sound decent, after hearing a set of Eminent Technologies LFT-11s, you may dig deep into your wallet for the $500 it will cost you.

Even good speakers have gotten more compact over time because of the use of powered bass units ("subwoofers"), which allow satellite speakers to be quite compact, yet deliver greater bass fidelity. On the other hand, because of the burgeoning interest in game audio, there are some mediocre speakers out there, masquerading as good speakers.

I shop for speakers for computers the same way I shop for speakers for my home theater rig. I snag several music CDs, including some with good bass content, and head to the local stores. I also bring a portable CD player along because some shops have no provision for playing customer's content. I've found that most are willing, though, to open the packaging for you and give it a listen.

Of course, even the best computer speakers can't rival good home audio speakers. If you're willing to invest in an amplifier (or two, if you want high-fidelity rear speakers for 3D audio), then nothing beats a decent set of speakers from your local stereo shop. But it will cost you more in space and money, so that's not an option for everyone.

Also, invest in a decent set of headphones—and I don't mean $5 headphones for portable tape players. Get a decent set of phones, which can range from $30–$300 from Sennheiser, Koss, Grado, or other high-quality headphone makers. For you Internet gamers, Koss makes a superb headphone that has a boom microphone attached.

# Chapter 7

# Space to Play

## Making Space for Your Toys

A full install of the 5-CD *Baldur's Gate*, Interplay's fantasy role-playing game, takes up *2.2 gigabytes*. A full install of *Jagged Alliance 2* takes up over 800MB. Even average games these days take up several hundred megabytes per game.

Then there's save game files. Not long ago, I discovered that *Might and Magic VII* created save game files that were almost 512KB each. LucasArts *Grim Fandago* adventure game creates 800+ KB save game files.

This is on top of Windows. My Windows folder, which includes all the temporary Internet files, fonts, drivers, and other mysteries weighs in at 1.1 gigabytes. Let's not even discuss Microsoft Office.

There's also the performance issue. A big game, like *Falcon 4.0*, can take a long time to load. More importantly, if a game has to bring in audio or texture data from the hard drive, a slow drive can cause annoying pauses in the action.

Clearly, today's games eat up disc space. It wasn't all that long ago when game companies were proclaiming that all games would run off CD. But CD drives are simply too slow. The good news is that disc drivers are getting bigger, faster—and cheaper. Recent advances have dropped the cost per megabyte down to under a penny in some cases.

# The Magnetic Domain

The world of hard drives is perhaps the most mechanical and arcane inside your PC. It's a world of spinning platters, magnetic domains, and drive heads floating microns above polished surfaces. It sometimes seems like very much a black art. The good news is that hard drives are getting physically more compact, store more data, and cost less. We'll touch on the basics of magnetic storage media, and then explore the differences between SCSI and IDE. We'll close with some hints about maximizing performance.

Layered on the highly polished surface of a hard drive is a coating of ultrafine magnetic particles. When the drive head passes over the platter, data is stored by altering the orientation of the magnetic particles (if you remember your high school or college physics courses, you know I'm talking about electromagnetism). When a particle is oriented one direction, the bit is on (set to a value of 1). When oriented the other direction, a particular magnetic particle represents a value of 0.

Flying over these billions of tiny bits are the flying heads. These heads use aerodynamic techniques to "fly" just above the platter, much the way the airflow over an aircraft wing creates lift. In reality, it's the platters that are moving (spinning), and the heads float above the rapidly spinning discs. Because today's drives can rotate 5,400 revolutions per minute or more, the surface of the disc is moving at a high rate of speed under the head. Hard drives using flying heads used to be called "Winchester drives," after the first drive of this type, but you hardly see that terminology any more.

The heads themselves also move laterally across the platters. Because hard drives are random access devices, the heads move very rapidly for short distances when locating the correct data track.

There have been numerous predictions over the years of the obsolescence of Winchester-style magnetic hard drives. The pundits have suggested several times that the practical limits of bit density on the drive platters have been reached, and that new methods for storage, such as optical disks, were the wave of the future. So far, they've been proven wrong every time. Recently, Seagate announced a record 23.8 *billion* bits per square inch had been achieved in the lab, which equates to 32 gigabytes on a single, 3.5-inch platter. Even today, there are drives shipping that pack 6.8GB on a single platter. In fact, the capacity of hard drives has exceeded the needs of most consumers, though demanding applications like digital video and MP3 audio still need huge drive capacities.

As we saw in the intro, modern games can also take up prodigious amounts of disc space. Although CD speeds have steadily increased, the storage requirements for games have increased dramatically. 3D games now have much larger texture sets, sophisticated 3D sound requires more storage needed for audio files, and support for high resolution modes means more space is needed. Even very fast CD drives just can't keep up with the data rates needed by 3D games.

# Hard Disc Structure

The modern hard drive consists of a sealed container with a spindle that's spun by a motor. Drive motors have gotten better over the years, and current drive motors can spin for years without a glitch. Current generation hard drives spin at rates ranging from 4,000RPM for the slowest drives to as fast as 10,000RPM for high-end, server drives. There's even a drive that spins at 12,000RPM, though it's limited in other ways.

Mounted on the spindle are anywhere from one to 10 platters (but usually four or less). Above and below each platter is the head, floating above the disc surface. Multiple read/write heads are mounted in a single assembly so they stay aligned and minimize moving parts. When the drive is powered down, the head assembly usually locks to one side to minimize the potential for touching the surface of the disc (this is known as *head parking*).

There's a lot of technology that goes into that head assembly. Current hard drives use *magnetoresistive* head technology (MR). Older head technology would pass over the surface and detect the magnetic domains inductively, but MR heads use a more active method. Current passes through the head constantly, and changes slightly as the head passes over the magnetic domains. MR heads (and their newer cousins, giant MR heads) can read much more closely packed bit densities than the older inductive heads. The heads float over the disc surface at a height of 3 microns (3 millionths of a meter) or less.

This brings us to the coating on the discs themselves. This is the domain of the materials scientist, who is constantly trying to develop coatings that pack more bits per square inch. The tighter the bit density, the faster the hard drive will be, all other things equal. That's because the greater the density, the more bits pass under the drive heads per second. The platters themselves are usually made of some rigid material that doesn't expand when it heats up—and fast hard drives can get pretty warm. Platter materials can vary from glass-ceramic composites to metallic alloys.

# Hard Disk Logical Structure

Inside the hard drive, the data is laid out in such a way that the onboard microcontroller chip that's part of the drive electronics can quickly find a particular piece of data. In truth, the hard drive knows nothing about "data." But it does understand locations and geometry.

Making it all work are the drive electronics, which handle the translation of data from the magnetic media to the electrical form needed for the computer. There's usually a fixed amount of cache on a hard drive to help buffer data transfers; cache amounts can range from 128KB to a whopping 4MB. This buffer is a two-way street. The PC can keep pulling data out of the cache while the drive heads are hunting for data. When data comes into the drive for storage, the buffer holds it temporarily while the drive heads finish their current operations.

The minimum unit of drive storage is the *sector*. Each sector contains 512 bytes of data (plus a little more for error correction information). That's pretty simple, but it gets a little more complex at this point.

Every hard drive is arranged as a series of discrete *tracks*. These are akin to the tracks on an audio CD, though much narrower. In fact, a typical hard drive has many thousands of tracks per inch. Each track contains a certain number of sectors per track—but that number of sectors isn't necessarily the same across all tracks.

All hard drives are *constant angular velocity* (CAV) devices, which means that they spin at a steady number of revolutions per minute. If you've ever watched a tire on a car spin, you may have noticed that the outside of the tire moves at a much faster *linear speed* than the innermost part of the tire because any point on the outside of the tire has to travel a greater distance to make it around one revolution.

Hard drive makers are very aware of this phenomenon, and tend to pack more sectors in a track on the *outside* of the platter than on the innermost track. Not every track has a different number of sectors; rather, tracks are grouped into *zones*, and every track in that zone may have the same number of sectors. This is called *zone bit recording*. There are two reasons to pack more sectors in the outer tracks: size and performance. A track on the outside of the disc is obviously longer than the ones on the inside of the platter, and so can physically hold more sectors. Also, the outer part of the drive moves at a faster *linear* velocity than the inner track. That is, more disc surface passes under the head in a given second when the head is on the outside of the drive than on the inside. Packing more sectors into a part of the drive that moves faster under the heads means that data gets moved much more quickly, and increases general performance. Windows 98 is also aware of this idea of zone bit recording, and tends to organize the most commonly used files so they reside on the outer tracks of a hard drive.

Most hard drives have more than one platter (see Figure 7.1). Because the drive heads are actually built into a single assembly, there's also a vertical organization. A particular track on a particular platter is logically organized with any track on a platter below or above it. Each set of vertically organized tracks across all platters is called a *cylinder*.

# The PC and the Hard Drive

Getting all that data from the hard drive to the computer isn't trivial, either. It wasn't that long ago when you had to understand about cylinders and heads, because you had to manually enter those parameters into the BIOS setup program (known as *Manual Drive Typing*). Now, however, smarter hard drives and better BIOSes mean that drive parameters are automatically set up (this is known as *Automatic Drive Typing*). Although some BIOS setup programs still allow you to manually enter hard drive parameters, many no longer allow manual setup.

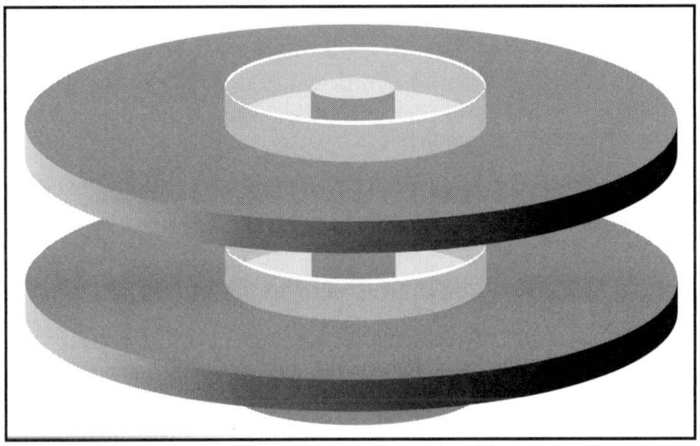

**Figure 7.1**
Most drives have at least three platters, but for simplicity, the drive pictured here shows two.

Still, there are some subtleties to be aware of. Really huge hard drives, with capacities in excess of 8 gigabytes, only arrived on the scene a couple of years ago. Some BIOSes simply don't understand drive sizes of greater than 8.4GB. To support larger drives, you either need to upgrade the PC's BIOS or use a disk manager program that's supplied by the drive maker.

Of the two choices, upgrading the BIOS is the preferable one. Upgrading a BIOS usually means downloading both the new BIOS and a program to "flash" it into your BIOS chip. Most BIOSes are stored on flash memory chips these days, and the data on-board can be altered.

The main BIOS companies are Award, Phoenix, and AMI. The AMI BIOS used to be quite popular, but these days, you only find it on a few motherboards. Phoenix is used on Intel motherboards. Because so many systems use Intel boards, the Phoenix BIOS has a huge presence. Award BIOSes are used in the majority of motherboards made in Taiwan by companies like Asus, Abit, Gigabyte, and others.

To properly upgrade the flash BIOS on a PC, you have to make sure the BIOS file and the BIOS upload program are in the same folder. You boot to the DOS prompt and run the flash memory utility. These flash memory upload utilities vary in complexity. With some, you just append the name of the BIOS file in the command line. Others are menu-driven. The best of them offer a way to back up the existing BIOS, if you should need to return to an older revision.

Just be *very* careful that there's no power interruption during the flash process (which takes only a couple of minutes), or you may have an unusable computer. So, a simple rule of thumb is, don't go upgrading your BIOS during a thunderstorm. The motherboard companies will replace the flash chip, but it does cost a few dollars, and you have to wait for the chip to arrive before you have a usable system.

Disk manager programs reside in the boot sector of the hard drive, and fools the PC hardware into thinking that the drive has an understandable configuration. Then, a driver is loaded when the PC boots up so that Windows knows what's really there. It's a pain to reconfigure a hard drive that has a disk manager installed, so avoid it if you can.

## When a Megabyte Is Not a Megabyte

This brings us to an interesting problem. Let's say you've just gotten that spanking new 9.1GB hard drive. You set it up, format it, and when you're done, Windows reports it as an 8.6GB drive. What gives?

As it turns out, drive manufacturers believe that a megabyte is one million bytes (10 to the sixth power). PCs and operating systems believe that one megabyte is 1024×1024 bytes, or 1,048,576 bytes. It's this mismatch that accounts for the difference between the manufacturer's specified capacity and the one you see after the drive is formatted. It's a historical quirk, not an attempt on drive makers to cheat you out of a few megabytes of storage space.

## Hard Drives and Windows

Now, vlet's cover how Windows and hard drives interact.

In the bad old days of DOS, there was the *FAT (file allocation table)*. The FAT was essentially a giant index of locations on the hard drive, organized by *clusters*. By the time Windows 95 rolled around, the FAT address length was 16 bits. This was a problem because the 16-bit FAT meant that the largest hard drive size could be 2GB. I don't know about you, but the idea of formatting a 22GB hard drive into 11 partitions, and trying to keep track of 11 drive letters, seems daunting. Besides, you couldn't do a full install of *Baldur's Gate* on a FAT16 volume.

There's another problem: cluster size. To get to 2GB, the cluster size has to expand to 32KB. That way, the 16-bit FAT, which has 65,535 entries, times the 32KB cluster size, can create a 2GB volume. This means that the *smallest* file on the volume is 32KB. Because many game files can be smaller than 32KB, that's a lot of wasted space.

Microsoft enhanced the FAT by making the address size longer—32 bits, and named it, of all things, FAT32. You could, if you wanted, have a volume as large as 2000 *gigabytes* (given a 32KB cluster size), but there's no single drive that large. Accesses would probably be pretty slow. Table 7.1 gives a list of drive sizes versus cluster sizes with FAT32.

**Table 7.1—FAT32 partition sizes versus cluster sizes**

| *Partition Size* | *Cluster Size* |
|---|---|
| 16MB–256MB | 4KB |
| 256MB–8GB | 8KB |
| 8GB–60GB | 16KB |
| 60GB–2000GB | 32KB |

As you can see, FAT32 is much more efficient—even a single, 60GB partition will only have cluster sizes of 16KB. So, if you've upgraded to Windows 98, it may behoove you to convert your drives to FAT32 just to avoid wasting space—and then you can also have larger drive partitions.

There are two major ways that hard drives interface with your PC: IDE and SCSI. The trade-offs between the two used to be performance versus price. That's still true, to a degree, but IDE drives have moved up the performance curve, and the gap isn't as great as it used to be. We'll touch on the differences in a bit.

# IDE

IDE stands for *integrated drive electronics*, and was pioneered by Compaq and Conner Peripherals (now a part of Seagate) in the early 1990s. Until that time, attaching a hard drive to a PC meant inserting an expansion card into your system. Not only that, but there were a number of competing interface standards: MFM, RLL, SCSI, and more. Most of the intelligence resided on the controller board. IDE turned that idea on its head, and most of the smarts moved to the hard drive electronics. The IDE interface, which acted mostly as a data conduit, could be either a very low-cost expansion board, or made a part of the motherboard itself with very little cost. In fact, all modern motherboards ship with IDE connectors on board.

The original IDE had some limitations. First, it only supported a maximum of two devices. Secondly, due to limitations in the specification, the largest hard drive could only be 528MB. When it first came out, the idea of 1GB of total disk storage seemed remarkable. Now, it seems almost miniscule.

## Enhanced IDE (EIDE)

IDE's limitations were soon realized, and work began on enhancing the spec. The new version was called, quite naturally, enhanced IDE or EIDE for short. Enhanced IDE added the potential for a second connector (although the second connector—secondary controller—requires its own IRQ), and can support up to four total devices. The maximum capacity increased to roughly 8GB. EIDE interfaces became ubiquitous on motherboards, and all the competing drive interface technologies, with the exception of SCSI, fell by the wayside.

EIDE isn't a monolithic standard; there are several flavors of EIDE, all with slightly different performance parameters. The fastest is mode 2 DMA, which improves EIDE drive performance in two ways. First, it cranks up the burst transfer rate to EIDE's theoretical maximum of 16.6 megabytes per second. Secondly, it uses direct memory access (DMA) to offload the CPU. Earlier EIDE drives used variations on PIO (programmed I/O) to transfer data. PIO is both slower and requires more CPU intervention.

# UltraDMA/UltraATA

As EIDE became more entrenched, SCSI became the purview of servers or those users desiring maximum hard drive performance. However, users were still demanding more performance out of the IDE interface, and drive capacities were growing. Several years ago, Quantum developed UltraDMA/33, which it released as a public standard. Also known as UltraATA, it was rapidly adopted by the industry (also known as Ultra-DMA).

UltraATA drives are backward-compatible with EIDE, so can work in systems that only have EIDE controllers. The maximum burst transfer rate was increased to 33MB per second, not far behind the fastest SCSI controllers. UltraATA is DMA-based, so it does offload the CPU somewhat. UltraATA made the advent of 7,200RPM IDE drives possible. Up until that point, IDE drives maxed out at 5,400RPM. Although a 7,200RPM EIDE drive could have been built, it would have made little difference—the EIDE interface itself was the bottleneck.

However, UltraATA uses much tighter tolerances on the signals that carry the data. Some drives interacted poorly with some motherboards, even though both ostensibly supported UltraATA. The problem lies not with the drive or the motherboard, but with the cheap IDE cables that come with most hard drives or motherboards. Not all drive/motherboard combinations have this problem, but it's common enough that the drive makers have started recommending higher-quality, 80 conductor ribbon cables.

# UltraATA/66

Lately, a newer, quicker flavor of UltraATA has emerged, doubling the maximum possible data rate once again. In the process, better error correction has been added, but the drive makers are more strongly recommending 80 conductor cables with UltraATA/66 drives.

Although UltraATA/66 drives are theoretically backward-compatible, some drives simply do not work in UltraATA/33 or EIDE systems unless the drive is put into the slower mode. Check the drive manufacturer for ,details.

# Limitations of IDE

Although the performance and capacity of IDE drives have steadily increased, IDE still has some limitations. First, there's that four device limit—two devices on the master controller and two devices on the secondary controller. That limit includes *all* IDE devices, so if you have a CD-ROM drive and an IDE Zip drive, that's two of the four, which limits you to two hard drives. With the huge capacities available in current drives, that's not that big a limitation.

There's also very limited support for external devices on the IDE interface due to the very short cable lengths—24" maximum per connector, or 12" in the case of some UltraATA/66 devices. Finally, even DMA-based IDE drives stall when a second device on the same interface is accessing the bus. For example, if you have a CD-ROM drive and a hard drive on the same IDE connector, and the slower CD is transferring data, the hard drive must wait.

Overall, however, EIDE or better drives make for a very solid solution for most users. The drive capacities and performance of today's hard drives enable games to load that much faster, and users to wait less.

# The Many Flavors of SCSI

SCSI stands for *small computer systems interface,* and is a very general interface that can be used for things other than mass storage devices. I've seen SCSI scanners, SCSI tape drives, and even a SCSI printer or two. SCSI is also a parallel interface, meaning that multiple bits of data are moved across the bus simultaneously. If the different variants of IDE seem confusing, then SCSI, with all its variations and multiple connector types, must be utterly baffling. But if you really want to eake out the maximum possible performance from your storage subsystem, then SCSI is still the best way to go today.

Most current SCSI host adapters can support up to fifteen devices on a single SCSI bus, using a single IRQ (some narrow-SCSI only controllers support up to six devices). Also, SCSI is a smart interface, so adding a CD drive to the same chain as a hard drive won't result in a bottleneck. The host adapter manages transfers so that both devices coexist peacefully, and with the best possible performance.

## Fast and Fast/Wide SCSI

Fast SCSI uses a 50-pin ribbon cable for internal connections, and moves data in 8-bit chunks. Connections to external devices vary, though, which can add to the confusion. There are two primary types of fast SCSI external connectors. There's one that looks a lot like the type of connectors on most parallel printers, and is in fact called a Centronics-style connector. The second type is a more compact, 50-pin high-density connector (see Figure 7.2).

Fast SCSI maxes out at around 10 megabytes per second, so wide SCSI was invented. Wide SCSI drives use a 68-pin connector, and move data in 16-bit chunks (as opposed to the 8-bit-wide data transfers for fast SCSI). Fast/wide SCSI can move data at up to 20MB per second. There's a 6 meter limit on cable length, which is ample for most applications.

Note that there's a variant called SCA (system connection architecture) that uses an 80-pin connector. This is used almost exclusively for servers and RAID arrays, which often require "hot-swapping" of drives. You should probably avoid SCA connectors because they require additional adapters for most desktop SCSI adapters.

Also, there's another SCSI variant called *differential SCSI*. Differential SCSI requires specialized host adapter cards and differential SCSI drives are not compatible with standard SCSI controllers. The advantage is that the cable lengths can be very long, so differential drives are used in specialized applications in which the drives need to be placed at some distance from the computer.

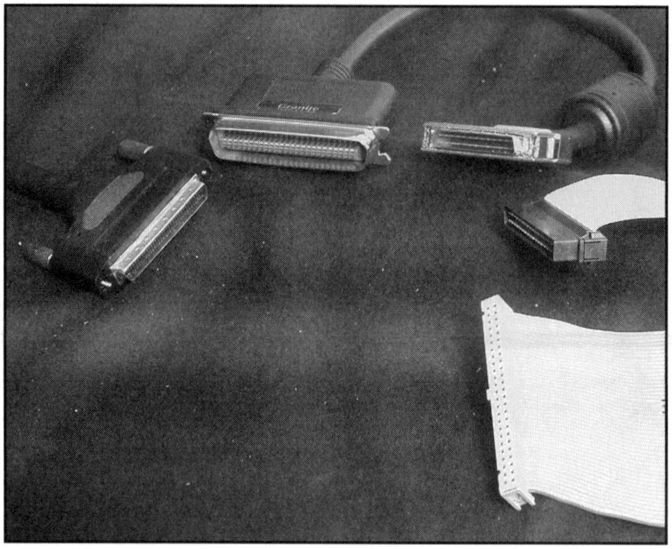

**Figure 7.2**

Here are various SCSI connectors: 50-pin internal, 50-pin Centronics, 50-pin high density and 68-pin. Not shown are SCA connectors used in RAID arrays or servers for hot swap drives.

# Ultra SCSI and Ultrawide SCSI

Large servers and video capture applications can require huge data rates, so ultra SCSI was created. Like fast SCSI, ultra SCSI supports both 8-bit (narrow) and 16-bit (wide) interfaces. Thankfully, the connectors are the same as with fast SCSI. However, the cable lengths were shortened to 1.5 meters in some cases, and 3M in others. Ultra SCSI maxes out at 20MB per second, whereas the best transfer rate of Ultrawide SCSI is 40MB per second.

# Ultra2 LVD SCSI

Ultra2 LVD (LVD stands for *low voltage differential*) is somewhat different from other SCSI flavors. First, it is a differential SCSI technology, which means that the cables must have double the number of wires for full performance. Unlike the older differential technology, LVD drives can exist on a standard-wide or Ultrawide SCSI bus, but defaults to the slower speeds and shorter cable lengths. Care must be taken with LVD drives because they have no provision for electrical termination, as most other SCSI devices do. Instead, the LVD cable itself must be terminated. (We'll discuss more about termination in the section on installing hard drives.)

When attached to an LVD controller, the maximum transfer rate is 80MB per second. Certainly, no single magnetic hard drive, no matter how speedy, can saturate an LVD bus.

Recently, the LVD standard has been expanded to include Ultra/160, which doubles the maximum speed once again. It's very unlikely that you'll ever use an Ultra/160 drive in a desktop computer.

# IDE or SCSI?

The choice between IDE and SCSI is a choice between performance, flexibility, and cost. Most motherboards do not have a SCSI host adapter built into them, and adding a SCSI interface will cost $150 to $350, depending on the capability of the controller. SCSI hard drives cost more, too. An 18GB, 7,200RPM SCSI hard drive costs about $650, versus about $350 for an 18GB UltraATA hard drive. However, comparing those specs are a little deceptive. The SCSI hard drive usually has more robust motors, and the average access time (the average time the heads take to move to a given spot on the drive) is usually lower. Also, the very highest performing, 10,000RPM drives are currently available only as SCSI drives.

Table 7.2 provides some basics about the different flavors of IDE and SCSI to help you decide what is right for you.

**Table 7.2—IDE and SCSI formats**

| *Drive Interface Type* | *Type of Devices* | *Maximum Speed* | *Maximum Connections* | *Cost* |
|---|---|---|---|---|
| UltraATA/33 | Hard drives, CD/DVD drives, removable discs, tape drives | 33MB/sec | 2 per port | Low; controllers built into motherboards |
| UltraATA/66 | Hard drives, CD/DVD drives, removable discs, tape drives | 66MB/sec | 2 per port | Low; controllers built into newest motherboards |
| UltraSCSI/ Ultrawide SCSI | Hard drives, CD/DVD drives, removable discs, | 20MB/sec (ultraSCSI), 40MB/sec (Ultrawide) | 14 per host adapter | Expensive; controller usually purchased separately. |

*continues*

**Table 7.2—IDE and SCSI formats** Continued

| *Drive Interface Type* | *Type of Devices* | *Maximum Speed* | *Maximum Connections* | *Cost* |
|---|---|---|---|---|
| | DVD-R, DVD-RW, scanners, tape drives | | | |
| Ultra2 LVD SCSI | Hard drives, CD/DVD drives, removable discs, DVD-R, DVD-RW, scanners, tape drives | 80MB/sec | 14 per host adapter | Expensive; host adapter usually purchased separately. Highest-speed drives are very pricey. |

Then, there's the issue of flexibility. Being able to chain together a dozen devices on a single SCSI bus can be very handy. On my production system, I have three SCSI hard drives, a CD-ROM drive, a CD-R (recordable CD) drive, a SCSI Zip drive, and an external SCSI DVD-RAM drive. All that connects into a single controller, using one IRQ.

On the other hand, the advent of the USB bus means that devices like scanners and even tape drives no longer need to have SCSI as a connection. In the end, it comes down to your desire for somewhat better performance and flexibility, versus cost. For most gaming purposes, a good, 7,200RPM A UltraATA drive is a very good solution.

# Other Hard Drive Interfaces

You may occasionally come across references to other hard drive interfaces. We'll touch on them briefly, but it's unlikely you'll need to worry about them in the near future.

## Fibre Channel

Fibre channel drives use a serial optical interface to move data at very high bit rates. It's generally used in large server installation and in *storage area networks (SAN)*. Fibre channel drives are quite a bit more expensive than SCSI drives, and the fibre channel adapters can cost $1,000 or more.

## Firewire (IEEE 1394)

Firewire holds the promise of replacing both IDE and SCSI as the future interface for hard drives. It uses elements of the SCSI protocols for managing data transfers, but is a serial interface. Firewire performance can exceed 800 megabits per second (about 100 megabytes/sec). Initially, it was thought that IEEE 1394 would be available in the Intel 820J (Camino) chipset, but that's not the case now. Earlier this year, Apple Computer, which invented Firewire, announced an onerous licensing arrangement of $1 *per port*. After much outcry—and Intel's defensive announcement of USB 2.0—Apple backed off and the licensing terms are now more reasonable. However, the whole affair delayed widespread adoption of Firewire. Firewire's killer applications may not be so much for games, but for easily connecting A/V devices like camcorders to your system to get data from them into your PC. Musical gear like synthesizers and samplers may also benefit from Firewire in the near future.

## Device Bay

Device Bay is a standard co-created by Compaq and Microsoft to allow easy upgrade and swapping of hard drives. We may see Device Bay computers in early 2000. Think of it as a "plug and go" hard drive interface—the underlying transfer technology could be IDE or Firewire. It means no more having to pop open your computer case and align fussy cable connectors to install a hard drive.

# Other Drive Types

Following is a quick listing of other drive types common to PCs today.

## The Floppy Disc Drive

The good old, 1.44MB, 3.5-inch floppy drive is still the mainstay for secondary storage in most PCs, and is handy for "sneaker-net" transfers (walking a file on floppy down the hall to your friend's PC). It's a good idea to always have a standard 3.5" floppy in your system because it's such a trouble-free device, and the floppy disc interface on the motherboard isn't used for anything else.

There are alternatives to the floppy, but none are perfect in their own right.

## Zip Drives

The Iomega Zip drive is probably the most ubiquitous removable storage medium next to the floppy disc drive. The Zip is available in capacities of 100 and 250MB. The Zip cartridge looks a lot like a floppy disc on steroids, and is more robust. The drive itself is faster than a floppy drive, though it won't win any speed contests.

Zip drives are available in IDE, SCSI, and parallel interface versions. They cannot read or write standard 3.5" floppy discs. Although you could theoretically use an IDE Zip drive to replace a floppy, you'd have to do all the setup yourself to create an emergency boot disc. Norton Utilities also lets you create a Zip recovery disc in an automated way.

## LS-120 SuperDisk

The Superfloppy, formerly known as the LS-120, is a magneto-optical drive that can read and write either its own 120MB cartridges or standard 1.44MB, 3.5" floppies. The problem is that it requires an IDE connection, rather than connecting to the floppy port. Unfortunately, it's not really that much faster than a floppy. Finally, it does require that the system have a BIOS that supports a bootable IDE removable device—most recent BIOSes do. Best support exists under Windows 98, but it does have drivers for Windows 95.

## Sony HiFD

The HiFD is a perfect example of an undelivered promise. It sounds great: a 230MB cartridge drive that's nearly as fast as a hard drive, and will read and write standard 3.5" floppy disks. Unfortunately, the drive was a year late. When Sony finally shipped it, it only shipped a parallel port version (!) that was not a bootable device. Then, it pulled it off the market because of "performance issues." It may make a comeback, but don't hold your breath.

## Cartridge Drives

Removable hard drives, like the Iomega Jaz series and the newer Castlewood Orb drives make interesting offline backup. The Castlewood drive is an interesting device because the 2.2GB cartridges only sell for around $30. Note that they are too slow to be hard drive replacements, but can augment your storage. The Jaz is a SCSI-only device, whereas the Orb is available in either SCSI or IDE formats.

# Maximizing Hard Drive Performance

There are several things you can do to be sure your hard drive is well tuned and running happily. First, be sure you keep the drive defragged. You can simply use the Defrag utility that comes with Windows, or use a more sophisticated tool like the ones that ship with Norton Utilities or McAffee's Nuts and Bolts.

Games in particular can benefit from a good defrag. Many games use hundreds of small files. The more time the hard drive heads have to spend hunting for file fragments, the more pauses and hesitations you may see in your game. Game loads and file saves will take longer, too.

Secondly, play around with the settings of the Windows 98 swap file. The swap file kicks in when your system memory fills up. Windows uses a chunk of the disk just as if it were part of memory (this is called *virtual memory* or *VM*). Most of the time, the Windows swap file can be left at its default setting. But if you have two *physical* drives (*not* two partitions on the same physical drive), you may want to move the swap file to the least-used drive, or at least to the drive that's not the drive with Windows. Moving the swap file to a second, less-used drive means that the heads on the main drive are free to handle real data, like loading a new level or map.

The best cure for frequent swap file accesses, though, is to add more RAM.

Then, there's the Windows 98 disc cache, called VCACHE. If you like, you can add settings to your SYSTEM.INI file to change the amount of memory allocated to the Windows disc cache. I generally don't recommend it because it can get you into trouble. But occasionally, the disc cache grows so that some applications begin swapping to virtual memory, even though you may have a lot of RAM. In that case, the best thing to do is reboot.

If your drive starts mysteriously churning for no good reason, check your startup folder. Some Microsoft applications install a utility called FASTFIND in your startup folder. Periodically, FASTFIND will index the contents of your hard drive so that searches for specific files can occur more quickly. The problem is that FASTFIND often thinks that Windows is inactive when a game is running. The best thing to do is move FASTFIND out of the startup folder.

# Buying a Hard Drive

Whether you're buying an A UltraATA hard drive or a SCSI drive, there are some things you should consider when buying. The first one is: retail or OEM. OEM (which stands for *original equipment manufacturer*) refers to parts sold to system builders in bulk packages), often in plain boxes. OEM hard drives are the same as their retail counterparts, and the warranties are usually the same. However, you get just the bare drive, with perhaps a flyleaf for documentation and a floppy disk with a disc manager program. Retail packaged drives often come with better manuals, cables, mounting hardware, and, occasionally, a bundled application. If you need some handholding, get the retail drives, but bare drives are fine if you know what you're doing.

Hard drives are very much commodity items, so do search for the best price. If installing a drive seems daunting, most local dealers will install them for you for a fee. I generally recommend buying size over performance. The difference in speed between a good 5,400RPM drive and a 7,200RPM drive is noticeable, but if the choice is between 9 and 17GB, then the bigger drive will be more useful. However, if you do have a few dollars more, spend the money to get a big, 7,200RPM drive.

If you're shopping for SCSI drives, first determine your controller type. If you have a SCSI controller capable of supporting Ultra2 LVD drives, make sure you get LVD drives. Configuring LVD drives is less of a headache, and you'll get somewhat better performance. The cost difference between an LVD drive and an Ultrawide drive is minor.

Finally, always make sure you buy the drive from someone with a good return policy. Hard drives are mechanical devices, and you do occasionally get a dead one. If the dealer won't accept returns or exchanges, you have to contact the drive maker. Swapping a hard drive with the manufacturer usually takes a few days.

Modern hard drives now offer good speed, huge capacities, and relatively low cost. Of all the upgrades you'll buy, a good new hard drive is probably the most useful one in many cases. After all, a slower 3D graphics card will simply run the game a bit more slowly, but if your hard drive is too small to even install the game, you're out of luck.

# Chapter 8

# CD and DVD

## Evolution of the CD

A CD-ROM drive is now a critical part of any modern PC. Almost no one ships software on floppy discs any more. Given the size of some games—or even business applications—the publishers would have to ship dozens or even hundreds of floppies. I once recall being 35 floppies into a 36-disc install of Microsoft Office for the Macintosh when I encountered an error and had to start all over again. CDs are definitely more efficient.

Until recently, CDs were *read-only* medium. Even if you had a CD recorder—prohibitively expensive for most users until late 1998—you could only use media once. But a new twist known as CD-RW has been added.

CDs used to be the capacity champ, too. A standard CD-ROM is capable of holding 74 minutes of 44.1KHz, 16-ibt audio (plus some error correction) or 650MB of data. There are lower capacity discs capable of holding only about 540MB, but those are usually used in CD audio recorders for home stereo systems. Recently, Teac announced that it would be shipping a *higher* capacity CD disc capable of storing a little over 700MB, but it's unclear whether current generation drives will be able to read them.

If CDs have become a floppy disc replacement for shipping software, DVD-ROM may very well become the CD replacement on computers. With a base capacity of 4.7GB for a single-sided, single-layered disc, and the capability to handle 17GB with a double-sided, double-layered disc, DVD shows a lot of promise.

We'll briefly check out both technologies, then examine some of the more practical issues, such as performance.

# It's the Pits

Underneath the plastic protective layer of a CD-ROM are millions of tiny pits created during the pressing of the CD. The layer containing the pits is known as the *substrate*. Each pit represents a binary one; the absence of a pit represents a binary zero. A low-power laser shines onto the substrate and some of the light is reflected back. The intensity of the reflected light varies depending on whether the beam is shone onto a pit or not, and that's how the binary 1's and 0's are interpreted.

DVD-ROM drives work in a very similar manner, but the laser actually uses a higher frequency light than the CD-ROM laser. The pits on the DVD substrate are also packed much more tightly. Just like hard drives, this higher areal density means that the data will stream off the disc that much faster. The rate at which data is transferred for a standard audio CD-ROM drive is 176,400 bytes per second. This is the minimum you need to stream out 16-bit, 44.1KHz stereo audio. The native data rate for DVD-ROM drives is 1.231 *mega*bytes per second. This level of performance is the minimum needed for DVD movies, which stream video and up to 7 channels of audio data simultaneously. However, this base rate is for consumer players, not CD-ROM or DVD-ROM drives, which often run much faster.

# X Marks the Spot

When you buy a CD-ROM or DVD drive, it's often labeled a "40x CD-ROM drive," or a "6x DVD drive." In theory, that means that a 40x CD-ROM drive should move data at 40 times a single-speed CD-ROM drive. (Note that a 1x CD-ROM drive moves data at 150 kilobytes per second for data, although slightly faster for audio). This would mean that data is moved off the drive at 6000 kilobytes per second (about 5.9MB/sec)—a data rate that's almost never achieved.

In fact, these "X" speeds are really an ideal speed, based on the maximum transfer rate from the outer tracks of the CD. That's because current high-speed CD-ROM drives are CAV (constant angular velocity) devices, just like hard drives. That means that the linear speed of a particular spot on the CD-ROM drive will vary, depending on whether you're looking closer to the inner part of the disc, near the spindle, or the outer part.

### Note

Early CD-ROM drives were CLV—constant *linear* velocity drives that actually spun at different rates, depending on the location of the head. The stream of bits under the data head was always at the same rate. However, it proved impossible to build a CD-ROM drive much faster than 12x with CLV technology—the motors became too expensive.

Unfortunately, data is not written on CD-ROM drives on the outer tracks first—it's written from the inner tracks. So, there's a good chance that, in most applications, you'll never see the maximum throughput of the CD-ROM drive.

DVD-ROM drives behave the same way. A "6x" DVD-ROM drive can move data at 7.8 megabytes per second from the outer tracks, but less from the inner. Because DVD-ROM drives can read standard CD-ROM discs, the CD speed is also often stated.

Except for applications in which raw data transfer is important—streaming video and installing large applications—the transfer rate isn't all that critical. A more useful measurement is access time. Ideally, you want the head of the drive to move as quickly as possible across the disc. While most games install some of the content on your hard drive, some data is often left on the CD itself. Access times measure how fast the head moves from one location to another. Ideally, you'd like to have an average access time of less than 150ms. Some current generation CD-ROM drives have sub-80 millisecond access times.

# CD-ROM Particulars

Unless you have a very old drive, most CD-ROM drives can now read all flavors of CD discs, including the new rewriteable CD format (CD-RW). (If you have a drive more than 18 months old, it may not be able to read CD-RW discs.) That means you can ignore the jumble of acronyms that accompany CD technology: CD-XA, Video CD, Enhanced CD, and so on. CD-ROM technology has matured to the point that it generally just works.

CD-ROM drives come in several flavors, with IDE and SCSI drives as the primary connection type. IDE drives are often called *ATAPI* drives; ATAPI stands for *AT Attachment Packet Interface*. The "AT" refers to the original IBM PC-AT, and is sometimes used as a synonym for industry standard personal computers. ATAPI is an extension of the IDE interface for removable drives, such as CD-ROM drives.

You can get CD-ROM drives in tray format (most common) or, occasionally, slot drive. The old CD caddy has pretty much fallen by the wayside, though you may find it in a few industrial-strength drives, where corporations may want to protect expensive CDs from being mishandled. By far, the most common format is the tray drive, in which a tray pops out of the drive, much like the tray on an audio CD-ROM drive. Pioneer makes a slot drive CD-ROM, which sucks the CD into a slot, much like a car CD audio player. It never had much market penetration, which is really unfortunate; if you've ever broken the fragile CD tray, a slot drive CD suddenly seems like a great idea.

The choice between IDE and SCSI CD-ROM drives is pretty similar to that of hard drives. The highest performing CD-ROM drives on the market are from Plextor, and use SCSI nearly exclusively—but they cost substantially more.

If you take a bare CD-ROM drive and look at the back, you'll see three or four connectors (depending on the drive), plus some jumpers (see Figure 8.1). We'll look into drive setup in the section on building a PC, but note the two smaller connectors to one side. The slightly larger connector is for analog audio, and typically connects to your sound card.

The smaller, but similar, connector is for extracting the digital audio stream directly from the CD disc. Known as a SPDIF connector (short for Sony/Phillips Digital Interface), it's a common feature on most ATAPI drives. (Plextor drives can extract digital audio data directly over the SCSI bus.) This feature is called Digital Audio Extraction (DAE), and you can find a similar feature on EIDE drives.

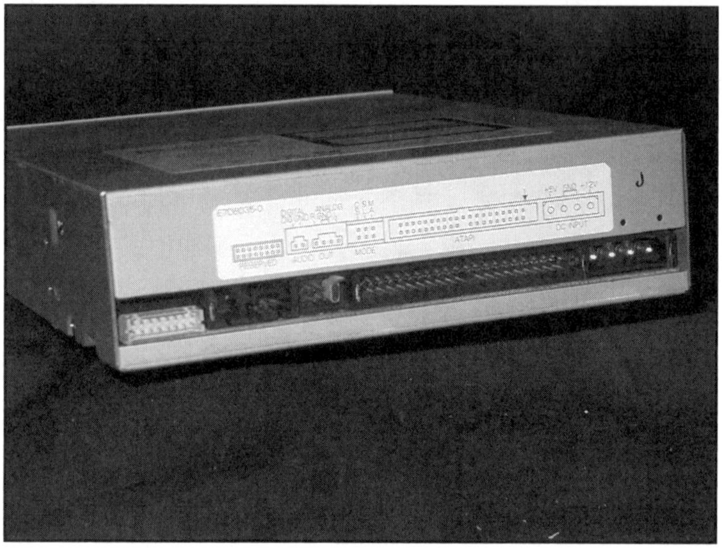

**Figure 8.1**
The two connectors shown here are for analog and digital audio, respectively.

# MultiBeam Technology

In the past year, a twist on standard CD technology has emerged, pioneered by Zen Research. Many high-speed CD-ROM drives rotate at very high speeds. However, not all CD discs are created equal. The elaborate, silk-screened labels on some discs actually cause the CD to be unbalanced at high speeds. This can create a very loud and annoying vibration, as if the drive itself was about to come apart. Some companies, such as Plextor, have done some clever engineering to balance these CDs, but it can be a pretty substantial problem with low-cost drives.

On top of that, Zen noticed that even high-speed CAV drives didn't work at their maximum speeds most of the time (see above for the reason). So they developed a way of splitting the CD laser into as many as seven beams, through either a prism or a mirror assembly. The head reads seven tracks simultaneously, and the drive electronics makes sure that the data is sent in the right order to the computer (see Figure 8.2).

When it works, it's great. Kenwood took a standard, 10x CLV drive mechanism and added the Zen Research technology. The result was a drive that behaved like a 40x drive at all locations on the disc. Because of the larger head assembly, the Zen drive did have a somewhat slower access time. All of this sounds great, but there have been a few warts along the way.

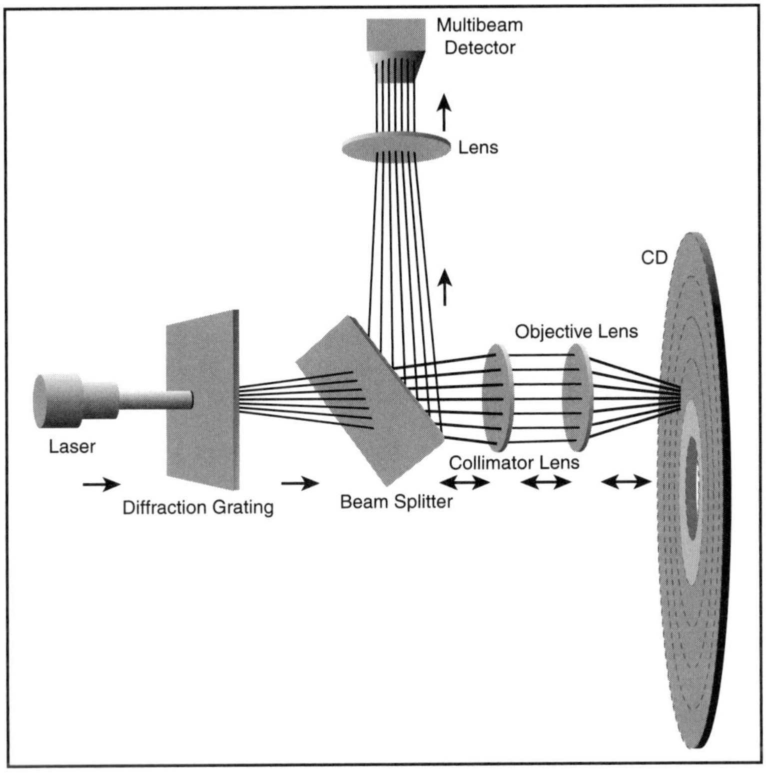


**Figure 8.2**

Zen Research's new method for reading CDs. Multiple tracks can be read simultaneously.

The most serious problem is that the Zen drives have difficulty reading CD recordable media. Some CD-R media simply refuse to work with the somewhat more diffuse laser beam generated by the Kenwood head assembly. CD-R discs use a dye substrate, rather than physical pits on the disc. When data is "burned" on to the media, the dye changes color in spots to represent 1's or 0's. For some reason, the Kenwood drives have difficulty reading the color changes. The other problem is that some motherboards don't like the drives. They will occasionally "lose" the drive, and only a power down and power up will cure the problem.

Most of the time, though, the Zen Research drives work fairly well. Just be aware that you may need to use your CD-R drive to play back discs that have been recorded on.

# Recordable CDs

In the past 18 months, the price of recordable CD-ROM drives—known colloquially as CD "burners"—has plummeted while performance has steadily improved. You can now get a drive that behaves like a 24x CD-ROM reader, 6x CD-R and 4x CD-RW drive for well under $400. Less capable drives are even cheaper. These drives are used in corporations to burn custom CDs and for backup.

The immediate question for end users is: Can I copy my game CDs?

The answer is: sure—for personal use only, as a backup. CDs are fragile media, and can be scratched. Burning a backup is a nice insurance policy—in fact, using the backup leaves the original in pristine condition. However, when you have a second copy of a game running from a backup *at the same time you have the original running*, you have broken the law. The most common use for this is to hand out copies to your friends. That's strictly illegal, and there are big fines if you get caught. In fact, if you "loan" a copy to a friend, and never run both simultaneously, you've still broken the law. "Personal use" means for your use, only, and never on more than one computer at a time.

Having said that, CD-R and CD-RW drives are handy for making backups of important data on your hard drive. Both types of discs work by altering a dye that's embedded on the substrate of the disc, under the protective plastic layer. Some recordable drives are fast enough to use as primary CD-ROM drives. Usually, CD-RW is slower than CD-R, but you can reuse the media. CD-RW discs are also more expensive. I've seen CD recordable media capable of burning discs at 4x speeds cost as little as $0.75 apiece in bulk quantities.

The game publishers have taken note of the low cost of both CD-R media and burners and have taken action. Copy protection has once again reared its ugly head. In the old days of floppy discs, publishers went to elaborate lengths to prevent illegal copies of games from being distributed. The schemes ranged from oddball floppy formats to strange code wheels you had to use during parts of the game. In fact, most game publishers breathed a sigh of relief, thinking that CD-ROM would minimize game piracy.

That lasted several years, until burners got cheap. Some companies have noted that sales of certain popular games would plummet after the first week or two in certain regions of the world. Yet, tech support calls and Internet newsgroup traffic would indicate that there were far more players than officially sold copies. So, the publishers brought back copy protection. Now, no copy protection scheme is perfect, and most do get broken over time—but copy protection does prevent casual piracy. Remember, a game company has to make money to keep creating the titles we love to play.

The problem with CD copy protection is incompatibility. One of the more common methods of copy protection is Macrovision's SafeDisc scheme. But some computer BIOSes had problems with SafeDisc-protected CDs in some drives. In other cases, DVD-ROM drives refused to read the protected media. These problems are being ironed out over time, but it's possible you may run into it with some aggressively protected CDs. You may need a new drive, but it's more likely a BIOS upgrade will fix the problem.

## Packet Recording

One of the interesting new technologies to emerge recently is CD packet recording. Installing a packet driver on your system allows you to access a recordable CD as if it were a hard drive. You can just drag and drop files onto the CD-ROM drive. It's especially handy with CD-RW discs, but even works with standard CD-R media. Note that it's not particularly fast (especially on CD-R), but makes backing up individual files easier.

# DVD

Okay, here's a quiz: What does "DVD" stand for?

Answer: Nothing at all—officially, anyway.

Until 1998, there were actually two competing standards for DVD formats. The two competing organizations finally kissed and made up. But one group wanted DVD to mean "digital video disc," while the other wanted it to mean "digital versatile disc." They agreed to let it drop, and DVD is an acronym with no meaning. However, it seems the "digital versatile disc" seems to be slowly entering the common lexicon.

The primary reason for the creation of DVD was to have a format similar to audio CDs for playing back video information. However, even 4.7GB of space isn't enough to adequately store an entire movie, so compression becomes a necessary evil. DVD uses MPEG-2 compression for movie storage and playback. MPEG-2 (MPEG stands for *Motion Picture Expert Group*) is a robust, lossy compression standard. *Lossy* means that some data—usually redundant information—is thrown away during the compression process. In fact, good compression is something of a black art. You don't just take a two-hour movie and feed it into a compressor and expect the result to be any good. If you want the best quality, a trained professional manages the compression process, compressing some sections of video more than others. There's a whole host of other issues with regards to MPEG-2 compression best left for a different book.

DVD movies are also outside the scope of this tome, but web sites like *The Digital Bits* (`www.digitalbits.com`) and *The DVD Resource Page* (`www.dvdresource.com`) are good places to start. However, I'll touch on MPEG-2 decompression for a moment, because it brings up the issue of DVD decoding.

If you have a DVD-ROM drive in your PC, it's almost inevitable that you'll want to play back a movie occasionally. The question I get asked most often is: Should I use a hardware DVD decoder or a software decoder? The answer is: It depends on your system, and on what you want to use it for.

A hardware decoder offloads the decompression and copy protection process from the CPU. This is a boon for a slower computer, whose CPU can't keep up with the strenuous computational requirements of decoding MPEG-2 video. Also, almost all DVD movies are copy protected in one form or another, and regionalized. This means that if you buy a DVD disc in Europe, *you may not be able to play it in a player bought in the U.S.*

If you have a fast Pentium III or Athlon computer, a software DVD decoder may be perfectly adequate for playing back movies. But you may still want a DVD decoder. There aren't very many DVD games out, but the ones I've seen require a hardware DVD decoder to be installed. A soft DVD player doesn't work in those circumstances, so the cool, high-resolution DVD playback of DVD games like *Journeyman Project* and *Wing Commander IV* don't work. It's uncertain as to what will happen as DVD-only games start to emerge. Windows 98 second edition has better support for MPEG-2, but it's not clear how DVD video on a game disc will be played back.

On the other hand, better support for DVD video is being built into current-generation graphics chips, so the solution on a fast PC may just be additions to the video card driver.

# Recordable DVD

The state of recordable DVD is, frankly, a mess. First, the only way to record a full, 4.7GB DVD that is readable with DVD players is with some very expensive units—in excess of $5,000. There's also DVD-RAM, DVD-RW, and DVD-R+W. If that doesn't confuse you, nothing will. The different writeable DVD formats have two problems: They are not compatible with each other, and currently, no DVD-ROM drive can read them. So, they're really only useful for specialized backup operations.

# Buying a CD or DVD Drive

CD-ROM drives—particularly ATAPI drives—are even more commodity items than hard drives. The name-brand drives from companies like Toshiba, Pioneer, Samsung, Plextor, and Creative Labs are probably a little more reliable than the no-name brands, but it's sometimes hard to find a truly no-name drive. Companies such as Pacific Digital and HiVal repackage name-brand drives under their own names.

I generally don't recommend multimedia kits these days. Kits usually come with a CD-ROM drive, a sound card, some speakers, and sometimes, bundled software. But most kits package fairly mediocre sound cards or speakers. The exceptions are a couple of the pricier kits from Creative Labs. Nonetheless, I prefer to mix and match my multimedia gear.

Be wary when you come across deals for older DVD-ROM drives. Under no circumstance should you get a first generation DVD drive. First, they're dog-slow as CD-ROM drives—8x or slower. Secondly, they cannot read CD-R media and often have problems with copy protected CD-ROM discs. Second generation (2–3x DVD/16–24x CD) drives are fine. If you do have need for frequent backup, consider a CD-RW drive—one of the newer ones, that will do double duty as a CD-ROM reader.

Finally, with the progress that DVD-ROM drives have made, I now almost always recommend a DVD drive. While DVD-ROM drives are more expensive, many 3rd generation bare drives are now well under $150, and will soon be under $100. Even if you don't get a hardware decoder, you're prepared for future growth. By the end of 1999, we'll probably be seeing the first DVD-only games—and they will certainly arrive in 2000.

# Chapter 9

# Control Your World

## You're in Control

Perhaps the most personal choice of any game player, short of the games themselves, is their choice of game controller. There seems to be little correlation between genre and game controllers, although it's rather difficult to play a turn-based strategy game with a joystick. There are also a host of different types of controllers, ranging from the simple, two-axis joystick to the elaborate, virtual cockpit setups of some of the hard-core users of automobile racing simulations. On the other hand, a lot of users still simply use the keyboard and mouse. The problem is that all the reviews in the world won't necessarily tell you what *you* like. Relying on the advice of others can certainly help, but ultimately, you'll have to experiment with different styles for different games.

Joysticks have been with us since the early days of personal computers. The Apple II supported joysticks, even before the advent of the mouse on the Macintosh. More specialized controllers, such as steering wheels and yokes, have only appeared in the past five years.

Still, it helps to understand how game controllers function, and we'll race through a variety of topics, ranging from keyboard input to sophisticated flight controllers. So strap in, hold on, and let's launch into it.

# The Keyboard as Game Controller

The IBM-PC keyboard has gone through some minor revisions over the years, but it still works much the way it did when the original PC came out in 1980. Each time you press a key, a *scan code* is generated. The keyboard controller chip passes this on to the computer, which interprets it as a letter. However, it's possible for games to read the raw scan codes themselves, and work directly at that level, rather than waiting for the signal to be interpreted by the operating system. Many games that use the keyboard in a more complex fashion bypass the operating system and BIOS altogether, although that's less common in the Windows 9x world.

At its heart, the keyboard controller detects when a key has been pressed or released. Note that the keyboard controller is also capable of detecting *chorded* key combinations—that is, keys that are held down simultaneously. The classic chorded combination is the trusty Ctrl+Alt+Del key combo that reboots your system, but many games make use of differing sets of chorded keys.

Although almost every game, from flight sim to role-playing, has a default keyboard setup, first person shooters such as *Unreal*, *Quake III: Arena*, and others seem tuned for the keyboard/mouse combo. Some heavy online players of shooters use the keyboard exclusively. If you're into that genre, it behooves you to get a keyboard that is solid, durable, and offers a reliable response.

My personal preference for keyboards is ergonomic keyboards like the original Microsoft Natural Keyboard or the new Natural Keyboard Deluxe. (I bypassed the Elite—it was ill-suited for gamers due to Microsoft's attempt to rearrange and shrink some of the keys.) That's partly because I'm a writer by trade—you may not desire or need an ergonomic keyboard. If you're used to a standard, flat keyboard, using even the modestly ergonomic Natural (Logitech makes a similar keyboard, as does Memorex and a few other makers) takes a little learning. I find that I can no longer type for any length of time on a standard keyboard. Microsoft has recently updated the Natural Keyboard with the USB-equipped Natural Keyboard Pro (see Figure 9.1).

One legendary keyboard is the original Northgate Omnikey. There are still users who have clung to their cherished Omnikeys. These keyboards were quite heavy, and had a distinctive, mechanical click when pressing the keys—you never doubted when a key was pressed. The keys themselves used heavy-duty, Alps mechanical contact switches. They were also built like M1A2 tanks. The good news is that, although the original Omnikey is no longer made, another company got the molds and is making exact replicas that have the added feature of being programmable.

There are also a host of weird, ergonomic keyboards that are far more eccentric than the Microsoft Natural Keyboard, and are generally ill-suited for gaming.

**Figure 9.1**
Microsoft's updated Natural Keyboard Pro adds some additional function keys and now supports USB. Photo used by permission of Microsoft.

A recent twist on keyboards has been the USB keyboard. This keyboard doesn't really behave any differently, but I've seen at least two that allow you to daisy-chain a USB mouse—a very handy thing, as most Macintosh users will tell you.

# Mousing Around

Most of us have become quite facile at using a mouse, and if you've played a lot of 3D shooters, mouse-look has become impossible to live without. Mouse-look is where you can view the 3D environment in all directions by moving the mouse. Moving the mouse left and right turns your view left and right. Moving the mouse forward looks up, whereas pulling it back looks down. It's invaluable to me, at least, though there are some hotshot players who swear by the keyboard only.

The mouse was invented by Doug Englebart back in the 1960s at SRI (then Stanford Research Institute). Since then, Englebart's crude mouse has undergone considerable evolution, with the latest twist being Microsoft's ball-free mouse (see Figure 9.2).

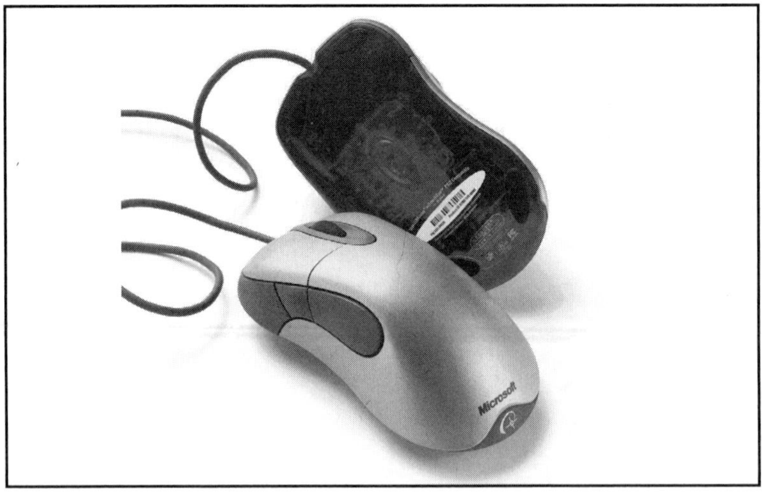

**Figure 9.2**
Microsoft's new mouse uses reflective LEDs to detect movement, rather than a mechanical ball. Photo used by permission of Microsoft.

The interest in 3D and Windows gaming has generated a whole new market for the gaming mouse. Game controller companies like Saitek and Thrustmaster now sell *gaming mice*. For the most part, these are capable mice with some additional features, like the four-way hat switch on the Saitek mouse. Another company with a successful line of computer rodents is Logitech. I've long preferred the Logitech Mouseman Plus (see Figure 9.3), but the new ball-free mouse from the boys in Redmond has me intrigued.

# Mouse Innards

With the exception of the new Microsoft mouse, most mice have a ball that sits on the underside of the device, nestled in a small compartment so that only about a quarter of it touches the desktop or mouse pad. As the ball spins, electromechanical or optical sensors measure the movement of the ball and send that to the appropriate mouse driver installed in Windows. Windows detects the movement of the mouse, which is a *relative* pointing device. For example, if I pick the mouse up from the table and move it several inches, then set it down again, the mouse pointer doesn't move. Contrast that with a penpad—lift the pen up, and put it down somewhere else on the pad, and the cursor moves there. The penpad is an *absolute* pointing device.

In addition to detecting movement, the mouse driver needs to know when a button is pressed or, in the case of mice with wheels or other controls, when those are used. Windows polls for mouse events roughly 25–30 times each second.

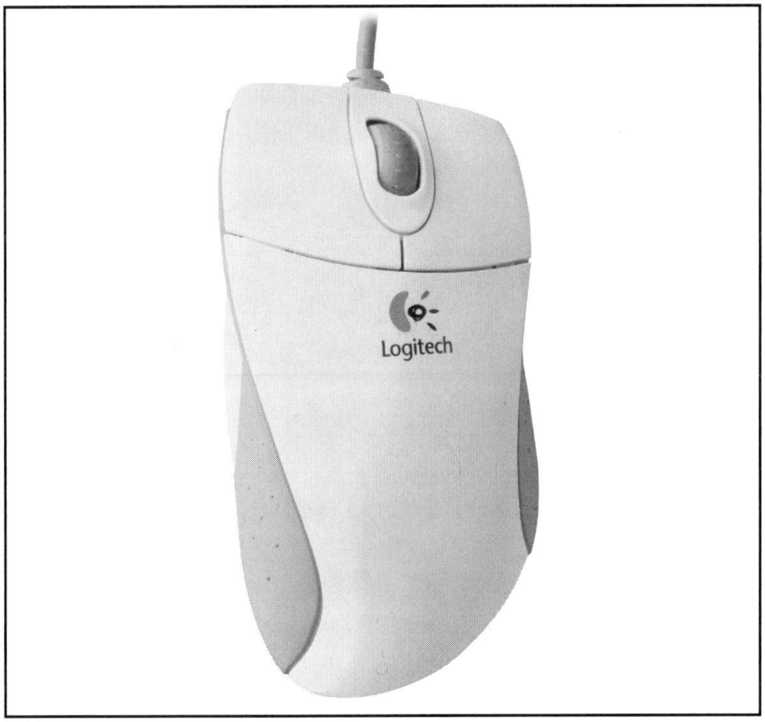


**Figure 9.3**

The Logitech Mouseman Wheel has long been one my favorites. It's been recently updated with a slip-free grip and USB support. Photo used by permission of Logitech.

There are several different ways to plug a mouse into the computer. These days, the most common way is the now-traditional PS/2 style mouse port. Some people still use serial mice, which plug into one of the PC's serial ports. Some older mice required expansion cards to be plugged into the PC for connecting the mouse. The latest twist is USB mice, and they may actually be better for gaming.

As mice have gotten more elaborate, so has the driver software. The software that comes with most current mice is quite complex, and allows you to adjust a variety of mouse parameters, ranging from double-click rate to assigning particular functions to a particular mouse button (see Figure 9.4).

The natural result of this complexity is bugs. Some games don't work correctly with older mouse drivers—and it's more often the mouse driver causing problems, not the game. Usually, upgrading the mouse software fixes the problem. You can avoid a lot of problems by just using the mouse driver that comes with Windows 98, but then you'll lose some functionality, like middle button support.

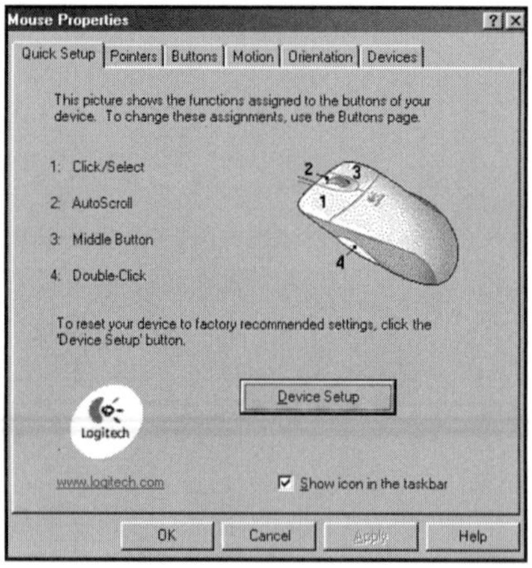


**Figure 9.4**

The Logitech Mouseman control panel allows a seemingly infinite number of different settings.

If you've seen most of the shaped mice, you've no doubt noticed that they are all designed for right-handed folk. The southpaws of the universe don't need to despair, though. Logitech makes a very decent mouse in the Wheel Mouse, which has a wheel and three buttons (the wheel also acts as a button) and is symmetric—meaning that it is not shaped for a right- or left-handed user (see Figure 9.5). It's relatively compact, too, so it is fairly comfortable for all but those with the largest hands. If you're a southpaw, you might want to give this mouse a try. Use the mouse control panel to swap the right and left button controls.

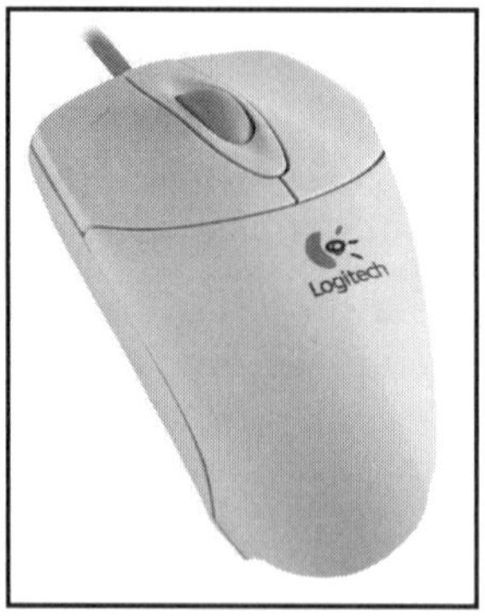


**Figure 9.5**

The Logitech Wheel Mouse is ideal for left-handed users, or ambidextrous households. Photo used by permission of Logitech.

There are one or two left-handed mice available, but my southpaw friends tell me the Logitech is actually more comfortable.

# Mouse Alternatives

Some people simply can't use mice. There may be an ergonomic reason, or simple preference. The most common mouse alternative is the trackball. The trackball is essentially a mouse with a ball on steroids, flipped on its back. Trackballs come in a huge variety of shapes and layouts, so if you have a hankering to try a trackball, head to a computer store and spin a few before choosing. I've had emails from readers who feel strongly that trackballs are better for first-person shooters than mice.

Other mouse alternatives include the pointing stick (generally available only on notebook computers) and the trackpad. I've had reports from quadriplegics who use the trackpad in conjunction with a mouth stick as a mouse. It's not well suited to action games, but it goes to show how human ingenuity, coupled with a little engineering, can solve a seemingly intractable problem.

# The Mouse and Game Performance

The 40Hz polling rate for Windows 98 is fine if you're just moving the mouse to select characters in a word processor, but if you have a hotrod gaming system capable of generating 60fps or more in an action game, the slower polling rate can actually affect performance. The granularity of the mouse movement isn't as fine as the movement through the virtual world at high frame rates. The result is that you can actually miss when firing at enemies, even though it may look like you've got a solid bead on them. This is especially noticeable when trying to move through a 3D world at high speed, as is often the case in online deathmatch games.

There are two solutions to the problem.

The first is a freeware program called PS2RATE. You can easily find it on the Internet by bringing up your Web browser's search function and searching on PS2RATE. As the name indicates, PS2RATE works with mice that plug into a PS/2 style mouse port. It increases the polling rate of the PS/2 mouse port at a user selectable rate of up to 200Hz. Interestingly, it seems to adversely affect the frame rate of the game, but only slightly, and the added precision makes it invaluable in many cases.

The other solution, if you have Windows 98 and the right hardware, is a USB mouse. It seems that Windows polls USB mice at a higher rate (120Hz), so the smoothing out of mouse movements is built-in, and you don't need a hack like PS2RATE. In either case, the improved granularity of mouse movement is a great boost to weapons accuracy in certain cases.

And you thought it was just that you had lousy aim....

# The Game Port

Before we dive into joysticks, game pads, and even more exotic controllers, we need to understand something about the workings of the traditional game port. Even though USB is the wave of the future, there are quite a number of legacy game port controllers out there—and many are very good and may never see a USB equivalent. Or, it may be that you have a couple of old DOS game titles that are near and dear to your heart, so you want to keep a game port-compatible controller around for the memories.

When IBM shipped the very first IBM-PC, it made the analog game port an optional accessory. The game port of today is very much like that original game port, though the controllers that attach to it have evolved beyond its capabilities.

The first thing to understand about the analog game port is that it's just that: analog. Unlike other PC devices, it is not ever remotely a digital device. The second thing to realize is that it's not an active device, but a passive one. In every standard joystick is a pair of potentiometers, called *pots* for short. Pushing the joystick forward or pulling it backwards activates the y-axis pot, whereas pushing the joystick left or right uses the x-axis pot. A pot is an odd device because when you move it, the only thing that happens is that its measured resistance value changes. There is no current or signal generated. Instead, the game itself constantly polls the game port to detect changes in resistance values generated by the moving potentiometers.

If it sounds like an arcane way to handle game input, it is. But the beauty of the game port at the time it was invented was that joysticks could be built very cheaply.

A pot is a very low-cost device, unlike devices that may have required some current from the PC to operate properly. A standard analog joystick is a much dumber device than a keyboard, or even a mouse.

The downside of all this is that there's no standard resolution for potentiometers, nor is there a standard way for a game to poll the game port. Microsoft has tried to wrap some consistency around the game port through its DirectInput controller API (a part of DirectX), but even DirectInput can be thrown for a loop by a slightly oddball game or game port configuration. USB anyone?

Still, the game port will probably be around for some time, so a little understanding of its nature is useful when troubleshooting exactly why the $#@%&$ joystick won't stay calibrated.

## Calibration and Variation with the Game Port

If you've ever played a flight simulator with a joystick or flight yoke attached to the game port on a sound card, you may have noticed some odd behavior. The game will behave just fine for a period of time, and then suddenly your control of the aircraft gets whacked. The plane begins drifting to the left for no reason, or the throttle won't completely reduce to zero. Welcome to the game port.

The problem may reside with the sound card, or with the game controller. When you calibrate a joystick, the resistance values generated by the potentiometers are compared to resistors that are part of the game port electronics. In the case of many sound cards, the game port is often an afterthought, and the cheapest possible components go into the game port electronics, which consists mostly of resistors. As the PC runs for awhile, the resistors actually change value as the PC heats up, which throws the calibration off (this is known as *thermal drift*). If you're lucky enough to have a joystick with trim wheels, you can recalibrate on the fly. In most cases, though, you'll have to exit the game and recalibrate the joystick.

Another part of the problem may lie in the joystick. Cheap joysticks have cheap pots. As you use the stick, the resistance values from the potentiometer may actually shift over time. Again, the result is that you have to recalibrate. The good news is that *most* newer PCI sound cards have decent game ports—though there may be other issues, which we'll touch on in a moment.

If you use more expensive joysticks, and encounter problems with calibration drift, you may consider getting a dedicated game port card. There are several available from companies like CH Products, but the Rolls Royce is probably the PDPI PCI game port card. The PDPI game card, in both its ISA and PCI configurations, has some intelligence, and can actually offload the CPU from its polling chores somewhat.

## Game Ports and Game Performance

Several years ago, Diamond Multimedia shipped the original Diamond Monster Sound card. It was one of the first PCI sound cards to support Aureal's A3D positional audio API, but Diamond also claimed it was a *game port accelerator*. To understand what this means, let's revisit the lowly analog game port again.

As we noted earlier, the game port is polled by the game itself. There is no intelligence on the original game port. Polling the game port requires CPU cycles. Depending on how frequently the game port is polled, it can eat up anywhere from 5–15% of the CPU cycles of a 300MHz Pentium II. Some poorly written games can lose even more CPU to game port polling. This can have a fairly serious performance impact on a demanding game.

The Monster Sound had some intelligence built into it, and it would collect changes in potentiometer values and buffer them up. Then, its game port driver would respond very quickly to any polling request from the game, reducing wait time and decreasing the CPU cycles needed. Unfortunately, the Monster Sound had some compatibility issues with digital game controllers, but it was a good first attempt.

Most newer PCI sound cards also respond quickly when faced with game port polling requests, and do offload the CPU somewhat. The PDPI dedicated game cards probably are the most efficient at reducing the load on the CPU.

## Other Game Port Limitations

Most people don't realize it, but the game port on most sound cards is actually *two* game ports. If you want to, you can hook up a special splitter cable and attach two joysticks. A more practical use may be to hang a separate throttle or rudder pedal set off the game port. The real limitation, though, is that each game port is limited to *two* axes—x and y for each. For example, Thrustmaster makes a joystick that has the joystick, an analog throttle wheel, and a hat switch on top that uses one of the axes. That's four total axes—and you can't attach a set of rudder pedals, as you might want to do with flight simulators.

If used as analog game ports, each port can support two buttons each (or four buttons maximum for a single joystick using both ports). Any additional buttons require custom software to work properly (or a special DirectInput driver). If you do attach a splitter, each controller can only have two axes and two buttons.

## Digital Game Controllers and the Game Port

Digital game controllers arrived on the scene even before USB controllers. Like many joysticks, they plug into the game port, but that's where the similarity ends. A digital game controller uses something other than potentiometers to measure changes in stick movement.

Digital game controllers work by having sensors in the controller that measure the movement of the axis. They typically sample this movement at a fairly high rate, so the user can't tell the difference between the fluidity of an analog joystick and a digital one.

The catch is in getting that digital data into the PC via the game port. Some Microsoft game controllers use a quirk in sound card game ports to transfer digital data to the driver. The vast majority of sound cards on the market use a scheme originally developed by Creative Labs for the original Sound Blaster in that MIDI digital data is transferred through a data pin on the 15-pin game controller that's normally unused by the game port. Digital data from the game controller is often transmitted and received through the MIDI pin.

Other game controllers do other hacks to get digital data in and out of the game port. All of these devices work well with most sound cards, but some occasionally do not. Thrustmaster uses a technology it calls DirectConnect to directly send digital data through any game port, but if you try to discuss DirectConnect with some sound card manufacturers, they just moan and shake their collective heads. USB anyone?

# Universal Serial Bus

The.era of the USB game controller is still very much in its infancy. The majority of USB controllers currently on the market are low-to-mid-range controllers. Really high-end flight and driving controllers still are mostly analog game port devices.

We touched on USB earlier, but it's worth revisiting some of the basics. Intel created USB as a replacement for the legacy RS-232 serial port. But the spec is robust enough for a variety of other functions, including printers, scanners, modems—and game controllers. USB is strictly a serial, digital I/O spec without a hint of the quirkiness of the old game port.

There are two "speed grades" for USB. Low-speed USB moves data at roughly 1.5 megabits per second, while high-speed USB transfers data at 12 megabits per second.

You can daisy-chain up to 127 USB devices on a single bus, though power requirements and compatibility issues often conspire to prevent this from being attained. There are also powered and unpowered USB devices. For example, Multitech makes a USB modem that draws power from the USB bus—no power brick required.

## Note

At first, the thought of hanging, say, a dozen controllers off your joystick port sounds very attractive. But even passive devices like joysticks draw some power over the USB interface. Also, as you start adding USB devices of other types—like modems—the power draw can start to tax the USB port. The solution is to get a powered hub, which can supply power to USB.

Modern, high-performance PCs have two USB ports on the back. As your collection of USB peripherals grows, you'll probably add one or two USB hubs. Entrega, a company formed to market USB devices, makes a nifty, 7-port USB hub (see Figure 9.6). Microsoft will have an extra port or two on its USB Natural Keyboard Deluxe.

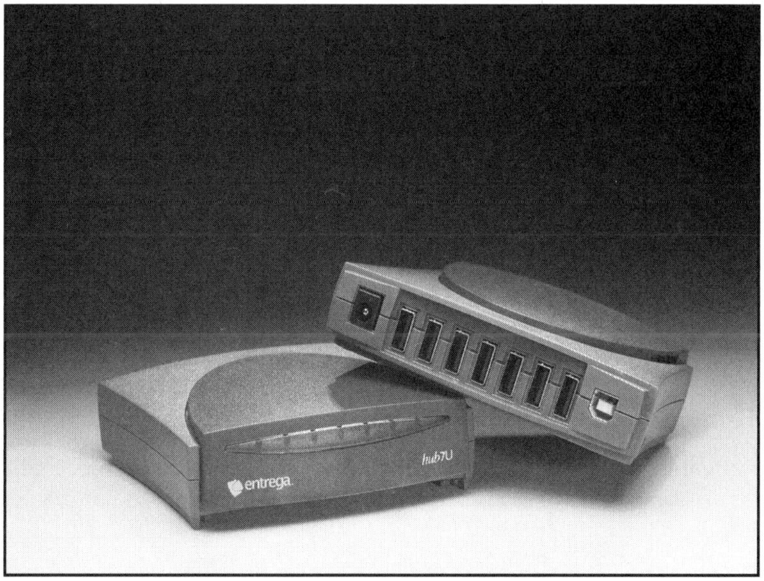


**Figure 9.6**

The Entrega 7 port USB hub should meet most USB needs. It's powered, and is also stackable, so you can add more hubs if needed. Photo used by permission of Entrega.

For more on HID, see page 167.

Windows 98 has a driver for a standard HID device (*human interface device*) built in. Many USB joysticks—even those with multiple buttons—don't need custom drivers, and instead can use the standard HID driver (we'll talk about HID a bit more in the DirectX discussion). It's hard to communicate the benefits of USB, but the first time you plug a USB joystick into a Windows 98 system—and it comes up preconfigured, with no software to install—will make you a convert.

It is an unfortunate truth that not all USB joysticks are digital devices, though you'd think they would be. A few still use potentiometers, converting the data to serial format before sending it out. Games still have to poll for inputs, and some USB sticks require calibration—a sure sign that they're not purely digital in nature.

There's no limitation to the number of axes—USB can support as many axes as needed by the game controller or the game. That, in itself, makes USB *the* way to go for controllers in the future.

USB isn't perfect, though. There have been reported compatibility issues with some hubs, depending on what USB controller chip is used. Also, only Windows 98, Windows 2000, and Macintosh OS 8.5 or later support USB. Although Windows 95 OSR2 (Windows 95C) ostensibly supported USB, it was mostly broken.

**Note**

You can determine which version of Windows 95 you have by right-clicking on My Computer and selecting Properties.

Still, I can't wait until I have a full digital setup with USB joystick, throttle, and rudder pedals.

# Force Feedback

One of the intriguing new technologies that has emerged in the past 18 months is force feedback. Force feedback controllers use a small electric motor and some electronic circuitry to make the joystick or wheel "active." Imagine firing a gun and feeling the recoil, or having the steering wheel suddenly go slack when your virtual car goes into a skid. That's what force feedback can give you.

On the software side, force feedback has been implemented as more of a gimmick in many titles. But as game designers get more expertise in force feedback, the effects can seem quite realistic.

There are two competing standards for force feedback. One is promoted by Microsoft's hardware group, and is built into its Force Feedback Pro and Force Feedback Wheel products; Saitek also uses it in its force feedback steering wheel. The other standard, I-Force, was developed by Immersion Corporation, and is used by most of the other force feedback products. All of the varying types work with Microsoft's DirectInput standard.

Although force feedback joysticks are interesting, the best use of force feedback so far has been in racing wheels for driving games (see Figure 9.7). But a good force feedback stick is a plus in some flight sims (see Figure 9.8).

**Figure 9.7**

The Force RS from ACT Labs is a solid force feedback wheel at a relatively low cost. Photo used by permission of ACT Labs.

Despite the added realism, force feedback can actually be detrimental to *winning* a game. The distraction of having the wheel vibrate in your hand, or even go slack, makes it more difficult to keep the wheel steady. There's a subculture of online car racing buffs who almost exclusively use very expensive analog (that is, non–force feedback) wheels. These are quite precise, and don't have the distraction of force feedback.

**Figure 9.8**

The Wingman force motor uses wires and pulleys, rather than gears, to drive the stick. Photo used by permission of Logitech.

# Controller Types

Controllers come in a multitude of flavors, as well as a dizzying variety of price points. We talked about the mouse and keyboard earlier. They're used for most strategy games and a number of action games. But there are times when only other types of controllers will do. Most people who play sports games, for example, like to use gamepads. Let's touch on each of the main controller types, but check out a few oddball controllers.

## Flight Joysticks

The joystick as it exists for computer games bears a strong resemblance to the flight sticks used in combat aircraft. Early joysticks looked more industrial, but as gamers demanded more verisimilitude, joysticks began to resemble aircraft sticks. In 1990, Thrustmaster burst onto the scene with its first throttle, soon followed by a joystick that was a replica of the actual flight stick used in the F4 Phantom fighter jet.

Flight sticks tend to be the most rugged of the various joystick types, but also the most expensive and often the most finicky. Setup can be a pain because almost all of them are old analog sticks—many of which also interface with the keyboard. However, the simpler flight sticks, such as the CH F16 Combat Stick (see Figure 9.9), are reliable and work well.

Flight simulation enthusiasts tend to value a realistic experience, so the gear often reflects this. Most fans of flight sims don't just have joysticks—they also have rudder pedals and throttles. People who play civil aviation flight sims will often substitute a yoke for a joystick because yokes are much more common in small and large civilian aircraft than flight sticks (see Figure 9.10).

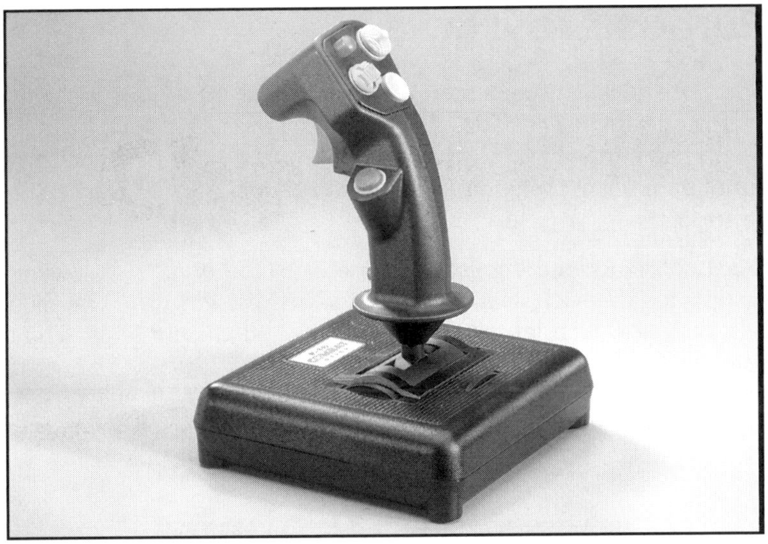

**Figure 9.9**

The CH F16 Combat Stick resembles the flight stick used on the F-16C fighter. It has a light, precise feel and is very durable. Photo used by permission of CH.

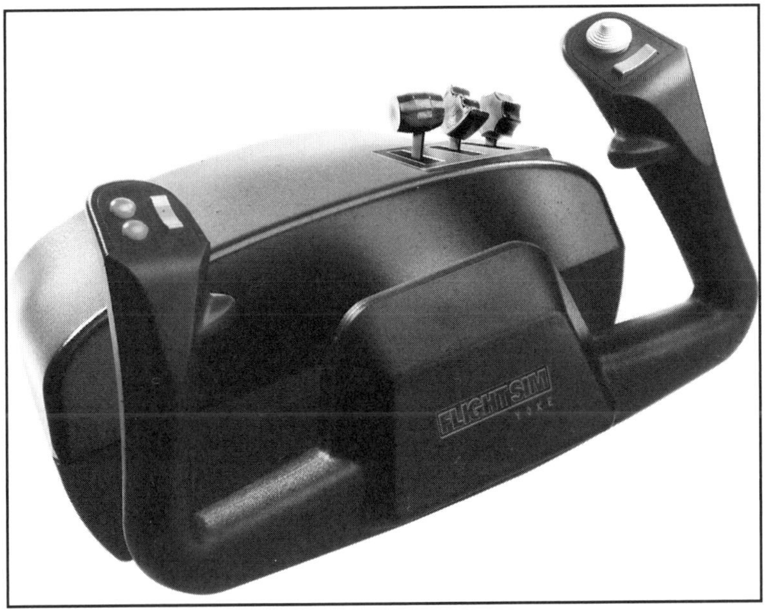


**Figure 9.10**

Civil aviation simulation buffs may prefer a yoke, similar to those used on small aircraft. Photo used by permission.

# General Purpose Joysticks

A general purpose stick is usually more compact than most flight sticks. It's often shaped more to conform to the users hand, than to model a realistic stick from an actual aircraft. These joysticks can certainly be used for flight sims, however. They also work well with a wide variety of game titles, ranging from *Mechwarrior 3* to the *Descent* series to even first-person shooters.

In 1997, Microsoft entered the joystick market with the original Sidewinder 3D. Since then, it has updated the stick with the Sidewinder Precision Pro. The Sidewinder 3D added a twist handle, which let the stick work through a fourth axis. The twist handle could be used for rudder pedals or other functionality that needed an extra axis (the third axis was used for the throttle). The Precision Pro is a purely digital stick, using optical detectors to measure stick movement rather than the far more primitive potentiometers (see Figure 9.11).

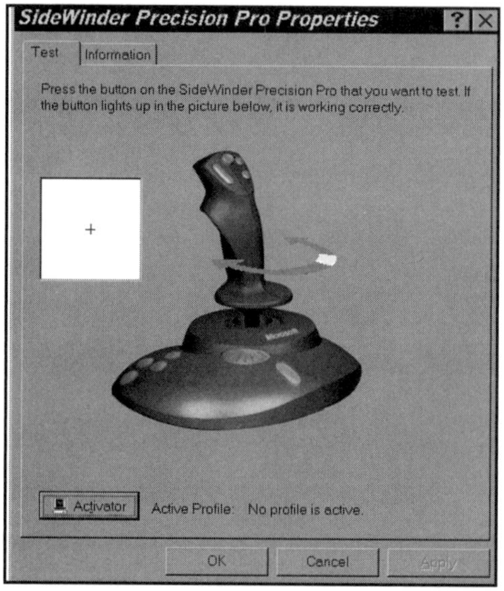


**Figure 9.11**
The Precision Pro is one of several sticks on the market with a twist handle.

Although the Sidewinder 3D wasn't the first stick on the market with a twist handle (some very early CH sticks used them), it was the first flight-style stick with the twist handle. Since then, the moniker *3D joystick* means a joystick with a twist handle. A number of companies, including Saitek, CH Products, and Thrustmaster have shipped 3D joysticks.

There are many joysticks on the market that don't have the twist handle, but are still perfectly decent joysticks. The twist handle does take some getting used to, and some people never warm up to it. When shopping for a good, general purpose stick, try it out in the store. If it feels flimsy, it probably is.

At a minimum, look for four buttons; a good USB stick should probably have at least eight buttons. The addition of a point-of-view hat is a useful feature. The *hat* is a switch that usually sits at the top of the stick that is multidirectional. It's often used to adjust views in games—the view switches direction, depending on which way you push the switch.

Finally, a throttle wheel or slider is a good thing to have as well. Many sticks also have trim wheels, which can be used for on-the-fly calibration, but these aren't a must-have feature.

Then, there's the issue of left- or right-handed users. Most sticks are biased towards right-handed users. However, CH and Guillemot make symmetrically shaped sticks suitable for either hand, whereas Saitek's Cyborg stick can be configured for either left- or right-handed users.

## Gamepads

Gamepads on PCs closely resemble those found on console game units like the Sony Playstation or Sega Dreamcast. There's a huge variety of gamepads for the PC, and it becomes a matter of taste as to which one you prefer. Gamepads have a jargon all their own. For example, the *D-pad* is the flat pad on the left side of the stick that's typically operated by a thumb—perhaps as revenge on all the right-handed people in the world. Gamepads also vary considerably in shape and size, which allows you to find one that's the best shape and fit for your hands (see Figure 9.12).

Although gamepads can work in a variety of action games, they seem to really shine in sports games, such as FIFA 2000 and NHL 99 from Electronic Arts. The D-pad and button layout allows you to easily jump from player to player, and allows quick changes in direction or movement. If you're an experienced console game player, you might start out with a gamepad for most PC gaming.

## Racing Controllers

If you're into car racing games, nothing beats having the feel of a good steering wheel. It's very tough to translate the motion of a joystick into a racing game because we're all so familiar with driving cars. Interestingly, my 8-year old daughter does much better with something like the Freestyle Pro game pad, but then she's never driven a car. For most of us, the steering wheel paradigm is so ingrained by now, it's difficult to drive with anything else.

Force feedback wheels have been all the rage, and are great fun in a good arcade racer, such as *Need for Speed III*. But if you're into serious online competition, a good high-end wheel like the CDDS series is a must-have. The larger wheel size and very precise feel let you better steer the more realistic racing simulations, such as *Grand Prix Legends*.

Of course, you may not want to spend a thousand bucks or more on a wheel. When looking for a good racing wheel, check for a solid feel and good shifters. A multitude of buttons isn't really necessary, and is often distracting. A padded, no-slip grip is a real plus.

**Figure 9.12**
Here are four typical gamepads from Saitek, Thrustmaster, Microsoft, and CH Products (clockwise from the left). The Microsoft Freestyle Pro has an accelerometer, so it can actually detect the orientation of the pad. This allows your physical movements (such as tilting the pad) to translate to game motion.

## Miscellaneous Controllers

Every year, I see a host of bizarre game controllers cross my desk. They range from the ill-fated, like the Titan Sphere, to the sometimes useful, like the SpaceOrb, to the really cool, like the Panther XL from Madcatz. Most of them are directed at 3D action games, and there seems to be an underground movement of inventors trying to create the perfect 3D game controller, just like there were scores of inventors trying to create airplanes at the turn of the century. Even Microsoft has gotten bit by the bug, having recently released its Dual Strike, which looks like an articulated gamepad, and actually works fairly well. All of these are a matter of taste, but a few simply don't work. Tread carefully when looking at an alternative controller—and wait for the reviews.

Then, there are the extreme controllers. I briefly mentioned the high-cost wheels because those are actually used in on-line competition. But the flight simmers aren't immune to the extreme controller bug, either. There are actually full cockpits you can get, as well as yoke/console combinations that have multiple working switches and other devices. These are often labors of love by serious enthusiasts, and if you are a real hard-core sim buff, you may want to check some of them out.

But make sure you warn your spouse or other roommates before you order a full F-16 cockpit....

# Part 3

# Software

# Chapter 10

# Gaming Under Windows

## A Brief Overview of Windows

A long time ago, in a place far, far away, I booted up a system with something called Microsoft Windows 1.0. It was an underwhelming experience, to say the least. Microsoft, being Microsoft, never gave up, and kept improving it. When Windows 3.0 came out, it rapidly left its chief competitor, IBM's OS/2, in the dust. Windows 3.0 went a long way toward making Windows a respectable choice as a graphical environment for running applications. By the time Windows 3.11 rolled around, networking got much easier as well.

Windows 3.0 was really just a glorified shell for MS-DOS, albeit a pretty slick one. So Microsoft developed a fully 32-bit operating system it called Windows NT. NT was much more stable than the DOS/Windows 3.0 combination, so it was useful as a small department server or with certain vertical applications. However, any application that tried to directly access hardware would be shut down by the operating system. Windows NT was designed to prevent direct access to the hardware for two reasons: better security and greater stability.

Games of the era were mostly MS-DOS games, and absolutely required direct hardware access, whether it was to the graphics card or the audio hardware. Even Windows 3.x, with its 16-bit roots and DOS underpinnings, didn't like apps that tried to talk to the hardware directly. The problem was, game developers intensely disliked Windows. The reason they wanted to write applications "close to the metal" was purely for performance reasons. Through clever use of frame buffer flipping and color map animation, game programmers could eke out amazing performance from fairly primitive hardware. Early versions of Windows, however, prevented most games from running under Windows.

On the other hand, the smash success of Windows 3.0 laid the groundwork for an even more ambitious project. Microsoft really wanted to move away from DOS because the clunky command-line interface and 16-bit limitations couldn't take advantage of the emerging 32-bit processors. Also, innovation in graphics, audio, and networking were being stifled by the limitations of MS-DOS. So, the Redmond company embarked on a plan to make Windows a true operating system.

**Note**

In this chapter, we'll be discussing Windows itself, how to tweak it and how to set it up for maximum performance with games. However, we won't be covering DirectX—that will be covered in chapters immediately following this one. Likewise, networking for games (both local and Internet gaming) will be covered in Chapter 15, "Area Networks," and Chapter 16, "Internet Gaming."

# Windows 95

Code-named Chicago during its development, Windows 95 represented a sea change in Microsoft's thinking. Although some pundits like to claim that it's still DOS underneath, Windows was a significant step from the old, command-line operating system that set the boys from Redmond on the path to success. Windows was much easier to use than Windows 3.0. More importantly, it was much easier to set up. One of the key reasons for this was *plug-and-play*, a technology co-developed by Microsoft and Intel. Products developed to be plug-and-play would be automatically detected when Windows started up.

If Windows didn't already have the appropriate driver, it would prompt the user for it. If a new piece of hardware was installed after Windows was up and running, Windows and the system would detect the new hardware and walk the user through the driver installation process.

Although there are other solid advances that came with Windows 95, plug-and-play (PnP) was the breakthrough that made PCs much easier for consumers. Sales of Windows 95 systems skyrocketed in the next several years. Other advances in Windows 95 included much easier network setup, easier access to online services and the Internet, a better help system, and a more consistent user interface. Because Windows was now the dominant operating system of choice, all hardware vendors with an interest in developing hardware for PCs had to develop some software expertise, even if it was only to write drivers.

Windows 95 improved on Windows 3.1 in a number of other ways, as well. Software that was fully 32-bit could avoid worrying about the DOS underpinnings, which enhanced stability and improved multitasking (the ability to run multiple applications in the background simultaneously). The 640KB memory barrier, which had become an albatross for programmers forced to write code for MS-DOS applications, became a thing of the past. System resources were increased, which meant that more applications and larger applications could be run.

All of this didn't come for free, of course. Memory requirements went up, and you needed at least 32MB of RAM to run Windows 95 efficiently. And although Windows could run on a 486, it didn't run particularly well on that CPU—you needed at least a Pentium class system for optimal performance. Windows needed more hard drive space, too. As Windows 95 native applications began arriving on the scene, the need for additional memory and hard drive space were exacerbated. The only mitigating factor was the precipitous decline in both memory and hard disc prices.

## Games and Windows 95

There were very few Windows 95 games early on. DirectX, the games API for Windows, hadn't fully taken hold in the game developer community. There had been a few games written for Windows 3.1, but the vast majority of computer games were DOS-based.

Unlike Intel at the time, Microsoft was keenly aware of the importance of games, particularly to home computer users. In fact, the company had dipped a toe in the game waters by selling Bruce Artwick's *Flight Simulator* for a number of years. *Flight Simulator* has always been a steady seller for Microsoft. As the PC grew in market share, revenues from PC games became increasingly important to companies like Sierra, Electronic Arts, Activision, and others. They were running into serious support problems with DOS-based PC games—two support calls would completely wipe out the profit from a game sale. The increasingly jury-rigged nature of DOS games was a cause of concern at the game companies and Microsoft.

Because most games that users would be running under Windows 95 were still DOS games, Microsoft had to be sure that they would run under the new operating system. A lot of effort went into Windows 95 to ensure a high degree of compatibility for DOS titles. By the time Windows 95 actually hit the streets, more than 80 percent of all DOS games could run under Windows 95 from the Windows desktop by simply double-clicking on the application. An additional 10 percent could be run from the desktop with just a little tuning. The rest did require a shutdown to the DOS prompt, but the ability to run DOS games, which often behaved poorly and demanded complete access to the underlying hardware, was remarkable.

## Tip

Some DOS games are difficult to run under Windows 95 or Windows 98. The majority of these are those that require a large amount of lower DOS memory. Lower DOS memory is that first 640KB that was so important for DOS programs. A number of games required high amounts of DOS memory to run. One example is *Falcon 3.0*, which required 604KB of lower DOS memory in order to run. Even on a vanilla MS-DOS 6.0 system, this was hard to reach. Today, *Falcon 4.0* is a Windows 9x game that uses DirectX.

Although you can use utilities like the Windows-supplied EMM386.EXE or Symantec's QEMM 97 to maximize lower memory performance, it may simply be time to move on to Windows games. Only a handful of DOS games needed a lot of tweaking to run, and those are getting very long in the tooth.

There were several service releases to Windows 95. Although you could download parts of them from the Microsoft Web site, a good chunk of them were available only if you bought a system with the updated version installed, or if you cajoled a local PC shop to sell you one. Table 10.1 presents a list of the service releases and their changes.

**Table 10.1—Windows 95 updates**

| *Windows 95 Update* | *Version Number* | *Additions* |
|---|---|---|
| Service release 1 (OSR2) | Windows 95b, 950b | Internet Explorer 3.0, Personal Web Server, FAT32 file system |
| Service release 2 (OSR2.1) | Windows 95c, 950c | Everything in 95b, plus USB support and AGP support |
| Service release 3 (OSR2.5) | Windows 95d, 950d | All of the above, plus Internet Explorer 4.01 and DirectX 5.0 |

# Windows 98

Windows 98 was a more evolutionary upgrade to Windows 95. By the time Windows 98 arrived on the scene, nearly every new game title shipping for the PC was a Windows game. The last DOS title I can think of that shipped was Bethesda's *Redguard* (in 1998), and even it had an intimate knowledge of Windows that allowed it to play well without resorting to the DOS prompt.

In fact, Windows 98 was the first retail release of Windows that shipped with the DirectX API integrated into the operating system. However, Windows 98 removed some useful tools, such as MEMMAKER, a DOS tool that made use of EMM386.EXE to maximize lower DOS memory. With Windows 98, Microsoft was making an even stronger statement that DOS was a thing of the past.

In 1999, Windows 98 Second Edition hit the streets. Windows 98 Second Edition was really an incremental update that fixed a lot of bugs, and added Internet Explorer 5.0 and DirectX 6.1a. Also in Windows 98 Second Edition was a tool allowing users to share a single Internet connection with more than one computer. Microsoft was becoming increasingly cognizant of the fact that many households were becoming multiple computer homes.

## Upgrading to Windows 98

I get a lot of email asking me why a Windows 95 user should upgrade to Windows 98. There are several very good reasons, particularly if you have recently completed a hardware upgrade:

- Making Windows 95 understand AGP is a pain. In fact, making the original version of Windows 95 really understand AGP is impossible because you need the USB update, which only runs on Windows 95 OSR2 and later versions.
- USB support. Although Windows 95 OSR2.1 and later ostensibly support USB, USB support is minimal at best. Many current USB products only work with Windows 98.
- Windows 98 comes with some nifty utilities, like MSCONFIG (the Microsoft Configuration Utility) and MSINFO32, a very useful diagnostic tool.

For more on MSINFO32 and MSCONFIG, see page 158.

- The OEM full install version is a bootable CD. Installs on systems with a boot-capable CD-ROM drive go much easier.

### Note

Note that the BIOS also has to be aware that the CD is bootable. Also, *only* the OEM full install version is bootable—the retail version is not.

# Windows 98 Performance Tips

Out of the box, Windows 98 runs surprisingly well, but there are still a number of things you can do to increase performance. Note that the tips we cover in this section apply to Windows 98—some may work with Windows 95, but there are no guarantees.

## Virtual Memory and Disk Caching

Virtual memory is the ability of an operating system to treat a chunk of the hard drive as if it were part of main memory. This can help in situations where you're running a large number of programs—software running in the background can swap out to the hard drive. Or, pieces of a running program can use the hard drive as if it were an extension of the memory pool. However, virtual memory is very slow.

The obvious inclination is to simply load up your system with lots of RAM and turn off virtual memory. This is a bad idea because programs often swap out to virtual memory even when there's available system RAM. The better solution is to maximize VM performance.

Windows 98 is more efficient at handling VM than Windows 95, so there's really only one thing to do to help performance, and that applies only if you have two physical hard drives. (This tip does *not* work if you have one physical hard drive with two partitions.) Let's say you have a C drive and a D drive. The C drive is bigger and faster than the D drive, so you put most of your applications and Windows on the C drive. Why not have virtual memory be on the D drive (see Figure 10.1)?

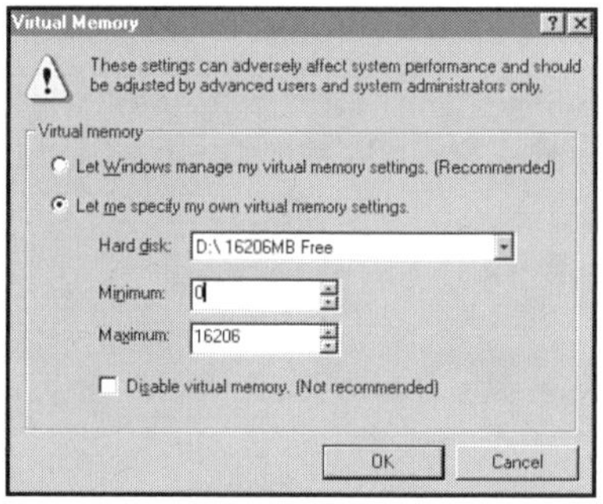


**Figure 10.1**

Place the virtual memory swap file on the second physical drive (other than the boot drive).

Disk caching is used by Windows to speed up access to the hard drive. Think of disk caching as the complementary opposite of virtual memory. Instead of using a piece of the hard drive as if it were memory, we're storing data normally on the hard drive in main memory for faster access.

The problem is that the disk cache can grow ad infinitum. If you've had Windows running for many hours, running numerous different programs, you may have noticed that it becomes increasingly sluggish. In some cases, you may even get an "insufficient memory to run" error when trying to open an application—even if you have nothing else running. You may also see some serious disk thrashing (hard drive runs continuously, even when there's no user input), because programs that should fit into memory attempt to use virtual memory instead.

You can actually control the amount of cache allocated by Windows. Oddly, it's a setting in the SYSTEM.INI file, rather than the system Registry. The SYSTEM.INI file is really a holdover from the old Windows 3.1 days. SYSTEM.INI is just a text file, however, and is easy to edit.

## Caution

The Windows 98 system Registry is a database used to store configuration data for Windows and a host of applications. You can look at the Registry by running the Registry editor, REGEDIT. Most of the entries will be arcane gobbledygook, though. Editing the Registry (in either Windows 95 or 98) is a dicey proposition, and can wreak great havoc if not done carefully. On rare occasions, you may be called on to edit the Registry, but for the most part, I recommend avoiding it if possible. Use uninstall or setup programs instead. If you do decide to edit the Registry, be sure to create a backup first.

To edit SYSTEM.INI:

1. First, make a backup of SYSTEM.INI by selecting the Start menu and choosing Run. In the Run dialog box, type **copy c:\windows\system.ini c:\windows\system.old**.
2. Then, run Notepad and load SYSTEM.INI. (It's in \windows.) Look for an entry that looks like this:

   ```
   [vcache]
   ```

   If there isn't one, you can create it anywhere below the section labeled `[386enh]`.
3. Add the following two lines below the `[vcache]` divider:

   ```
   MinFileCache=xxxxx
   MaxFileCache=xxxxx
   ```

   The five `x`'s represent the number of kilobytes of memory allocated to the file cache. If you have 64 or more megabytes of RAM, go ahead and make both numbers the same: `16384`. If you have less than 64MB of memory, set MinFileCache to something lower, like `4096`. You really don't need a disk cache bigger than 16MB.

There's one more thing you can do to improve disk performance. In the system control panel, change the system type to "network server" (see Figure 10.2).

This setting increases the size of the filename cache in Windows. Caching filenames and file addresses doesn't take up much memory, but can speed up the process of locating files on the hard drive.

Although we're looking at the file system, let's touch on CD-ROM drive performance for a moment. If you look at the CD-ROM tab, you'll see that it's already maxed out for quad speed or higher CD drives and as large a supplemental cache as possible (see Figure 10.3).

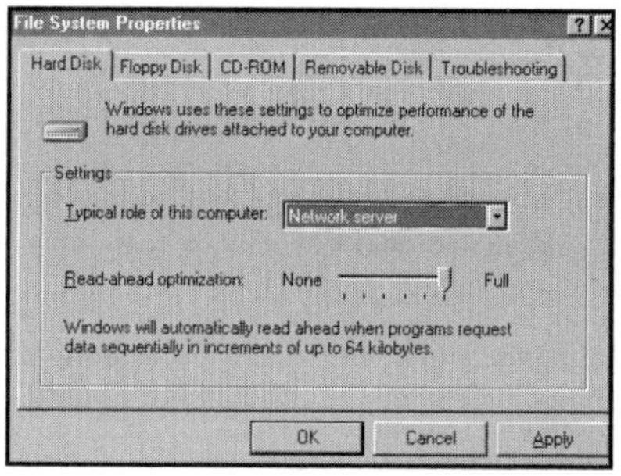


**Figure 10.2**

Changing the system type to network server will improve file loading performance.

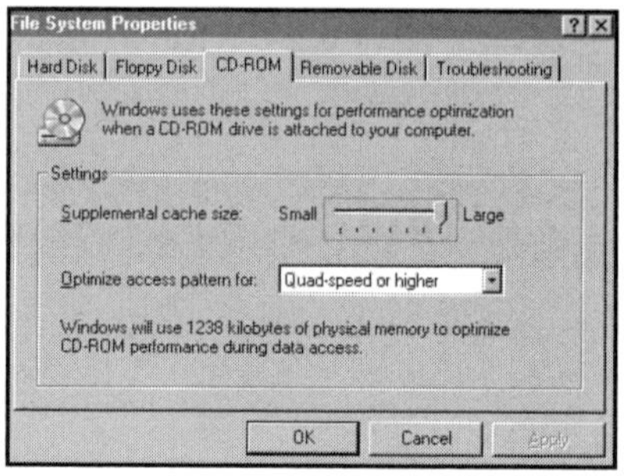


**Figure 10.3**

Most of the time, you should just leave the CD setting maxed out.

You should probably leave this alone most of the time. However, there are a few games that prefer to have the supplemental cache size set to small. Check the game's README for more information.

# Maximizing Windows Performance for Games

There you are, hot and heavy in a multiplayer action game. You're running your character like mad down the hallway, turn the corner, and see an enemy in the distance. Just as you're about to pull the trigger, the computer halts for just a split-second. That split second is enough, though, and you find an enemy rocket in your face when the computer finishes its hiccup.

What happened?

Minor system pauses can occur for a number of reasons. We'll touch on a couple of them here, but there are actually numerous reasons.

The most common culprit for a momentary system pause is stuff running in the background. If you've installed a number of applications over time, there's a good chance that something starts up when you boot up Windows. There are two places to check.

The first place is the startup folder. You can actually see the contents of the startup folder by popping up the Start menu. Right-clicking on the startup folder icon in the Start menu allows you to open a window. Culprits to remove include anything installed by Microsoft Office or utility programs like Norton Utilities. These suck CPU cycles like kids slurping popsicles on a hot day.

The other place to look is MSCONFIG (see Figure 10.4). A number of programs mysteriously start up when you boot, and there's no obvious source. Those programs are configured in the system Registry to start up. MSCONFIG allows you to check or uncheck any item that starts on bootup.

To bring up MSCONFIG, click on Start, select Run, and then type **MSCONFIG**. The menu to set startup items is found in the rightmost tab.

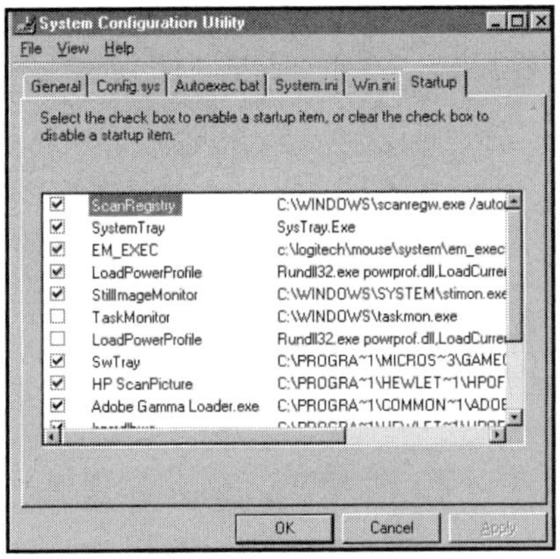


**Figure 10.4**

Look at all that junk that runs when you start Windows! You can probably turn most of it off.

You definitely want to have system tray start up on boot. Any utilities that are used by your game controller are probably useful, too. On the other hand, task scheduler and power profile can be unloaded—though, if you unload power profile, you'll lose some of the power-saving features of your system. It's a trade-off between a few more CPU cycles and the ability to save some electricity. Definitely uncheck anything loaded for Microsoft Office, Norton Utilities, or other similar applications.

Another source of system pauses is networking, particularly TCP/IP networking. We'll touch on a few networking tips in Chapters 15 and 16, but there is one key tip I'd like to hit here. If you have an Ethernet card (network interface card, or NIC for short) installed, you may be experiencing a momentary halt every 4–5 minutes. Check you network settings—it's likely that your TCP/IP binding for the NIC is set to retrieve an IP address from another source. If that source of IP addresses isn't present, Windows will pause every few minutes to search for it—it's very annoying, because these pauses can last 4–5 seconds. You need to assign a hard IP address, or have a live source of IP addresses for the network card.

For more on TCP/IP terms and TCP/IP setup, as well as other network setup issues for gaming, see page 269.

The final tip I offer is to defrag your hard drive. Do it at least once a week. There are a lot of games that use many small files, and if those files aren't contiguous, time is wasted hunting for them. Defragging will minimize this problem.

Configuring Windows 98 can be a headache, but taking just a few minutes to make a few changes can go a long way to enhancing Windows performance and improving your gaming experience.

# Chapter 11

# DirectX

## In the Beginning...

DirectX began life as a small, secretive project at Microsoft, but has now attained stature as a key part of the operating system. DirectX is a set of software services and APIs (Application Programming Interfaces) that can be used by programmers to write high-performance multimedia applications—to wit, games.

But DirectX can do much more these days. Audio editing packages like Sound Forge use DirectSound in some of their features. Lightwave3D and 3D Studio allow realtime previews of objects using Direct3D.

DirectX shortcuts many standard Windows programming methods to allow the game programmer to get close to the hardware. We'll take a closer look over the next few chapters on the inner workings of the various components of DirectX.

# A Brief History

## GDI

GDI stands for Graphics Device Interface, and is the standard method for developing Windows applications. GDI is great for moving windows, handling the mouse, creating menus, and so on. But GDI has a very high-level, abstract way of dealing with hardware, and gives little control of the hardware to the programmer. It's also far too slow for any type of sophisticated animation, and doesn't understand 3D graphics at all. GDI has evolved since the original Windows 1.0 era. As Microsoft moves into the next generation of Windows, it is completely re-architecting GDI. But for games, it's simply inadequate.

## WinG

Although Windows 95 was in development, Microsoft realized that a new way to write computer games was desperately needed. DOS games couldn't make full use of current generation 2D cards, much less the 3D accelerators that would be coming after Windows 95 hit the scene.

The first attempt to address the issue was something known as WinG, which actually ran under Windows 3.1 and allowed direct access to the frame buffer on the graphics card. It was limited to 2D graphics only—there was still no direct hardware support for sound cards, game controllers, and so on. A few WinG titles shipped, including one of the best PC games ever put out: Microprose's *Civilization II.*

## DirectX

As Windows 95 neared completion, Microsoft realized that WinG wasn't nearly enough—game programmers really did want access to other pieces of hardware. So the DirectX project was born. Code-named the Manhattan Project, the initial DirectX team was pretty small—almost an underground project in Microsoft—but moved pretty quickly. DirectX 1.0 was released in the fall of 1995. Shortly afterwards, Direct3D was added to the mix.

At first, many game developers were resistant. Even with DirectX, Windows programming was more complex and unfamiliar. And despite the efforts of the DirectX team, there was still some performance penalty when using Windows. Finally, many game developers were simply diehard DOS programmers, and slow to change. They viewed DirectX with skepticism—rightfully so, as WinG had been summarily replaced by DirectX. For all they knew, DirectX would be replaced by something equally different.

Microsoft stuck to the game plan, enhancing DirectX through six official versions (DirectX 4.0 was never released), and now we're at DirectX 7. There are no longer new DOS titles shipping, and Windows games are sophisticated in their use of 3D graphics, audio, and networking technologies. It has been a long, hard road for both programmers and users, but Windows games today, and DirectX, are much better than in the early days.

# DirectX Architecture

DirectX is actually a family of APIs (see Figure 11.1):

## Note

An *API (Application Programming Interface)* is a tool used by software developers to write programs in a standard way. APIs typically consist of libraries of prewritten software routines that software engineers can call from their programs to handle tasks like screen drawing, file I/O, and so on.

- DirectDraw handles all the 2D graphics and low level access to the hardware on the graphics card. DirectDraw is a layer below Direct3D, and is responsible for the final display of the image on your computer screen.
- Direct3D handles 3D graphics. Most games use the lowest level of Direct3D, which is just the pure rendering engine. Direct3D also has a transform and lighting engine, but few game developers have used it. Because DirectX 7.0 enables hardware acceleration of transform and lighting, we may see more games in the near future that make full use of Direct3D's graphics pipeline. We'll cover what transform and lighting is, along with a bunch of other 3D terms, in Chapter 13 "Direct 3D."
- DirectSound and DirectSound3D handle audio chores. DirectSound enables software emulation of some key functions, such as MIDI music and 3D audio, but at the expense of CPU cycles. DirectSound3D also has extensions capability, allowing games to easily use features of new 3D audio chips even if those features aren't supported by DirectSound API calls. We'll look at DirectSound in more detail in Chapter 12, "DirectSound and Audio."
- DirectMusic is an API that enables musicians to automate interactive scoring of in-game music. It has been little used, but does hold the promise of true, interactive music scores. See Chapter 12 for more on DirectMusic.
- DirectInput handles game controllers, such as joysticks, game pads, and other devices. DirectInput just keeps getting better, and with a generation of USB game controllers emerging, the nightmare of setting up joysticks may finally be a thing of the past.
- DirectPlay is actually a high-level networking API that enables game developers to easily create virtual "lobbies" where network game players can meet.

The key to understanding DirectX as it relates to you, the gamer, is not found in the vertical boxes that list the APIs in Figure 11.1. It's the two boxes underneath them: the HEL and the HAL.

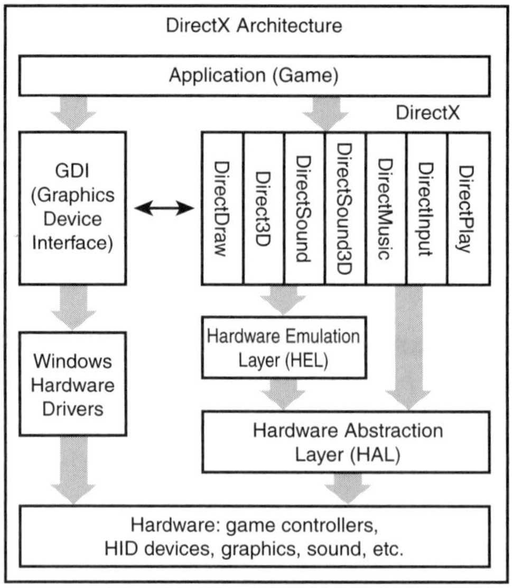


**Figure 11.1**

The DirectX architecture. The APIs talk to the hardware abstraction layer, which represents the underlying hardware.

The HEL is the *hardware emulation layer*. If, for example, a Direct3D application is run, but it doesn't find a Direct3D-compatible 3D accelerator present, it will instead do everything in software. This is less of an issue today than in the past, when 3D graphics cards weren't so commonplace. However, the HEL does kick in when you have a sound card that doesn't handle positional audio in its hardware. In reality, although the HEL is drawn as a kind of monolithic box, there's really an emulation layer for each piece of DirectX.

The other important box is the HAL, or *hardware abstraction layer*. The HAL is the face that the underlying hardware presents to DirectX. In other words, the HAL is what the application "sees"—but the HAL is really a piece of software. The program never talks directly to the hardware itself. Another way to look at it is that the HAL is a kind of virtual representation of the underlying hardware. One of the key parts of the HAL is the *capability bit*, or *cap bit* for short. The cap bits are simply toggles that tell DirectX what the hardware can do. Can the 3D accelerator do bilinear filtering? If the cap bit for bilinear filtering is flipped on, DirectX assumes it can be done. DirectX will blindly accept what the cap bits tell it—it believes that all driver writers are honest.

But, in the past, some drivers have not presented a completely honest face to DirectX. They will tell DirectX that a capability exists when it doesn't. This can be benign or annoying. A benign example is the RIVA TNT2 telling DirectX that it can do trilinear filtering. In fact, the TNT2 emulates trilinear filtering with anisotropic filtering. Because there's only a small performance hit, that's not a big deal. Other accelerators have exposed features to the API when, in fact, they either emulated them in the software driver (resulting in a major performance hit), or couldn't handle two of the capabilities simultaneously.

Various filtering techniques, including trilinear and anisotropic filtering, are discussed on page 72.

The good news is that these little tricks are rapidly becoming a thing of the past, as hardware truly becomes more capable.

# Why Annual Releases?

A new version of DirectX comes out roughly every year. The DirectX team at Microsoft has been aggressive at meeting the schedule, ruthlessly dropping or delaying features that can't make it in. Many gamers wonder: Why the push for an annual release?

Many gamers dread a new release of DirectX. Backward-compatibility is generally good, and drivers developed for a previous version of DirectX work correctly the vast majority of the time. However, there are so many different possible hardware combinations—including systems that include some fairly ancient technology—that something is bound to break.

But annual releases are a fact of life. Conspiracy theories to the contrary, there is a simple reason for such regular updates: New hardware keeps coming out. For example, DirectX 7.0 exposes the transform and lighting part of Direct3D to the hardware—because now there is hardware capable of accelerating transforms and lighting. If Microsoft didn't keep up the speedy DirectX releases, hardware vendors would be tempted to create their own, proprietary APIs (as in 3dfx's Glide). The result would be the same type of chaos that ensued in the bad old days of DOS. (Yes, there is an alternative to Direct3D: OpenGL. But there are no alternatives to DirectSound, DirectInput, and so on).

# DirectDraw

DirectDraw is the core graphics subsystem under DirectX. Even Direct3D eventually sends its results to DirectDraw for final display. DirectDraw takes care of a number of graphics issues, including moving bitmaps around quickly (called *blitting,* which stands for *block image transfer*) and handling the chores of animation through page flipping.

DirectDraw is really a very simple tool for programmers. Its real purpose is to give them direct access to the graphics card frame buffer, plus accelerate changes in bitmaps if the hardware supports it. Think of DirectDraw as a sort of programmer's representation of a graphics card. DirectDraw allows games to talk to any graphics card in a standard way.

The term "frame buffer" has been used a lot, but now it's time to describe what it really is. The frame buffer is a portion of memory on your graphics card that holds the current displayed image. Remember, it is *memory*. For example, if the game is displaying an 800×600 image in 16-bit color, then 800×600×2 (16 bits equals 2 bytes) or 960,000 bytes of graphics memory must be set aside. Another way to look at this is that each line on your 800×600 graphics display is using 800×2 bytes of data, or 1600 bytes. This is only the front buffer.

## Surface Tension

At the core of DirectDraw is an idea known as a "surface." A surface is simply a chunk of memory that holds graphics data. The *primary surface* is that part of memory that corresponds to your graphics display. Secondary surfaces are the blank slates into which graphics data is written. When the time is right, they are copied or flipped onto the primary surface to display the new frame.

There are also offscreen surfaces used to store graphics data, whether it's unused sprites, texture maps, or other graphical elements that need to be loaded quickly. Given the graphical richness of today's games, you can begin to appreciate why some games require 64MB of RAM to run effectively—and why some games require a huge amount of disk space for an install.

# DirectInput

Another key component of DirectX is DirectInput. DirectInput, as the name implies, gives game programmers access to input devices. These can range from simple keyboard and mouse inputs to sophisticated HOTAS *(hands on throttle and stick)* controllers used by high-end flight sim buffs.

When standard Microsoft Windows programs handle inputs from a mouse or keyboard, they do it by using *messages*. An input generates a message, which is passed through the operating system to the application, which then returns a message to the input device. The problem is that this is quite slow. If you're playing a 3D shooter at 60 frames per second, the last thing you want is to have "mouse lag."

DirectInput, then, allows direct access at the driver level to input hardware. In addition, DirectInput has mechanisms for devices undreamed of by normal Windows applications, such as force feedback joysticks.

## Game Ports

DirectInput is quite aware of the legacy game port.

We covered the arcane workings of the game port in great detail, beginning at page 138.

However, game ports being what they are, DirectInput has no knowledge of the quality of the game port. It could be a cheap knockoff sound card that never holds calibration or an expensive PDPI digital game port card that is rock solid.

Most PCI sound cards today have decent analog game ports. More importantly, most of them have a MIDI data pin, which is used by some digital game controllers to transmit data back to the system.

But the days of game ports are numbered. The reason is simple: USB.

# USB and Multiple Controllers

As of DirectX 6.0, DirectInput understands a class of hardware called *human input devices* or *HIDs* for short. USB game controllers are HID devices, and both Windows 98 and DirectInput know this. In fact, DirectInput can ask the HID device what its capabilities are (such as number of buttons, axes, and force effects) and list them automatically in the control panel. If you've ever wrestled with trying to get a four-axis joystick working, you'll come to appreciate HID devices in a hurry. Whenever I plug a USB controller into a system to someone new to USB devices, you can almost see the light bulb light up over their heads when the controller practically installs itself (see Figure 11.2).

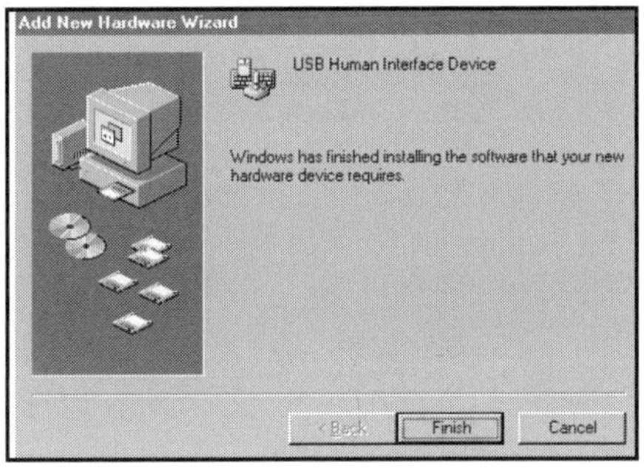


**Figure 11.2**

USB devices can be nearly self-installing because both Windows 98 and DirectInput automatically configure HID devices.

One thing that's not well known by most users—and seemingly by many game programmers—is that DirectInput can support multiple input devices from several sources. If you've ever wondered why the controller you want to use has to be at the top of the list in the joystick control panel, blame the game programmer, not DirectX (see Figure 11.3).

Note that in Figure 11.3, the two controllers have five axes between them—something that an analog game port couldn't support. But a game could, theoretically, support these two USB devices simultaneously. This is stretching the point a bit, but flight sim users will soon have the capability to have a split throttle (two axes), joystick (two axes, and rudder pedals (another axis), all on USB.

The bottom line is that USB is the future of game controllers, and gamers will be much better off because of it. DirectInput is ready—now the games have to take advantage of it.

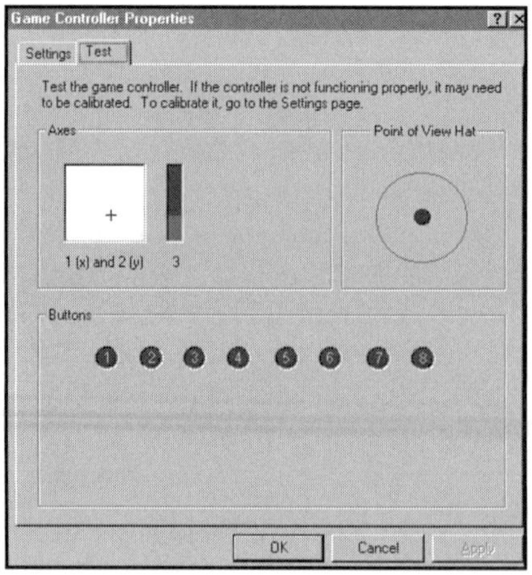


## Figure 11.3

This figure illustrates the ability to use a second joystick device, which works without problems. Most games don't take advantage of the multiple controller capability.

# Chapter 12

# DirectSound and Audio

## The Birth of DirectSound

I can recall two games that really hooked me on computer gaming. The first one was *Their Finest Hour*, the World War II combat flight simulator based on the Battle of Britain. Larry Holland, the game's designer, added support for the Adlib sound card. The Adlib had a primitive FM tone generator, but it was still light years ahead of the crude PC speaker. I had recently added an Adlib to my system, and when I heard the sound of aircraft engines and machine gun fire, I was totally hooked.

The other game that put the cap on it was *Wing Commander II*. *Wing Commander II* added support for voice through the use of a seven-floppy add-on that needed to be purchased separately. But each pilot came alive, with his or her own personality, so it was worth it.

In those days, putting sound into games was a difficult art. As the sophistication of DOS games increased, the industry settled on the Sound Blaster as a sort of *de-facto* standard. However, the Sound Blaster had some limitations. Its dependence on using DMA through the ISA bus created a lot of headaches for users and game programmers. The FM synthesizer, so amazing when it first came out, was soon scorned for its limitations. By the same token, Sound Blaster was so firmly entrenched in the market that game publishers were loath to support anything else. Products like the API libraries from John Miles helped, but they weren't widely used.

In many ways, DirectSound was as significant to the game industry as the graphics side of DirectX. After DirectSound was firmly entrenched, new audio technologies emerged, including immersive "3D" sound that can actually make use of the world geometry inside a 3D title.

In this chapter, we'll explore DirectSound a bit, so you can understand its workings. At the least, you may be better equipped to troubleshoot audio problems in your games.

# Static Versus Streaming

DirectSound makes use of buffers to temporarily store audio data. The primary buffer is always the sound hardware itself, in much the same way that the frame buffer represents the actual displayed image with a graphics card. Buffers can be either static or streaming. A static buffer is simply one that stores an entire audio sample for future use. A streaming buffer is one in which the audio data is being constantly updated. This is useful for dynamic audio effects, but can adversely affect performance in a slow system, or one with a sound card that doesn't have audio acceleration.

A few games are designed so that the user can actually choose which type of sound buffer to use, but in most cases, the game developer makes the decision. The more channels of streaming audio your sound card can handle, the less the CPU will be involved when game audio gets intense.

## Mixing Audio

One way that DirectSound differs from DirectDraw/Direct3D is with regards to supported hardware. If a graphics card can't handle a particular capability, that function isn't performed. Audio functions, however, can be handed over to the Windows sound management system. It will be slower, and not accelerated, but it does work.

One of the trickiest arts is to mix sound. If you have a sound card and a sound editor, like Sound Forge XP, you can play around with mixing sound yourself (see Figure 12.1). You'll rapidly discover that mixing audio can have surprising and unpredictable results, and it may give you some appreciation of the difficulties sound designers face in games. DirectSound does a great job of mixing sounds, but if the game tries to mix too many sounds, or mix audio of different resolutions, performance problems can occur.

Even if we take a pair of very simple sounds and try to mix them, we'd get results that look completely counterintuitive, as in Figure 12.1. And if we tried mixing audio that was captured at different resolutions or sampled at different rates, the problems only get worse. Now, imagine trying to mix eight different sounds to get a pleasing, balanced result.

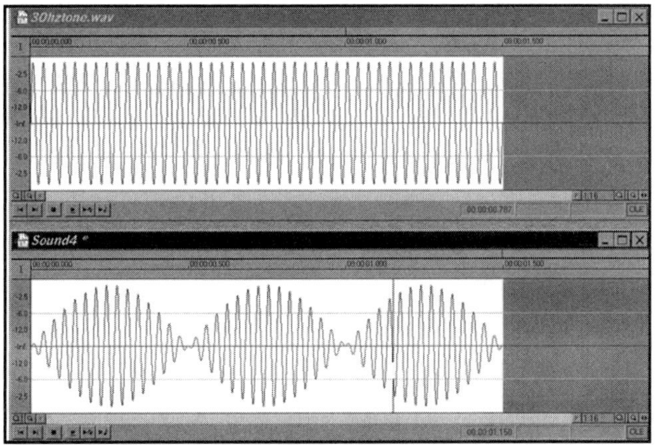


**Figure 12.1**

Here's a very simple example of mixing two sound files. The result isn't what most people might predict—and these are very simple tones, recorded at the same resolution.

Speaking of resolution, now that we have all this great hardware capable of 44.1KHz into multiple audio channels, why is it that all the sound files you've seen in games are 22KHz, monophonic? There are a couple of reasons. The 22KHz number is there because that's the native resolution accepted by DirectSound. A game programmer can change that, but then there's the problem of space. As we noted earlier, a CD audio stream takes up roughly 176KB per second. An Audio CD itself can hold a maximum of 74 minutes of CD-quality audio. Game publishers want to limit the number of CDs they have to ship, so the audio budget is often pretty skinny. Really, though, it's hard to distinguish whether a human voice or an explosion sound was recorded at 44.1KHz or 22KHz. Music is another matter, but these days, a lot of the game music is shipped as standard Audio CD tracks—you can often just pop a game CD into your CD player and play the audio tracks.

## Caution

When listening to the audio tracks from a game CD in your CD player, make sure you skip track 1, which is the game track, unless you want to hear something really strange and ugly that could damage your speakers.

The reason all audio files are monophonic (except maybe music) is subtler. If you think about it, all real-world sound is monophonic. If someone taps on a cowbell next to your right ear, that's a single sound source. It's our *ears* that hear stereophonically, and can distinguish direction and movement of sound. So it's natural that a single sound effect file will be mono. It's how that sound effect gets treated in a game that may give it some directionality. Again, that mixer built into DirectSound comes into play.

Game programmers like to use the mixer in DirectSound, rather than the standard Windows multimedia tools, for the same reason they like DirectDraw: It's faster, and allows closer access to the hardware. After all, the primary sound buffer *is* the hardware. Also, the DirectSound mixer has very low latency. Multiple sounds can be mixed and played back in realtime, with no perceptible delay.

But if all sound effects files are monophonic, how does 3D audio work?

# DirectSound3D

Let's take a look at how DirectSound3D actually works. DirectSound3D is closely tied to Direct3D itself. It uses the same coordinate system as Direct3D.

Coordinate systems are discussed on page 178.

However, unlike Direct3D, DirectSound3D has some knowledge of actual distance. In other words, the x-, y-, and z-axes are actually specified in units of meters (or other distance units, as specified by the programmer). You need that distance figure, because sound attenuates over distance. A sound that's farther away will sound dimmer than the same sound next to your ear.

People who design 3D sound for games have to take into account a number of factors:

- The distance from the listener. (Here, "listener" refers to the character in the game who is supposed to hear the sound.)
- Is the sound coming from the right or the left? If it's coming from the right, it will sound louder to the right ear than the left ear.

### Note

Sound engineers call the process of altering the sound volume based on the direction of the sound "interaural intensity difference."

- Similarly, that sound coming from the right takes about a millisecond longer to get to the left ear. So not only does the volume of the sound from the right sound less than the right ear, the sound arrives a little later. The time difference is too short to hear as an echo, but your brain can process it as a direction. (The technical term here is "interaural time difference.")
- Your head "gets in the way," too. Because of the way our ears are shaped, sounds that emanate directly from behind are slightly muffled because they actually travel through your head. Similarly, a sound coming from the right will sound somewhat muffled to the left ear because your head is in the way (see Figure 12.2).

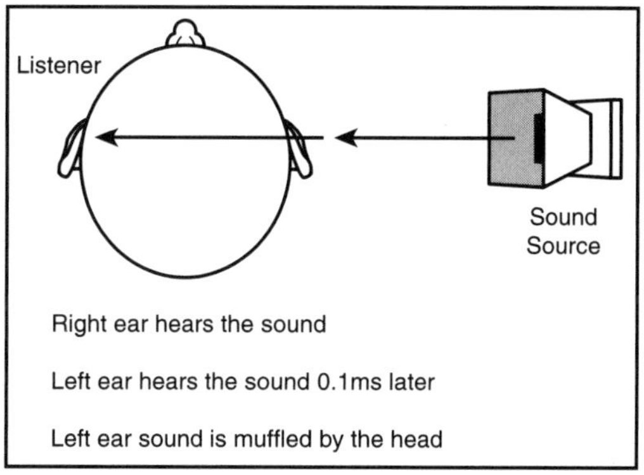


**Figure 12.2**
The human head both gets in the way of what we hear and enables us to assign directionality to a sound.

In fact, the human head proves to be a royal pain to 3D audio designers. Due to the differences in both the human head and to how well people are able to localize sound, various 3D effects may sound quite startling to some people and others will simply scratch their, uh, heads and wonder what the fuss is about.

A programmer using DirectSound3D can assign a bunch of attributes to a sound, such as how fast the sound is moving, how far away it is, and what direction it's moving. DirectSound3D also handles Doppler shifting quite well. If you've ever noticed how the sound of an approaching airplane can vary in both volume *and* pitch as it flies by, you've heard Doppler shifting. In fact, the sound signal itself can have a shape, by treating it like it was being broadcast through a cone, rather than simply being an omnidirectional sound source. This is much like light, in which a spotlight behaves much differently than a bare light bulb. Sound designers can get some interesting effects by shaping the sound source.

# How Other APIs Integrate with DirectSound

All in all, DirectSound3D is fairly flexible and sophisticated. However, it's not the end all and be all, so several sound card companies have developed technologies to enhance the gaming audio experience, such as Aureal's A3D and Creative Labs EAX.

A3D and EAX are discussed in more depth, starting on page 99.

A3D makes use of a number of advanced features not yet built into DirectSound3D, such as occlusions (walls or objects blocking sound) and wavetracing (following the path of the sound wave through space to model its reflections of walls and other surfaces). Aureal has created A3D 2.0 as its own discrete API. However, if an A3D-enabled game detects a sound card that doesn't use an Aureal audio chip, it will fall back to DirectSound3D.

Creative Labs EAX makes use of DirectSound 6.0's property set extensions. Property sets allow DirectX 6 audio to use hardware features that aren't directly supported by DirectSound3D. However, property sets only work with DirectSound3D. In DirectX 7.0, Microsoft has built in a more sophisticated capability called Voice Manager that can integrate new audio technology in both DirectSound and DirectSound 3D. Sensaura's 3D audio technology integrates into DirectSound3D in the same manner.

# DirectMusic

MIDI (Musical Instrument Digital Interface) has long been popular in the electronic music community as a standard way to tell synthesizers what type of instrument to play and what notes to play back. MIDI was also used on games in the DOS and early Windows era because MIDI music data was very compact and took little space. However, MIDI fell out of favor because of its inconsistent implementation in hardware. Musicians writing scores for games could never be sure if the audio would be reproduced on a Roland GS wavetable or an Adlib-compatible FM synthesizer. So, instead, many games use Red Book audio—the same type of sound used in standard audio CDs you buy at the local music store. In some cases, music consists of digital audio files similar to that used in games.

The problem is that this type of audio isn't responsive in an interactive way. Ideally, you'd want the score to react to what's occurring in the game—not just in a coarse way, but second-by-second. Canned digital audio doesn't allow this.

DirectMusic does. At its core, DirectMusic takes a set of themes that have been composed by a human composer and modifies them depending on what's going on in the game. The composer also creates a set of styles, chords, and tempos that can be used. The composer can be confident that the sound playback will be consistent because Microsoft now ships a high-quality software synthesizer that uses sound samples created by Roland Corporation for its SoundCanvas line of hardware wavetable synthesizers.

**Note**

Using the software synth does eat CPU cycles, though, so having a decent hardware synth engine—as any good PCI sound card would have—is essential.

DirectMusic has yet to really prove itself, but the idea is intriguing, and a truly interactive score, properly done, could enhance the gaming experience.

# Making Audio Work

I get a lot of email from readers who have various problems with games. About 80 percent of the messages blame the graphics hardware, whereas the other 20 percent blame Windows or bugs in the game. Almost no one thinks about sound cards.

In my experience, though, about one-quarter of the game-related problems I run into have to do with the sound hardware. Here's a handy checklist you can use to check for sound-related problems.

- Check all your connections—not just the obvious connection to the speaker, but internal connections as well. If you hear sound from your speaker during parts of the game, but the game's music score doesn't work, it's possible that the CD audio connector isn't properly connected.
- Check the game capabilities or setup screen. Some games unwisely allow you to enable a capability that the sound hardware may not support because DirectSound will happily emulate them in software. This can cause some serious performance problems.
- Check the Windows mixer (see Figure 12.3). It shows up as a speaker icon in your system tray, in the lower-right corner. If the speaker icon isn't there, check the multimedia control panel—you can enable it there (see Figure 12.4). Sometimes, I've seen volume settings mysteriously reset to zero, or certain audio components disabled. Just turn them up or re-enable them.

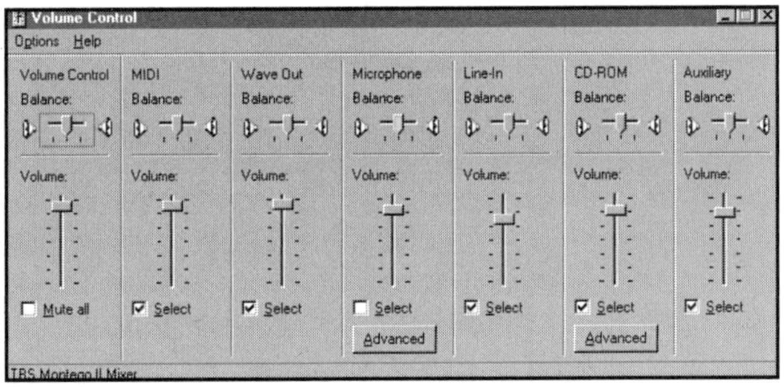


**Figure 12.3**

The Windows mixer allows you to adjust the volume of various input and output devices. However, sometimes your settings may be mysteriously reset.

- Make sure you have the latest driver for your sound card. It can make a big difference in both performance and stability. The CPU utilization of Aureal Vortex2 drivers has steadily decreased with each driver release.
- Check your speakers—and not just the obvious things, like the volume controls or cable connections. Many speakers today have some form of power management built-in. They'll go into standby mode when there's no sound signal present. But I've seen situations where they never come out of standby mode when you try to play a sound. I once spent hours ripping out and installing sound cards, only to discover that the problem was fixed by simply disconnecting and reconnecting the speaker's power supply.
- As a last resort, move the sound card to a different slot, if possible.

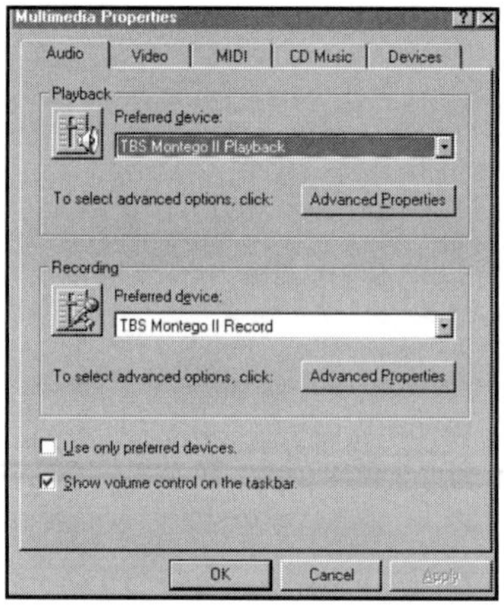


### Figure 12.4

If the speaker icon doesn't appear in your System Tray, use the Multimedia Control Panel to enable it.

The bottom line is that if you're having problems with games, don't assume it's the graphics or a buggy game. Check your audio subsystem, too.

# Chapter 13

# Direct3D

## Direct3D—A Love-Hate Relationship

If you put a legion of game programmers together in a small room and shout the word "Direct3D," you are likely to get a host of reactions. They'll range from "Cool stuff, I love execute buffers," to "it sucks less now" to the sounds of derisive snorts, followed by shouts of, "OpenGL rules!"

Some of it's historical. When Direct3D 1.0 finally shipped, a number of 3D game programmers had been using 3dfx's Glide API. Glide is fairly easy to bring up and use, from a programmer's perspective. Direct3D 1.0 used a method known as *execute buffers*. Execute buffers are packages of data that completely describe a 3D scene, plus the instructions to create that scene. However, execute buffers were not how most game developers from the days of DOS operated, so a lot of wailing and gnashing of teeth ensued. Other game programmers quietly used Direct3D, complete with execute buffers, to create some pretty cool game titles. Another problem was that Direct3D 1.0 was the descendant of the Reality Lab API, which Microsoft bought from a British outfit called RenderMorphics. This was originally a pretty good "software" renderer, using the CPU for all 3D calculations, but it didn't understand hardware acceleration very well, and its learning process was difficult for Microsoft, developers, and gamers alike.

Now, it's time to put on our thinking caps. Be prepared for some serious jargon ahead, as we explain a bit about how Direct3D works. We can't possibly cover it all in this chapter, but the goal is to give you a basic idea of the workings of Direct3D, and an appreciation for the complexities of writing a 3D game. One game developer I know estimated that a 3D game takes about twice as long to develop as a 2D game with the same overall complexity and scope of gameplay. Also, if you are equipped with an understanding of the jargon, you can also better judge the claims of the various makers of 3D graphics hardware.

# Direct3D Features Explained

Before we dive into how Direct3D—or any 3D API—works, we have to understand coordinate systems. Direct3D uses a *left-handed* coordinate system (see Figure 13.1). A handedness of a coordinate system is determined by wrapping a hand around the z-axis (depth axis), with the thumb pointing along the increasing direction of the z-value.

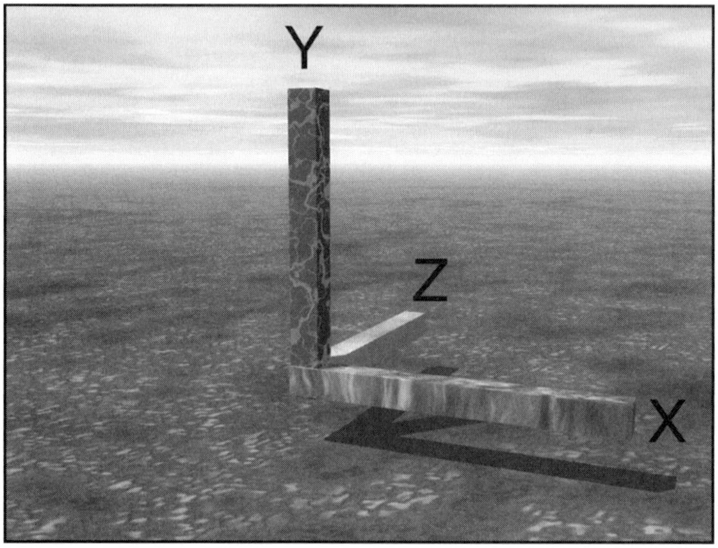


**Figure 13.1**

This depicts a left-handed coordinate system; the z-axis value gets larger as the object moves away from the viewer.

The coordinate system allows the programmer to specify the location of an object. For example, a helicopter hovering 30 feet above the ground, 30 feet directly to your right would have an x value of 30, a y value of 30, and a z value of 0.

### Note

Direct3D has no knowledge of units, like feet, inches, or meters. The programmer is responsible for figuring out distances. I'm using units here to make the examples a little clearer. Objects are created to the scale defined by the application, not Direct3D.

But there's more to coordinate systems. Each object has its very own coordinate system, known as *local coordinates*. At some point during the creation of a 3D scene, the local coordinates of each object must be translated to *world coordinates*, so that the objects can be properly placed in the world.

## The Vertex

Now that we have a coordinate system, it's time to create some objects. Objects are built out of *primitives*, usually polygons. Most often, objects are built out of one specific type of polygon: triangles. Why triangles? A triangle is created from three points, and only three points. A triangle will always consist of a flat surface. An object with four points could be a flat square—or it could be bent. It's easy to make complex objects out of a large number of triangles (see Figure 13.2).

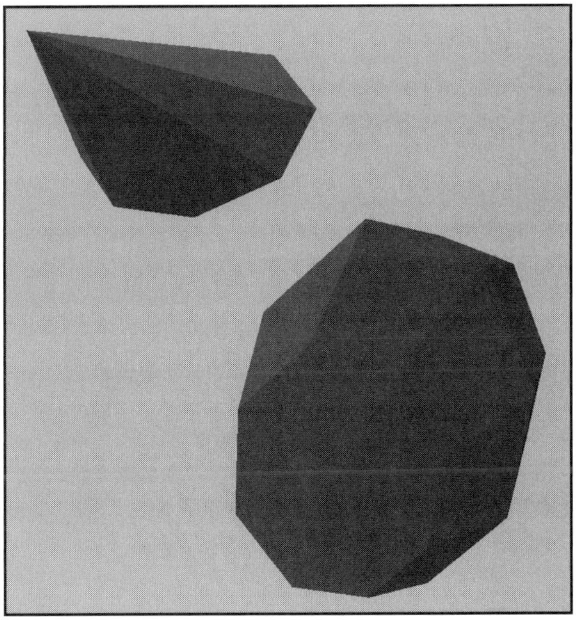

**Figure 13.2**

It's very easy to make 3D object out of a bunch of triangles.

Various hardware manufacturers are looking at ways of handling 3D objects using something other than triangles, but for the near future, most 3D games will use triangles as the base primitive.

There's kind of a golden rule of 3D graphics: Do the least amount of computation to describe the most detailed scene possible. The reasons for this rule are pretty straightforward; by being clever about eliminating redundant operations, 3D programmers can create a more convincing virtual world, and their game will still run at a decent frame rate on older systems.

A square or rectangle is formed out of two triangles, and the seam between those two is the *vertex*. This vertex is now a single line, not two lines (as it was when there were two separate triangles). As we join more triangles to create complex objects, the vertex data becomes critical in describing the object (see Figure 13.3). As we join triangles, the number of vertices decreases. In fact, most 3D objects are made of *strips* of triangles. This minimizes the number of vertices.

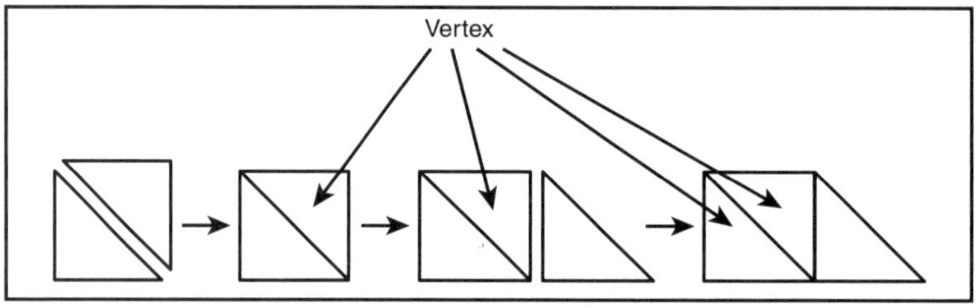


**Figure 13.3**

An object is made from three triangles, but the final object has only two vertices.

The reason for all the effort in reducing the number of vertices is reduce the amount of data that has to be moved around in memory or onto the graphics card. Because one frame of one scene can consist of thousands of triangles, minimizing vertex data can improve performance.

After we have our objects in the scene, the next thing to do is begin the animation process. It's all well and good to render a static scene, but we want things to move. That's where transforms come into play. Transforms, well, transform the 3D objects, by either moving them, rotating them, or making them bigger or smaller.

Transforms are defined on page 64.

I've spent some time describing what a vertex is because it is such a critical component of Direct3D. Direct3D has a number of different vertex formats, depending on what the programmer is doing. It's the vertex data that describes a 3D object to Direct3D. How a 3D graphics card and its associated software drivers handle vertex data can make quite a difference in performance.

In fact, if you think about it, you suddenly realize what a shell game any 3D graphics card specification really is. When you're reading the specs on the back of a box, and it says "ten million triangles per second," what does that really mean? Ten million discrete triangles? Ten million triangles joined as a huge strip of triangles? How big are the triangles? Always be wary of 3D performance numbers; 3D graphics cardmakers always place their products in the best possible light.

# Texture Mapping

Direct3D supports a variety of texture mapping modes, including texture wraps, texture blending, and multitexturing. Understanding a little about how texture mapping works can give you more of an appreciation of the effort 3D artists put into a game.

A texture map is a bitmap—that is, a computer picture of a surface. If you stop and think for a moment, a bitmap is simply a series of pixels, arranged in a line of pixels. The lines of pixels are stacked on top of each other. Each pixel is a single color. If you zoom into a single pixel on a bitmap, you'll see that it's one color.

This pattern of pixels needs to be applied to the surface of a polygon. Like polygons, texture maps need a coordinate system. Because texture maps are flat, however, they only need two coordinates, which are known as U and V. Texture coordinates are important, because the programmer can tell Direct3D exactly how much of a texture to apply. You see, textures are a fixed size, but the polygons they are applied to may be a wide variety of sizes. If you tried to squash a big texture onto a small polygon, or stretch a small texture to fit a large one, you could end up with a pretty strange looking image.

One type of texture commonly used in games is the *palettized* texture. Palettized textures are textures that use a limited number of colors. The palette of colors that the texture can use must be defined and accessible. Each pixel represents a color value defined in the color palette. Note that each texture may have its own color palette. The net result is that even though the final scene may be richly colored, each texture takes up less memory because it consists of a limited set of colors. But because each texture palette can be a *different* set of colors, you can end up with many more colors on the screen. Because of this, palettized textures have been called "poor man's texture compression."

A pixel in a polygon that has had a texture map applied to it is called a *texel* (or, textured pixel). You'd think that a single texel would directly correspond to a single pixel on your computer monitor. You'd be wrong. Let's say a brick texture is applied. During gameplay, you move your character very close to the wall. Suddenly, you're looking at a mass of huge, square blobs, each a single color. You're looking at a bunch of individual texels. Each texel now occupies many screen pixels.

To alleviate this visual mess, texture maps are filtered in various ways. After you dig through the jargon, all types of filtering—bilinear, trilinear, anisotropic, and so on—create their effects by blending the color values of nearby texels. On the one hand, the image can look somewhat blurred—but that blurring is often much better looking than huge, blocky texels.

MIP-Mapping is where textures are created in a variety of resolutions, and then applied depending on how far or near an object appears (see Figure 13.4). MIP maps are applied at distances defined by the 3D programmer. By using a series of discrete textures for different distances, performance is improved (at the expense of some memory) because the texture doesn't have to be constantly resized.

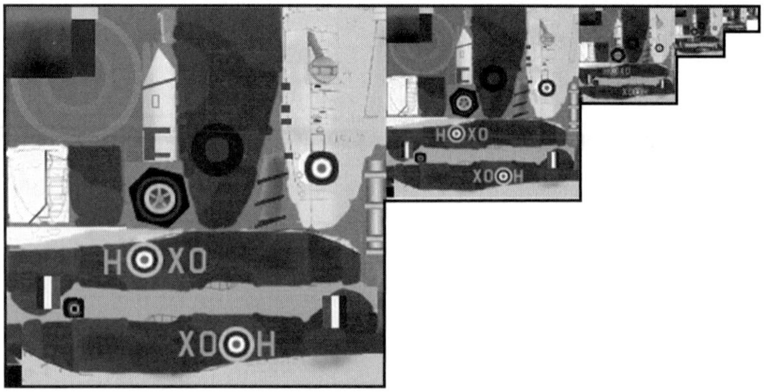


**Figure 13.4**

This is a MIP-map used to texture an aircraft in a combat flight simulator. *Trilinear filtering*, also called *Trilinear MIP-mapping*, filters within the different textures of the MIP map, but then filters between the MIP maps. This can minimize the sudden transitions you may see in places like long, straight roads or walls.

# Texture Blending and Multitexturing

More than one texture map can be combined in a process called texture blending. Texture blending can be used for a multitude of effects, ranging from transparency to lighting. In fact, most lighting you see in today's games uses light maps to create the effects, rather than mathematically calculating the light paths. Transparency effects are created using a process called *alpha texture blending*, or just *alpha blending*. Textures used in transparency effects have the usual set of colors (red, green, and blue), plus an *alpha channel*, which holds data that defines the degree of transparency.

# Constructing a 3D Scene

At this point, it might be useful to describe the steps in setting up a Direct3D scene. This should give you an appreciation for what game programmers have to consider.

1. Set up the infrastructure. This includes creating a window (we are in Windows, after all), making sure that DirectDraw is ready, set up some DirectDraw surfaces, and get Direct3D ready.

2. Set up a viewport. Remember, the monitor is our 2D "window" into the virtual world. The programmer has to define what can be seen—and what can't be seen. This is analogous to setting up a camera on a movie set. 3D programmers like to talk about something called a "viewing frustrum." You even see this term occasionally used in README files for games. The viewing frustrum is simply the visible area (see Figure 13.5). The clipping planes define the boundaries of what can be seen—only objects between the two clipping planes, and within the viewing frustrum, are visible.
3. After we've determined what objects are visible, we now need to determine what parts of the visible objects should be rendered. For example, if you're looking at the front of a house, there's no need to render the back of the house. This is called *hidden surface removal*. A part of hidden surface removal is *backface culling*. After all, if you're looking at a flat polygon head on, there's no need to render the backside.

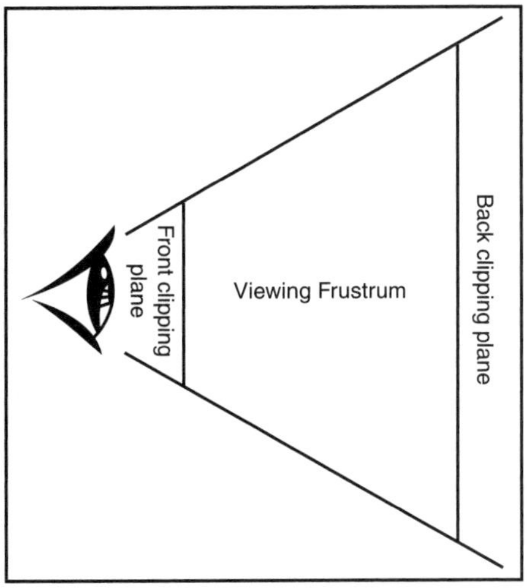


**Figure 13.5**

The viewing frustrum defines the volume that contains visible objects.

4. Describe the geometry. This is typically done with a lot of vertex data.
5. Set up the textures and map them to the various surfaces of the polygons. Initial lighting may be set up at this time.
6. Perform the transform and lighting steps.
7. Update the scene (there will be multiple frames, after all).
8. Render the scene onto a DirectDraw surface.
9. Update the display by flipping our just-rendered surface onto the primary surface.

This is an extremely abbreviated series of steps. In fact, step 3 above is worth a book unto itself. Think about keeping track of thousands of triangles that make up dozens of objects as they change from one frame to the next, and then the next. You begin to get an appreciation of why 3D games take so long to make.

# Transform and Lighting Acceleration

Direct3D has always had the capability to handle transform and lighting. But it's also set up so game programmers can create independent geometry engines; at that point, Direct3D is just used as a rendering engine.

*Transforms* describe how an object changes over time. There are several types of transforms: translation, rotation, and scaling. The simplest type is simply moving an object in a straight line. This is *translation*. A table hockey puck slides along a sawdust-covered wood surface—it is being *translated* down the length of the table.

Another important type of transform is *rotation*. Rotation is exactly what you think—an object is rotated in the 3D world. Think of an aircraft performing a barrel roll, for example. That object—the airplane—is being rotated around one axis.

Scaling, of course, is where the object is made bigger or smaller. As an object moves into the distance, it grows smaller. Note that in a real scene, all types of transforms may be used simultaneously (see Figure 13.6).

**Figure 13.6**

As the car moves along the banked curve, it is being translated, rotated, and scaled. (Artwork courtesy Nvidia Corp.)

Lighting is simply shading pixels so that the scene appears to have light sources. Those light sources may be visible—like a torch or searchlight—or not visible. Unless the game specifically wants you to be in the dark, all scenes in a game at least have some ambient light. In this instance, we are talking about geometric lights—light sources in which the effect of the light is actually calculated according to physical laws. Calculating the lights as they shine also results in the absence of light—shadows. (Many games use a trick called light maps, which are precalculated texture maps blended with the image to give the illusion of lighting.)

Figure 13.7 shows two images. The left image has only ambient light. The right-handed image has a directional light. Note how the column seems to be a part of the wall on the left. Add a directional light, and you suddenly see that the columns are discrete objects (see Figure 13.7).

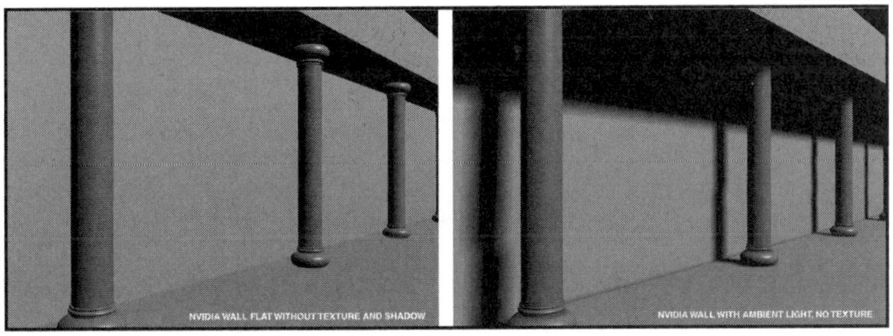


**Figure 13.7**

Realistic light sources add a strong feeling of depth to an otherwise flat scene. (Artwork courtesy Nvidia Corp.)

With DirectX 7, however, transform and lighting is "exposed to the hardware," as Microsoft likes to put it. Transform and lighting acceleration in hardware is poised to take 3D gaming to the next level. Objects can have much more detail than before, and we may finally have 3D characters that look realistic.

Of course, OpenGL has always exposed transform and lighting to the hardware. Which brings us to the next topic.

# OpenGL

OpenGL is an open, flexible 3D graphics API that was originally created by SGI (formerly Silicon Graphics). 3D graphics programmers praise OpenGL for its ease of programming and flexible extensions mechanism. The extensions mechanism allows makers of 3D graphics hardware to make a special feature in their hardware that isn't part of the API in a standard way. Unlike Direct3D, OpenGL was designed from the beginning to support 3D acceleration in hardware.

A number of games on the market make heavy use of OpenGL, most notably, games developed by id Software and its licensees. Games that have OpenGL support include *Quake II*, *Quake III: Arena*, *Sin*, *Half-Life,* and others. OpenGL is also used heavily by 3D modeling and CAD applications.

OpenGL hasn't been as widely accepted by the entire game developer community as Direct3D, but the games that use it are popular enough that most 3D graphics chip companies now have a fully functional OpenGL ICD (installable client driver).

There are actually two types of OpenGL drivers: the mini-client driver (MCD) and the installable client driver (ICD). The ICD is a full-1featured driver that supports the full OpenGL extensions mechanism. As such, it's much more complex than an MCD. In fact, the MCD is so limiting Microsoft refused to support one in Windows, so the graphics hardware companies spent the extra time and effort to develop an ICD.

## Note

Don't confuse MCD with a "mini-GL" driver. An MCD would support all defined OpenGL functions. A "mini-GL" driver only supports the subset of functions used in certain games. The most famous mini-GL is the one developed for 3dfx hardware to support *GL Quake*, *Quake II*, and games that use those game engines.

All the technical details we covered for Direct3D apply to OpenGL as well. Programmers conversant with both APIs say that OpenGL is much easier to use, requires fewer lines of programming code, and can be learned faster. New hardware features can be implemented in the accelerator's driver as an OpenGL extension.

Direct3D, with its annual updates, has pretty much caught up with OpenGL (and passed it in a couple of cases), but the ease of programming issue still exists. And there are a few things that OpenGL has that Direct3D hasn't quite attained yet, like support for *splines* (a type of curved line primitive). The other case for OpenGL is platform independence. A Direct3D title will only run on a Microsoft-based platform. An OpenGL game could theoretically run on Windows, Linux, BeOS, Macintosh OS, and various flavors of UNIX.

Tim Sweeney, the chief 3D architect for the *Unreal* game engine, has worked with OpenGL, Glide, and Direct3D. Of the three, the Direct3D version has improved the most. According to Sweeney, the Direct3D drivers are more stable and robust than the OpenGL drivers under Windows across a wider variety of graphics hardware. Some of that is no doubt due to the relative lack of experience on the part of some of the hardware companies. Most have been doing Direct3D drivers because of Direct3D version 1.0. As time goes by, and the drivers get more robust, OpenGL may be a bigger factor—but it's likely to always be second fiddle to Direct3D on Windows.

What is true is that OpenGL is no longer the purview only of games that use the Quake engine or its derivatives. Sierra's *Tribes* multiplayer game, as of version 1.7, has robust support for OpenGL. *Diablo II* also uses OpenGL. Also true is that an application, if written in a portable manner, can plug in any 3D API if necessary.

When using an OpenGL application, whether it's a modeling application or a game, there are several things you need to know.

First, a generic OpenGL implementation ships with Windows 98 and Windows NT 4.0. If you look in \windows\system, you'll see a file called OPENGL32.DLL residing there. If you tried to run, say, *Quake II* in OpenGL mode with no OpenGL hardware, you'd see a frame rate of around one frame every 1 or 2 seconds—on a fast system.

When you install an OpenGL-capable 3D accelerator, it copies some files into the \windows\system folder. For example, on my system, I have a RIVA TNT2-based graphics card, and there's a file called NV4OGL.DLL. This is the hardware enabler for OpenGL. What happens is that it "plugs into" Microsoft's OPENGL32.DLL and reroutes the calls from the software renderer to the hardware. A graphics card does *not* replace the Windows OpenGL library.

### Tip

If you've recently installed a new, OpenGL-capable card, and for some reason, it won't work with OpenGL games like *Quake II*, it may be that you have an errant "mini-GL" driver lying around. Look for files named OPENGL32.DLL that do live outside of \windows\system. If you find one—especially if it's in the game folder—delete it or rename it to something innocuous. Also, for *GL Quake* and *Quake II* and many *Quake* engine games, be sure that your desktop is either in 16- or 32-bit color. These games will not run in accelerated mode if the desktop is set to 256 colors.

For more on how 3D graphics works with hardware, see page 57.

# Making Graphics Work

Now, it's time to move away from the rarified environment of writing 3D games to the more practical world of actually making them work.

Probably the single biggest headache in PC games is getting graphics to work right. This section will contain a number of tips, divided by category, to help you keep your graphics setup running smoothly and with good performance. Problem symptoms include, but aren't limited to, the following:

- Inability to switch resolutions in Windows.
- The game won't run at all.
- The game starts, but all you see is a black screen.
- The game runs very slowly.
- The image doesn't look right. This can be seen as flashing during animation, incorrect colors, and other strange looking stuff.
- The game inexplicably crashes. This might or might not be a graphics issue.

The solution path to solving graphics problems fits into several categories:

- Hardware configuration problems
- Driver issues
- Game compatibility problems

- Mixed driver sets
- Other software causing .the problem

# Hardware Configuration Problems

Hardware configuration problems are myriad, but there are several that are more common. The first, and easiest, is an incorrect monitor configuration. If you can't seem to get a resolution higher than 800×600×256 after installing a driver, check to see that the monitor is configured properly. Choose Control Panel, Display and choose the Advanced tab (see Figure 13.8). Sometimes Windows will "lose" the monitor—even if it's a plug-and-play monitor—when a new set of graphics drivers are installed.

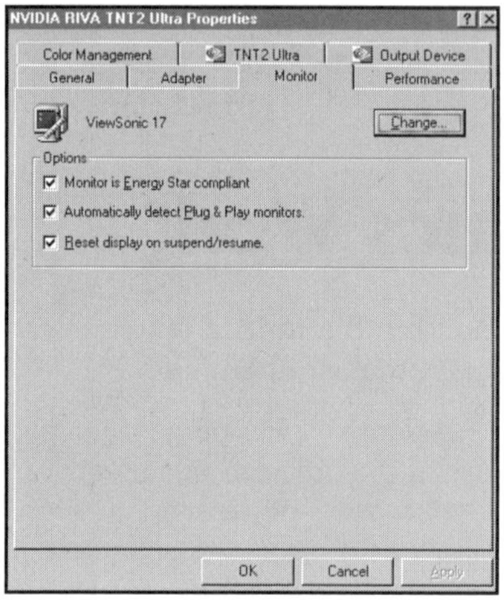


**Figure 13.8**

Check the Display control panel. If the monitor listed is "unknown," add the correct one.

Another common hardware configuration problem is an incorrect IRQ assignment, or a conflict with another piece of hardware. Choose Control Panel, System, select the Device Manager tab, and click the Properties button to see a list of IRQ assignments.

## Note

You will occasionally see "PCI IRQ Steering" listed, with an IRQ that's the same as one of your current expansion cards. If you have a fairly new motherboard or BIOS update, you can probably ignore this. IRQ steering is Windows 98's way of allowing PCI cards to share IRQs.

Almost every new AGP graphics card now requires its own IRQ. If it doesn't get an IRQ, you will likely be forced into VGA mode when you run Windows. You may even get the dreaded "Windows Protection Error," and the system will shut down. Some system BIOSes allow the user to disable IRQ assignment to AGP. Make sure that an IRQ is assigned to the AGP port. Also, make sure that the PCI card in the slot directly next to the AGP port is either friendly about IRQ sharing or doesn't require an IRQ. You may have to go so far as to rearrange the PCI cards in your system.

For more in IRQ (interrupt requests), see page 48.

One final problem that may crop up is incompatibilities between the graphics card and the motherboard itself. This was especially true of early Super 7 motherboards, which didn't properly support AGP 2x. More recently, some Nvidia TNT2 Ultra cards won't run properly on a few motherboards. These cards require the full 6 amps at 3.3 volts defined by the AGP specification—but a few motherboards cut corners on voltage regulation and delivered less than the optimum current. The only solution available is to clock back the card, replace it with something else, or replace the motherboard.

# Driver Issues

If you're running into graphics problems, the first thing you should check are the drivers for the graphics card. It's easy to check the driver revision. Hidden away in \program files\directx\setup is a nifty tool called DXDIAG. It first showed up in DirectX 6.0, and is there to help you troubleshoot DirectX problems. Launch it and click on the display tab (you may have two, if you have a Voodoo2 card installed). See Figure 13.9.

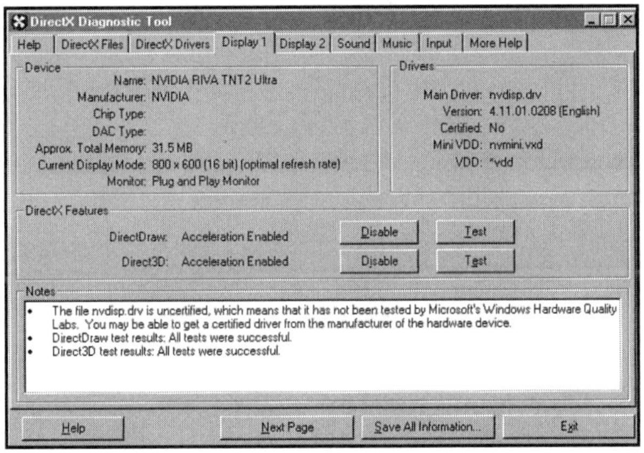


**Figure 13.9**
You can determine the current driver revision using DXDIAG, the DirectX diagnostic tool.

Updating the driver can solve a host of problems. Driver problems are often exhibited by symptoms like the game refusing to run, or frequent crashes or lockups within the game. But, software being what it is, a new driver can sometimes cause more problems than it fixes. In that case, you may have to uninstall the new driver and reinstall the old one. If the driver doesn't have an uninstall option, the easiest way to force an older driver install is to set up Windows with the standard PCI VGA driver (in the display control panel), and then install the new driver after rebooting.

### The "Driver du Jour" Phenomenon

Some graphics card companies seem to take forever to issue new driver releases; others seem to release updates practically every week. Although it's annoying to have to wait an excessively long time to update a buggy set of drivers, updating every week is equally onerous. If nothing else, your Registry gets bigger and messier.

The Internet has exacerbated the problem because beta or interim drivers often get leaked to fan sites of the various graphics hardware companies. My advice is: Don't update your driver until you need to do it. If you have a problem that can be solved by a driver update, go ahead and do it—but get the officially released version.

Independent graphics chip companies, like Nvidia, will often release reference drivers. Sometimes, the reference drivers work better than the official release from the company that made your card, and sometimes not. Again, make sure you have a problem that needs to be fixed, first.

## Texture Load Issues

If you see occasional pauses in a 3D game—especially when entering a new area of the game—you may be seeing texture management overhead. The problem can lie in any of several areas. The hardware itself may just be inefficient at fast loading of numerous or large texture sets. More likely, it's the driver, introducing overhead during the texture loading process. This can actually vary between the Direct3D and OpenGL drivers on the same piece of hardware, depending on the maturity of the individual driver. It may also be a bandwidth problem. Experimenting with settings like the BIOS setting for AGP aperture may help.

**Note**

The AGP aperture is simply the amount of system memory that *can* be allocated for AGP memory. The most common settings are 64MB and 256MB. Some boards have other settings as well.

Occasionally, it's the game. If the game has used DirectX's automatic texture management, problems can occur. DirectX has gotten better at texture management—especially in DirectX 7—but there are times when manual intervention on the part of the graphics programmer may be necessary. Of course, the problem could always lie in the game itself. You frequently see game patches released that address performance issues, not just bugs.

For example, the 220 patch for *Unreal* added Direct3D support, but the Direct3D implementation was fairly poor at texture handling. At 225f, the situation improved tremendously.

# Visual Quality Issues

Sometimes, the problems lie with image quality. If you're running an older graphics card with a limited feature set, there may be nothing you can do, short of upgrading the hardware.

However, there is a class of image quality problems that can be diagnosed and fixed. Here's what to look for:

- Image corruption, particularly odd behavior of distant objects. Solution: Go into the graphics card's Display Properties control panel and check to see if the card is trying to automatically generate MIP Maps. Some games that handle their own MIP mapping don't like this.
- "Tearing,"or mismatches between partial frames that appear as visual lines partway down the screen. This is likely due to flip-on-vsync being disabled. Check the 3D card's panel and see if you can re-enable vsync. If the control panel doesn't have it, you may need to resort to a third-party utility, like Powerstrip (`www.entechtaiwan.com`).
- You see mysterious white dots on the screen at random. This is often a problem with the memory on the graphics card. It may be that the card is failing. On the other hand, if you're overclocking the card, that may also be the culprit. It also could be heat related—a number of current cards run very warm, so make sure you have adequate cooling and try to leave empty slots next to graphics cards, if possible.
- Incorrect colors appearing in the game. If this is severe, you may have a heat-related problem. On the other hand, check to make sure that all your video connections are enabled.

Graphics problems can be complex and difficult to diagnose. If the solutions presented here don't help, check other resources. Begin with the manufacturer's Web site, but also check fan sites for the various cards. Another resource is the video newsgroup, `comp.sys.ibm.pc.hardware.video`. This is a forum of users who try to help each other out with technical problems.

# Chapter 14

# Windows 2000 and DirectX

## Striking Pure 32

Windows 98 has come a long way, but it still hasn't achieved complete 32-bit nirvana. Some compromises had to be made so Windows 98 could handle the plethora of 16-bit and DOS applications that are still out there. But the days of 16-bit applications are numbered.

It is looking like there will be one more version of Windows based on the guts of Windows 95, called the kernel. The code name is "Millenium," which means it will probably be out sometime in 2000.

However, if you're looking for pure 32-bit operation, with a fairly good degree of game compatibility, it looks like Windows 2000, which is based on the Windows NT kernel, will be your ticket.

### Note

Until Windows 2000, operating systems based on the Windows NT kernel have been ill-suited for gaming. Although DirectX became available in an NT 4.0 service pack, there was very little DirectX hardware device driver support. The net result was that most Windows 95/98 games didn't work under NT 4.0. A few did, such as *Quake II* and a number of strategy games. But for the most part, if you wanted to do some serious gaming on your NT platform, you had to install a dual-boot Windows 95/98 partition. This, of course, makes Windows 2000 attractive to NT users who are gamers.

# Hardware Support for DirectX

Several times a year, Microsoft hosts an event for developers called Meltdown. Software and hardware developers get together at Meltdown to test how well the new game titles run on the new hardware under the latest version of DirectX.

In the summer of 1999, Microsoft sent a clear message to game developers: Use Windows 2000 as your development tool.

That's good news for game players, too. Windows 2000 shipped with DirectX 6.1. Hardware driver support for DirectX 6.1 under Windows 2000 has been somewhat slow—particularly for advanced PCI sound cards. However, most 3D graphics accelerators already have Windows 2000 drivers available, and most USB game controllers are already supported in Windows 2000 (see Figure 14.1).

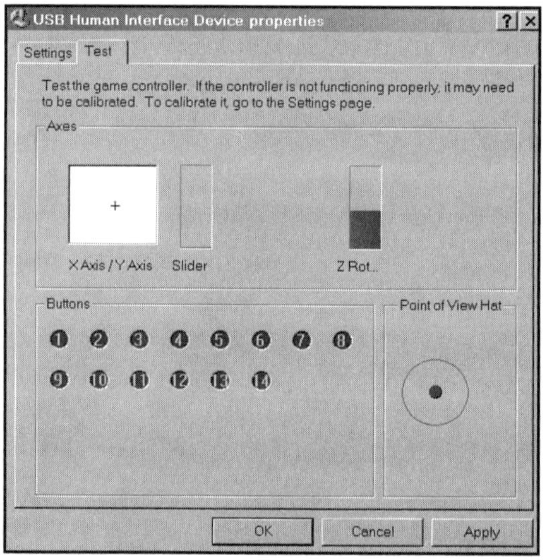


**Figure 14.1**
USB joysticks just plug in and work under Windows 2000. DirectInput now works as it should; DirectInput hardware wasn't available in previous versions of NT.

Currently, many Windows games don't work properly under Windows 2000, but more do work under Win2k than under Windows NT 4.0. That's a pretty good sign for a beta operating system.

# Windows 2000

The Windows 2000 Desktop resembles the one found in Windows 98 quite closely, with a few minor exceptions (see Figure 14.2).

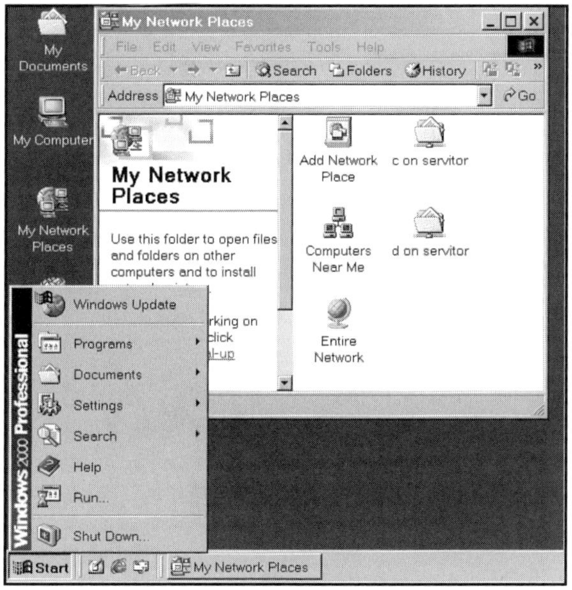


**Figure 14.2**
The Windows 2000 screen closely resembles that of Windows 98.

In fact, Windows 2000 is much friendlier toward its 9x sibling than Windows NT was. For one thing, Windows 2000 now has full support for the FAT32 file system, so file sharing and coexistence with Windows 98 are much easier.

## Note

Windows 2000 also supports the NTFS file system. Choosing which file system to use is a crucial choice if you are a power user or if you want to dual boot another operating system, such as Windows NT, Windows 9x, or Linux. For more help, see *Special Edition Using Microsoft Windows 2000 Professional*, published by Que.

It's also simpler to navigate around the environment. Key windows have hyperlinks to other related areas on the left side. When browsing the multimedia control panel, I found it quite easy to pop up the device properties for the sound card. Under Windows 98, I would have had to bring up the System Control Panel, click on Device Manager, and scroll down to find the device.

Hardware driver support is a little slow to come out—especially for sound cards. After some digging, I uncovered a driver for the Aureal Vortex 2–based sound card in the Windows 2000 system. However, that driver seemed to be comfortable only with .WAV files. If I actually ran a game that used DirectSound, the game would invariably lock up.

Swapping out the Vortex 2 board for a Sound Blaster AWE-64 made life much easier—games would run—but there was no positional audio, and the CPU hit was greater.

Speaking of CPU hit, it's a little easier to monitor performance in Windows 2000—it's built into task manager now. Just press Ctrl+Alt+Del and launch Task Manager. Click on the Performance tab, and you get a quick and dirty look at memory and CPU usage (see Figure 14.3).

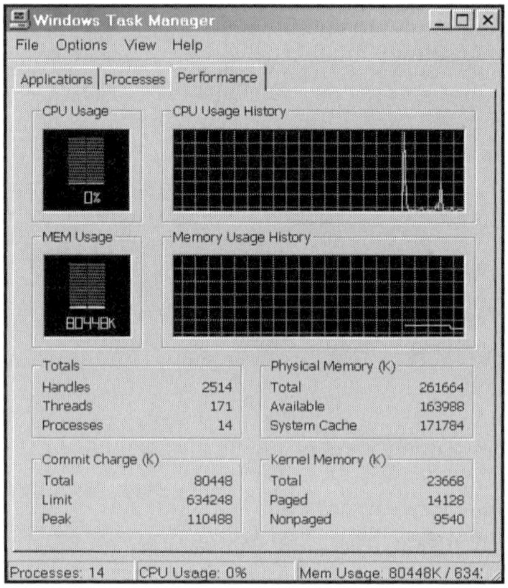


**Figure 14.3**

The Windows 2000 task manager has a mini-system monitor built into it.

## Note

If you are a Windows 9x convert, you might think it strange that I told you to press Ctrl+Alt+Del. In Windows 9x, this key combination brought up the close program box. In Windows NT and 2000 parlance, it launches the task manager. Trust me, you'll get used to it.

Note also in Figure 14.3 that there are two additional tabs: one labeled Applications, and another called Processes. Windows 2000 separates global processes from local applications—each application gets its own memory space, and can't step on another application or on Windows itself. Better memory protection, as it's called, makes Windows 2000 more stable because it can shut down a renegade application if that app tries to take memory not allocated to it. But this extra stability comes at a price: Memory protection overhead does slow overall performance down a bit.

## Caution

Windows 2000 Professional—the lowest level of Windows 2000 you can buy—will support up to two CPUs. Today, only a couple of games will benefit from multiple CPUs: *Quake III: Arena* and *Falcon 4.0*. This will probably change slowly over time—most games are still not built to take advantage of a second CPU, even in an operating system that supports it. So rushing out and buying a dual CPU system is probably a waste of your hard-earned dollars.

Windows 2000 really got my juices flowing when I plugged in a USB joystick. I tried to bring up a standard, game port joystick, but Win2k couldn't find the correct driver for the game port. So I plugged in a four-axis USB stick. It was quite a revelation. The joystick control panel interface was somewhat cleaner. But stepping through the calibration screens was a real eye-opener. At first blush, it looked like a bigger version of the Windows 98 calibration screen, but the ability to display the raw data gave you a more solid idea of when you were hitting the limits of the potentiometer (see Figure 14.4).

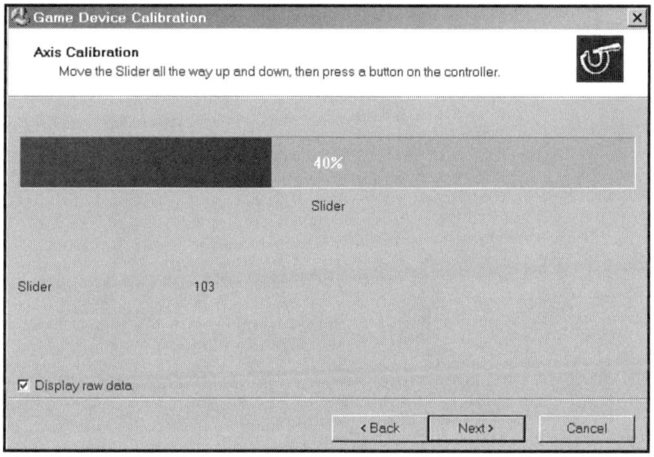


**Figure 14.4**

Windows 2000 joystick calibration is easier and friendlier.

Unlike Windows 98, Windows 2000 defaults to a logon screen when you boot up (Windows 98 only does this if you enable networking). But you can configure it to boot straight into the Windows desktop in the user control panel.

Only about half the games I tried would run out of the box (some—like *Mechwarrior 3*—wouldn't even install). A great deal of the problem lay in the less-than-robust sound support. Windows 2000 will require WDM drivers for sound cards. WDM—*windows driver model*—is different from the past Windows 95-style drivers.

The bottom line is that Windows 2000 looks very promising for most gaming applications. The only significant issue of concern is that DirectX hardware device driver support is trickling out at a slow pace. That is, however, a vast improvement over the almost nonexistent hardware support for DirectX in Windows NT 4.0. As hardware and game companies become more comfortable with this latest Microsoft OS, Windows 2000 looks to be a stable, robust gaming platform.

# Part 4

# Multiplayer Gaming

# Chapter 15

# Area Networks

## Social Gaming

It's a typical Friday night at the Case household. The sound of explosions, gunfire, raucous laughter, and screams emanate from the daylight basement. So far, though, the local constabulary hasn't seen fit to show up on my doorstep with a SWAT team.

It's a LAN party.

In my basement office, I have anywhere from four to seven PCs at any given time, all networked. Occasionally, buddies will show up, lugging their own systems. We spend most of Friday night and some of the wee hours of Saturday morning having a blast with LAN-based multiplayer games.

In fact, I've found such LAN parties to be a lot more fun than Internet gaming. Somehow, gaming over the Net seems anonymous, even when you're playing with a friend. There's something satisfying about being able to needle a friend in person after a particularly satisfying win. Cooperative play goes much more smoothly, too, because the proximity of players makes for easier coordination.

A LAN party uses a local area network instead of the Internet to connect multiple computers—much like the networks in most businesses. With Windows 98, setting up a small LAN for gaming is surprisingly easy. LAN parties can be found all over the country. Not everyone has multiple PCs, but a surprising number have more than one. Flight sim buffs have been doing this since the days of *Falcon 3.0*. If no one has a large enough house, they may rent a hotel ballroom for a weekend.

We'll look into the various network technologies available for home networking. In Chapter 22, "Getting Your Network Running," we'll talk about how to actually set up a network.

# Traditional Ethernet

The original Ethernet network was created at the Xerox PARC research labs in the early '70s. It was modified slightly, and turned into the IEEE 802 standard in the late '70s. Since then, ethernet (with a small "e") has gone through several different revisions, and you can now find ethernet LANs that support throughput of 100 megabits per second or more.

### Note

Another type of networking common in some companies is *Token Ring*, originally developed by IBM. You rarely find it these days (except in existing networks that were set up a long time ago), and it's very expensive. Ethernet is much more suitable for home networks.

There are several variants of ethernet currently available, sorted by speed and cable type. The older, once prevalent type is 10 megabit per second ethernet, which adheres to the IEEE 802.3 standard. 802.3 networks came in several flavors of cables. For our purposes, the most interesting types are 10base2 and 10base-T.

10base2 cuses a coax cable that closely resembles the cable used in cable TV connections. In the past, 10base2 was cheaper to set up because you didn't need a hub. The cable was somewhat fragile, though, and if you reconfigured a network, you had to worry about reconnecting small, 50 ohm terminators at the ends of the cable.

10base-T uses a twisted-pair cable, much like the cable used to connect telephone lines, but somewhat heavier. The cost of 10base-T is really not an issue anymore. Ethernet cards (called *NICs,* short for *network interface card*) supporting twisted pair can be had for as little as $20 apiece.

A 10base-T network requires hubs to operate (see Figure 15.1). A hub is a device that has a bunch of connections. You wire all the PCs to the hub, and the hub has electronics to manage all the interconnections. This type of network used to be called a *star topology,* but you hardly ever see that term anymore. Hubs have dropped substantially in price, and 10 megabit hubs can be found for $30.

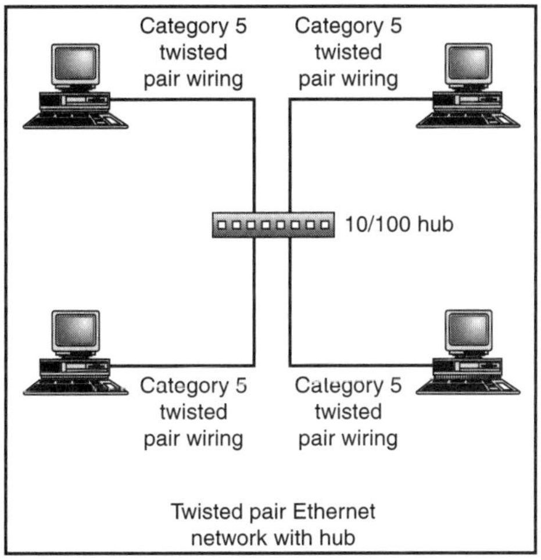


**Figure 15.1**

A typical layout for a 10baseT network. All the PCs are connected to the hub.

A higher-speed variant of 10base-T is *fast Ethernet*, which supports speeds of up to 100 megabits per second. For fast Ethernet, you need a more robust type of twisted pair cable, known as *category 5* cable. Also, the hubs must support the higher speed. Lately, hubs have appeared on the market that support both standard or fast Ethernet; a few can actually handle both types of connections simultaneously. A dual speed hub, that can connect 10mbps and 100mbps systems, is very handy if you're setting up a LAN party—you never know what kind of network card someone could have in his or her system. An 8-port, dual speed hub can be found for well under $150 (see Figure 15.2).

**Figure 15.2**

Here's the stack o' hubs at the Case house. There are two Netgear hubs (only one is dual-sensing), and a Linksys hub stacked on top.

If you are 100% sure you'll only be connecting two systems, all you need is a pair of NICs and a special twisted pair cable called a direct-connect ethernet cable, sometimes called an Ethernet crossover cable. This is simply a standard twisted pair cable with a couple of the wires reversed, so that a hub is unnecessary.

The price of fast Ethernet has dropped precipitously in the past several years, and you can find a kit with a four-port, dual-speed hub and a pair of fast Ethernet PCI cards for $100 now. You can even find category 5 cables in varying colors, which can aid in troubleshooting connections. A variety of networking kits are available, from companies like Netgear, 3Com, Hewlett-Packard, Linksys, D-Link, and others.

### Note

Networking your computers is an enormous topic and although the steps for doing so have gotten much easier for the home user, there's still almost no end to the snafus you can encounter along the way. If you want to learn a great deal more about networking, I suggest picking up copies of:

*Upgrading and Repairing Networks, Second Edition*, ISBN 0-7897-2034-5, Que

*Complete Idiot's Guide to Networking Your Home*, ISBN 0-7897-1963-0, Que

*Practical Network Cabling*, ISBN 0-7897-2247-X, Que

## Direct Connect

If you have only a pair of PCs, or just a laptop and a desktop system, going to the effort of setting up an ethernet network—even one with just two NICs and a direct ethernet cable—may seem like a big chore. One alternative is to use Windows own direct connect capability.

Direct connect allows you to connect two computers using a special parallel cable (sometimes called a laplink cable). The problem with this is that it will interfere with any other parallel port devices you may have, such as a printer. If that's not an issue, this may be a good answer if you only do a little, occasional two-player gaming.

To set up a direct connect network, you first need to install the protocols you want to use in the network control panel. Then, you open the Start menu, select Programs, Accessories, Communications, Direct Connect. After that, follow the onscreen instructions. One computer needs to be the "host" and the other is the "guest." You'll have to do this for both computers.

### Tip

If you don't have a Direct Connect option in Accessories, it wasn't installed during Windows setup. You can add it by running the Add/Remove Programs Control panel. Click on the Windows Setup tab, select Communications, and then click on the Details button.

For more information on how to set up protocols, see page 269.

Microsoft has licensed Parallel Technologies as a supplier of parallel cables for direct connect. It can be found at `www.lpt.com`.

# Phone Line Networks

The problem with ethernet is that you have to string the cable through your house. This may seem a little onerous if you have only two PCs, or if you have PCs scattered through different rooms in the house. One solution may be close at hand. In many houses—particularly houses that have PCs—there are multiple telephone jacks throughout the residence. Wouldn't it be great if those jacks could be used to network PCs?

As a matter of fact, they can. The Home phone-line Networking Alliance (HomePNA) was set up in 1998 for just that purpose. The HomePNA was originally founded by 11 companies, including industry heavyweights 3Com, Lucent Technologies, AMD, Hewlett-Packard, and Intel. The idea was to use all those spare telephone jacks in American households to connect PCs (see Figure 15.3). The actual technology for phone-line networking was developed by Tut Systems.

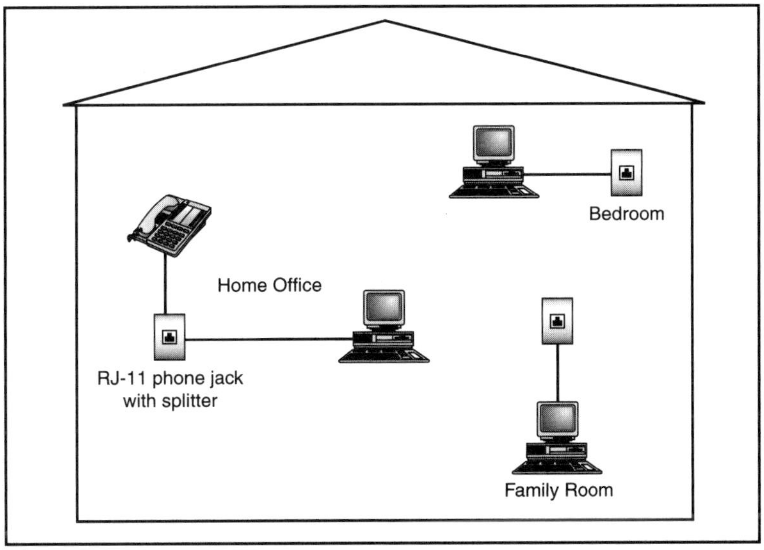


**Figure 15.3**

Telephone networking allows users to be spread out through a house.

## Note

At first blush, you might think this would be an easy way to wire an apartment building or dorm. It's not quite that simple. Phone-line networking kits I've tested don't seem to want to cross physical phone lines. They will network on jacks assigned to different numbers, but only if they're part of the same wire set.

There were obstacles to overcome. First, people don't want to give up an active phone line to connect PCs. This is shown by the huge demand for second phone lines by households that have Internet connections. Secondly, you wouldn't want to interfere with alternative Internet connections, such as DSL. The solution is to use a different set of frequencies for each discrete user type (see Figure 15.4).

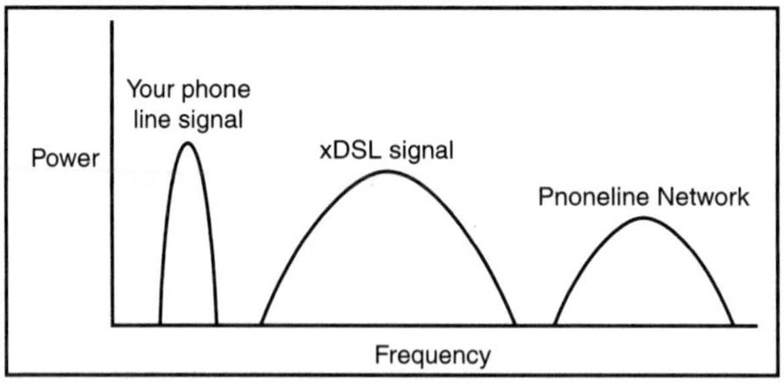


**Figure 15.4**

Because phone-line networking uses a completely different frequency band, it doesn't interfere with voice or data communications.

Of course, phone-line networking isn't a panacea. You do need those jacks in the rooms that have computers. The good news is that installing new telephone wiring and jacks is relatively inexpensive—much lower than hiring an electrician to string ethernet cable.

The other problem is that, as of the HomePNA 1.0 spec, it's pretty slow: 1 megabit per second. This actually is fine for multiplayer gaming (up to four or so players), but moving files around is painful. If you create large graphics or database files and plan to move them from machine to machine, 1 megabit could seem a bit like being transported back to the dark ages.

To that end, the HomePNA has recently signed off on the 2.0 standard, which boosts transfer speeds to 10 megabits per second, or as much as traditional ethernet. This makes phone-line networking more viable than most of the ethernet alternatives.

Phone-line kits are generally easier to set up than standard ethernet, too. In most cases, you do have to install a couple of cards into expansion slots in the PC. Recently, though, Intel has started shipping a kit with a dongle that plugs into the PC's parallel port. It works, but it's clunky and slower even than regular phone-line networking due to the parallel port overhead. It's too bad Intel didn't go with a USB connection.

Most kits also come with software that allows you to share an ethernet connection. This sounds like a gamer's dream, but it's not so simple. Most game servers require a discreet IP address per player. Internet sharing software generally presents only a single IP address to the outside world—because most home users only get one IP address from their service provider. So, trying to log on to a game server with two or three users through Internet sharing software is problematic at best.

# Other Home Networking Alternatives

There have been a number of other solutions developed to connect small networks of PCs. None are as viable as ethernet or phone-line networking, but they may be suited to your particular circumstances.

## Power-Line Networking

Every room in most houses is wired for electricity. So it's natural that someone would think of transmitting data over the power line. Intelogis, a Utah company, created its Passport power line networking kits. It consists of a huge device resembling a power brick that plugs into a wall outlet. You plug the attached cable to your parallel port. It installs very easily, works well, but is quite slow.

One possible use for the Passport is to connect PCs in different dorm rooms or apartments in a small apartment building. As long as all the connections are on the same side of a power transformer, up to twelve PCs can be networked. This also creates a natural security concern, so Intelogis has built levels of security into its software. Like the phone-line kits, the Passport comes with Internet sharing software.

## USB

The cool thing about a really fast serial bus, like USB, is that it's multipurpose. Several companies are now marketing USB networking kits. These take several forms. Entrega makes a network adapter that plugs into your PC's USB port. The other end is a standard RJ-45 jack, and it connects to any standard ethernet network at 10 megabits per second. The company also makes a three-port USB hub, with a fourth port that has an ethernet connection.

Anchor Chips makes a USB networking kit in which you daisy chain PCs via USB cables, but the cable length is somewhat limited. There are several appealing things about the Anchor Chips kit, however. First, the speed is a little better than most other alternative methods—about 2–3 megabits per second, or about one-third the speed of ethernet. Secondly, it's instantly configurable. You do have to configure the networking protocols the first time, but when you connect to the USB port (if it's been disconnected for some reason), it instantly reconfigures—without rebooting. True plug-and-play networking is a wonderful thing.

## Wireless

It's natural to wish for a wireless network. After all, if you didn't have to string any wires, that would be perfect. There are, in fact, wireless networking products out there. Diamond Multimedia sells a wireless kit that works via radio frequencies over relatively short (150 feet) distances between nodes. Anything that broadcasts over radio waves creates a natural concern for security, but the Diamond hardware uses both spread spectrum and encryption technology to maintain security.

Several companies have developed wireless LANs that use infrared repeaters, but the technology is quite expensive. Diamond's Homefree wireless kits are under $150 for two systems. The real downside is that they're pretty slow. Although rated at 1 megabit per second—the same as the HomePNA 1.0 standard—it actually is slower than that in practice. Speed seems to degrade over distance, too.

# No More Solitary Confinement

As personal computers get cheaper and cheaper, it's easy for a gamer to become tempted into adding a second system for multiplayer gaming. Participating in the LAN party movement is a lot of fun, too. In August, 1999, the largest LAN party ever assembled—over 300 users—took part in Fragapalooza, in Edmonton, Alberta, Canada. The four-day event had sessions for action games, flight sims, strategy games, and other genres. It was a true computer gaming convention for users.

Another way to add a second system is to simply keep an existing computer after you upgrade (assuming the upgrade was a new system). For all but the most demanding titles, this can be a good way to extend the life of your older system.

But whether it's LAN parties, the office network, or your own multi-PC setup, multiplayer is more fun than playing against a PC. Just remember to keep the windows closed....

# Chapter 16

# Internet Gaming

## Taking On the World

The Internet has now become as much a part of our way of life as automobiles and television. Although PCs don't have quite the market penetration of those older technologies, the Internet is rapidly reshaping the way we communicate and do business. It's also reshaping entertainment—including games.

Although LAN gaming is definitely more social, it's also more limiting in other ways. You're always limited in the number of PCs and players that can participate. *Quake III: Arena* supports a maximum of 64 players, whereas Microprose's *B-17II* flight simulator maxes out at 32 players.

Internet gaming, on the other hand, encompasses both games that support small or moderate player count (like *Quake III: Arena*) and other types of games. These can range from massively multiplayer, persistent worlds, like *Everquest* and *Ultima Online*, to text-based MUDs (multiuser dungeons), to team-based games like *Tribes*. A popular pastime is parlor games, like card games and backgammon.

One of the more interesting gaming phenomena recently was the world against Gary Kasparov. Kasparov, the world Chess champion, took part in a chess game against all comers on the Internet. His opponents would suggest moves and strategies, and the move that got the most votes would get the nod. It was an interesting, Internet spin on one of the oldest games known.

But to play on the Internet, you have to connect to the Internet. And to play well, you have to have a good connection. Which brings us to the next topic.

# Lag Is a Drag

High lag times in games take a variety of forms. One is sudden warping, in which a character or monster is seen in one place, then suddenly appears somewhere else—and not by design. Another symptom may be pauses or freezes in the action. Other odd problems can occur due to high lag, such as games crashing or players being dropped unexpectedly. Whatever the symptom, lag is a drag. But what causes it?

One cause is delays in getting the data from your PC to the game server. The Internet consists of thousands of servers, all interconnected over the telecommunications backbone. The Internet gets its name because it is a "network of networks"—the new buzzword is "Internetwork." The networks keep track of each other through routing tables that are essentially giant phone books for computers. If you send an email message to a friend halfway across the country, you have no idea how many servers it passes through (*hops*, as it's known). There might be only a couple of server hops, or dozens, as the various data packets that make up your message wind their way through the Net.

The other important thought is the idea of packets. Your message is broken up into discrete packets of data, which are reassembled into a coherent whole at the other end. The problem is, all the packets don't have to take the same route (see Figure 16.1). The Internet was originally designed to be able to do this so that no one machine would ever be the "nerve center" of the entire Net.

Another problem can crop up if the game server is overloaded. Trying to run a 32-player *Quake III* game is probably a fruitless endeavor if the server is only a 166MHz Pentium.

Another problem may be the connection to the Internet. That can be the modem or connection hardware itself, or it could be at the ISP side. If your ISP is several hops from a high-speed backbone, that can cause lag. Sometimes (early to mid-evenings), popular ISPs can get very busy, and that can show up as additional lag.

Lag time is often measured by looking at *ping times,* which are measured in milliseconds (ms). Ping is a utility that was originally developed for UNIX, and actually runs in DOS under Windows. *Ping* measures how long it takes to send a small amount of data to the destination machine, and for that machine to answer back. To check for ping times generically, you just pop up a DOS window and run it by typing:

```
ping <servername or ip address>
```

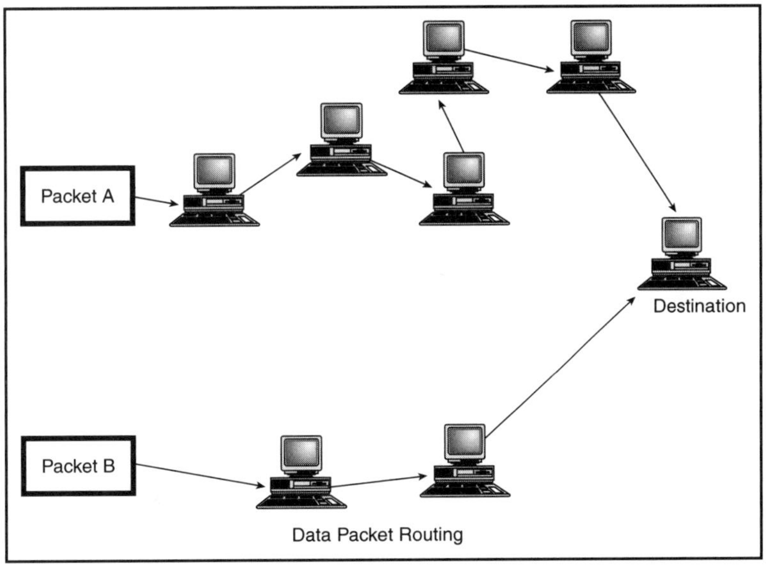


**Figure 16.1**
Messages—including data transmitted from games—are broken up into packets. The individual packets can take different routes to the final destination.

Many games that are designed to play over the Internet have built-in ability to check each game site for lag times. Figure 16.2 shows the server list for *Tribes*, which provides Ping information for each of its game sites.

As we explore the different technologies for connecting to the Internet, we'll talk about the possible solutions for lag, as each connectivity type may have different causes and solutions.

# Dial-Up (Analog Modems)

I got my first modem in 1985—a Hayes modem, which could connect at a whopping 1200 baud. It cost about $400 at the time. Now, you can get 56kbps modems for under $100. Times have definitely changed.

---

**Note**

Modem is actually a contraction for *modulator-demodulator*, which describes what it does. A modem takes a digital signal and converts it to an analog sound. When it receives the sound, it demodulates it into a digital signal again. Although most modems these days are specified in kilobits per second (kbps), you see the word *baud* used occasionally. Baud is short for Baudot code, a type of transmission code used in older teletype systems. Baud and bits per second (bps) are almost, but not quite the same. However, you can just think in terms of bits per second these days.

---

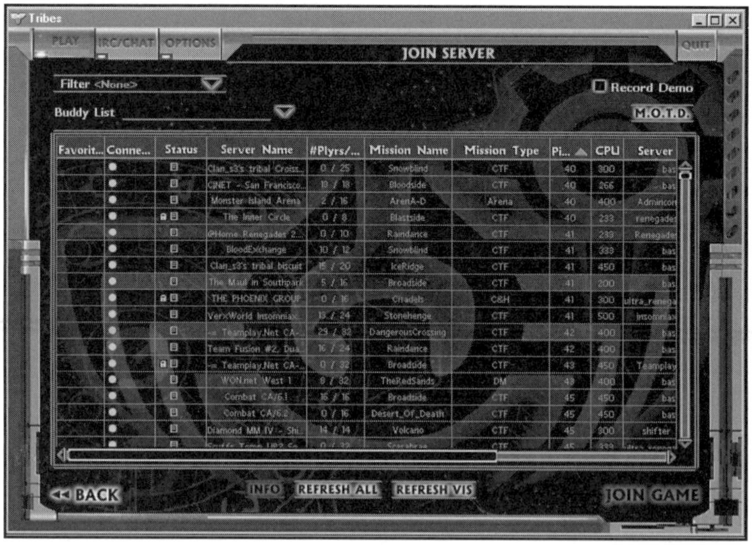

**Figure 16.2**

Internet-aware games, like **Tribes**, can help you find servers with lower lag times. Ideally, you want to play your game on a server with the lowest possible lag time.

As recently as early 1998, there were two competing standards for connecting modems at 56kbps, but now there's one universal standard: V.90. If you have an older modem that adheres to one of the older, proprietary standards—X2 or K56flex—you might contact the manufacturer. Most are offering free or very low cost flash ROM upgrades to V.90, which allow you to upgrade the modem's firmware with a software upgrade.

### Note

There are two points about 56kbps connection speeds. The first is that you can only really connect at about 53kbps in the U.S., due to electrical current limits on telephone lines. The second is that the 56kbps (or 53, if you will) number is good only for *downstream* data—that is, data that's coming into your system. 56k modems get their speed because of the capability of ISPs to connect their gear at digital speeds. But your modem can only really send data "upstream" at 33.6kbps.

# Internal Versus External Modems

Internal modems come as expansion cards that are plugged into the ISA or PCI slots. It used to be that internal modems were slower than external modems. The vast majority of external modems plugged into the faster PC serial port. Due to the way the serial port operated, its maximum transfer speed was 115kbps. But wait, you say, isn't the maximum speed of the modem 56kbps? True, but often connections are made and data is transferred using hardware compression techniques built into the modem itself. When the modem decompresses the incoming data, it can potentially generate data rates in excess of 115kbps.

### Tip

USB modems don't suffer from this limitation; we'll talk more about that a little later in this chapter.

However, internal modems have been historically difficult to configure. Older ones required jumpers to set the serial port IRQs, and even plug-and-play modems would often cause conflicts with the serial port, especially if a mouse was attached. Modern PCI modems don't have this problem—they can use or share any IRQ.

### Tip

A PCI modem first seems attractive, but you should be very wary. Check to see if the modem has its own onboard controller chip. Most (but not all) PCI modems are controllerless types. They are really just interfaces between the PC and the phone line—the CPU inside your system is really taking care of the modem duties. This is fine for Web surfing, but can result in severe lag time when gaming. Some ISA-based modems have this problem, too. Look for labels that say "Winmodem," which is a sure sign there's no onboard controller. Avoid them like the plague.

External modems are a lot easier to configure, but have been slower in the past. This is no longer true, as a new generation of USB modems has emerged. USB modems from Multitech, Diamond/Supra, and Actiontec are easier to set up than internal modems and offer better throughput rates than older external devices that connected to your serial port. The Multitech modem is a standout because it draws power from USB and doesn't even need a power connection.

As we noted previously, one source of lag time is the infamous "winmodems" or controllerless modems. Still, a modem is a complex device that translates digital data to analog signals and transmits them over a copper phone wire, where they are then reconverted upon arrival at the other end. There's an inherent delay right there. The best (lowest) lag times I've ever seen with a good modem and a good connection are in the 80ms range—but most of the time, I could only see best ping times of 110–120ms.

## ISDN

ISDN *(Integrated Services Digital Network)* was, for a long time, the only way for home users to connect to the Internet through a digital connection. Larger companies could afford products like fast T1 connections. ISDN wasn't nearly as cheap as an analog modem connection. Even today, there are places where your only option for a true digital connection is ISDN.

ISDN has been around for a long time. As noted, it is a true digital connection, but does use the metaphor of telephone numbers and dial-up. If you have an ISDN connection, you do have to take the time to connect, though it typically takes much less time than an analog modem.

A full ISDN setup actually has two phone lines and two phone numbers. Each line, called a *B-channel*, supports either 56kbps or 64kbps. The speed is dependent on the switch at the telco switching office. Most ISPs allow you to bond the two lines for a full 128kbps.

Most ISDN lines in the U.S. are capable of 64kbps per line. ISDN used to be a royal pain to set up, and had a weird jargon all its own (phone numbers are *SPIDs*, for example). But newer ISDN modems have fully automated connection programs these days. All you need to know is the two phone numbers.

### Note

Yes, we call it a "modem," even though it's digital. If you want to be completely correct, the right jargon is "terminal adapter," or TA for short.

The problem with ISDN today is that it's slow and expensive—not a great combo. Most ISPs charge more for an ISDN connection, and then charge you by the minute if you exceed a certain number of B-channel hours. On top of that, most telcos also charge by the minute after a set number of hours. So, your ISDN bill at the end of the month can be pretty hefty. Still, if you're a serious gamer, and there are no other options, you might want to explore it. Ping times for games over a typical ISDN connection can be as low as 45–50ms.

The same argument about external versus internal holds true for ISDN as well. However, when I had an ISDN link, I used an external 3Com ImpactIQ, mainly because it was easy to set up and I had a fax machine attached which needed to be always on (see Figure 16.3).

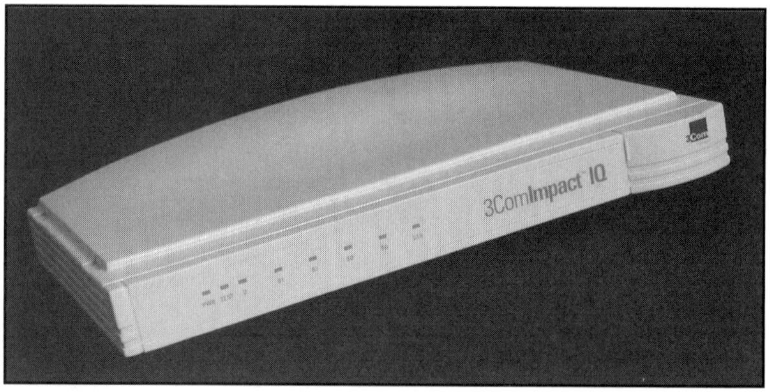


**Figure 16.3**

The 3Com ImpactIQ external ISDN Terminal Adapter. It's very flexible and easy to configure.

# DSL

DSL stands for *digital subscriber line*. DSL is a true digital connection to the Internet, and is always on—no dial-up hassle. DSL has some interesting advantages. First, it can work over standard copper wire—your phone line. It can even share a phone line. Second, DSL is cheaper than ISDN (for a personal connection) in most parts of the country. However, it is more expensive, typically, than an analog modem connection.

DSL, however, can be a confusing topic because there are a number of different versions—all incompatible with each other. This is somewhat mitigated by the fact that most telcos will support all the flavors of DSL—but you have to find an ISP that supports your particular type, assuming you even have a preference (see Table 16.1). This is not an exhaustive table (there are a multitude of DSL types), but it does list the most common types available for home users.

### Table 16.1—DSL types

| *DSL Type* | *Upstream Speed (Max)* | *Downstream Speed (Max)* | *Maximum Distance from Switch (Feet)* | *Splitter Required?* |
|---|---|---|---|---|
| ADSL | 640kbps | 6.1mbps | 18,000 | Yes |
| SDSL | 1.44mbps | 1.44mbps | 22,000 | Yes |
| G.Lite | 384kbps | 6.1mbps | 18,000 | No |
| IDSL | 144kbps | 144kbps | 18,000 | Yes |

## Note

Note that maximum speeds and maximum distances are often mutually incompatible—the farther from the switch, the slower the maximum data rate.

Here are a few things to keep in mind if you are shopping for DSL:

- ADSL is *asymmetric DSL*, which means that the upstream and downstream speeds are different.
- SDSL is *symmetric DSL*; the upstream and downstream speeds are identical.
- G.Lite (also known as UADSL, or Universal ADSL) doesn't require a splitter to be installed, so installation is much cheaper—but it has a slower maximum upstream speed. However, G.Lite has very wide support among computer vendors, and is now an ITU (International Telecommunications Union) standard, so it will likely spread pretty quickly.
- IDSL is really ISDN without voice services. Its only benefit is that it's cheaper than ISDN and is always on.

I've been running a symmetric DSL (SDSL) connection for several months now. Typical game ping times are down in the low 30–40ms for the best servers. Note that it costs more—but part of it is because I opted for a small business LAN service, and have 12 dedicated IP addresses.

For more on IP addresses and what they do for Internet connections, see page 270.

The DSL modem I use (primarily because my ISP, @Work, recommended it), is the CopperRocket 201 SDSL "modem" (see Figure 16.4). It's a very simple device whose real benefit is that you can connect it to a hub, as well as having a port to connect it directly to an ethernet NIC. That allows me to route multiple computers through the modem. (The 201 is *not* a router, for those of you who are telecomm savvy—it has no smarts of its own.)

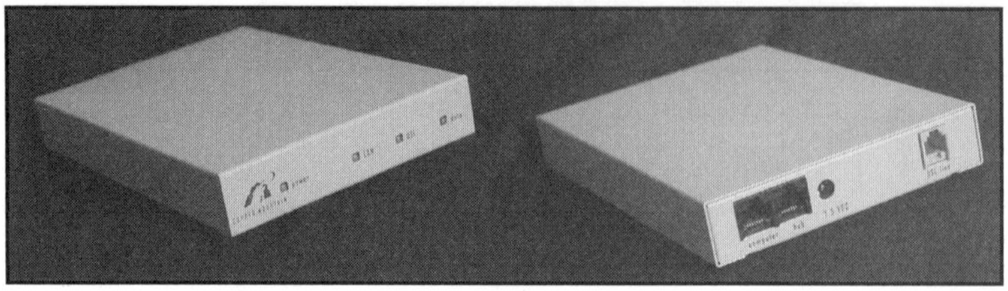

**Figure 16.4**
The CopperRocket 201 DSL adapter. It's extremely simple and requires no setup outside of making the correct connections.

Note that some DSL modems may either be directly installed inside your PC, or require a direct connection to an ethernet NIC in your PC.

DSL is still in its infancy, so don't be surprised if you run into some problems. In my case, I occasionally have the line drop on me; it usually comes back up in a few minutes. On the other hand, I'm near the distance limit from the switching office, so that's probably part of the problem. Still, with DSL, I've *never* had a lag time problem with nearby servers that can be attributed to connection issues.

# Cable Modems

Cable television wants your telecommunications business. Now that AT&T has jumped into the cable TV fray, there's an even greater impetus to connect households to cable data services.

The problem with cable modems is the cable infrastructure. Most of the cable technology (CATV networks) in the country is set up for downstream only—meaning that you can receive information at incredible speeds, but sending information is generally much slower. Cable companies back in the '60s and '70s never dreamed they'd be data-comm carriers. However, most are scrambling like mad to upgrade their existing infrastructure. It looks like most cable networks will be fully upgraded in the next one to four years.

Here in the heart of Silicon Valley, home of numerous computer and Internet-related companies, it's almost impossible to get cable modem service. Apparently, there's a crazy-quilt patchwork of incompatible technologies that need to be ripped out a piece at a time and replaced.

Still, if you can get cable, it's very speedy. Downstream speeds of up to 10 megabits per second are quite common. Note, however, that some cable ISPs are limiting upstream rates, sometimes to as little as 128kbps. The reason is that multiple users on the same head end (that is, users who share the same neighborhood cable box) share the bandwidth. The more users, the less speed everyone gets.

On the other hand, cable is very cheap—nearly as cheap as an analog modem connection. So, if you can get it in your area, it may definitely be worth checking out. And like DSL, cable connections are always on.

### Caution

One Internet service that looks very attractive on the surface is DirecPC. It uses the same satellite links used by the DirecTV satellite TV service. It does offer very fast download times. It is a poor choice for gaming, though, because the link is not two-way. The upstream data from your PC is still sent via a standard modem. This mismatch in connection type causes an inherent delay, exacerbated by the distances the wireless transmissions have to cover traveling to space and back to earth. The result is ping times in excess of 500ms—unacceptable for all but turn-based strategy games.

# Gaming Services

Okay, so you've just signed up for high-speed digital access. Now you want to do a little gaming. There are several different ways to do this, depending on the game or type of game.

## Squad Level Games

"Squad level" is a term I just made up to denote games that support no more than 64 players. They're typically designed for either competitive play, whether deathmatch style or teamplay. Some also support cooperative play within the story or against the computer.

Many of these games, such as *Unreal Tournament* and *Tribes*, have hosts of free servers. Find a server with a set of like-minded players, and have at it. It's anarchic good fun, very much in the spirit of the Net itself. These games also typically play very well over a LAN. Usually, the worlds are ephemeral—after the users log out, their character and accomplishments vanish. Games are often started and restarted with no real connection between them.

This is gradually changing. *Unreal Tournament* will have a way of tracking scores over a huge number of players. But still, each individual game is ephemeral.

# Massively Multiplayer Worlds

One type of game that has become popular (to the point of addiction with some people) are massively multiplayer games. These can range from flight simulators, like *Air Warrior III*, to huge, persistent world games like *Everquest* and the upcoming *Battletech 3025*.

Although these games can be tremendously absorbing and fun, they have a cost. You typically pay on an ongoing basis. Games that have ephemeral worlds, like *Air Warrior*, allow you to pay by the hour or day. Persistent world games typically are subscription services, so be sure that you really want to play it because your credit card gets dinged on a regular basis.

These games provide a terrific social environment, even though it's a virtual kind of society. With the advent of voice communication tools like *Roger Wilco*, the interactions can even be more personal. Many a friendship has blossomed in *Everquest* or *Ultima Online*.

The problem with these games is that you're there, online, with 30,000 of your closest friends. That usually means that there's a wide array of maturity levels. *Ultima Online* developed a bad reputation for "PKs" (player killers), who would lie in wait for newbies, kill the characters, and loot the virtual bodies. Verant's *Everquest* has solved the problem by making PK characters optional—if you choose not to have the ability to kill another player character, then another player can't kill your character.

# Gaming Services

There are a number of sites on the net that offer services as a sort of gaming matchmaker. Many also have games of their own, such as *Fighter Ace*, Microsoft's massively multiplayer flight sim featured on the company's Internet Gaming Zone (usually just called "the Zone").

Although the featured games at sites like HEAT.NET or MPath cost money, the matchmaking service for off-the-shelf games is usually free. The services make their revenues by a combination of fees generated by their exclusive content and by advertising.

There's another type of gaming service, represented by a one-time fee. These aren't services in the traditional sense, but offer a way to find servers that may be playing your favorite game. The granddaddy of all these is *Kali*. *Kali* was originally written as a way to play LAN games that only supported the IPX protocol over the Internet, which only supports TCP/IP. It was a sort of translation medium. *Kali* grew increasingly sophisticated, and developed into a kind of amorphous matchmaking service. More recently, *GameSpy*, with its native TCP/IP support, has taken a lot of mindshare from *Kali*. *GameSpy* has a slick user interface and allows users to configure filters so they can search for certain servers or game types (see Figure 16.5).

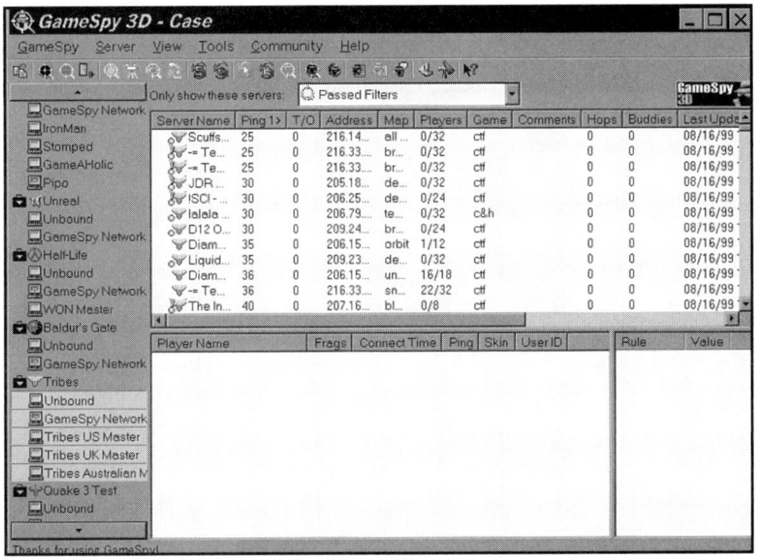

**Figure 16.5**
GameSpy is both a utility and a matchmaking service.

Table 16.2 contrasts some of the different Internet gaming services. This table is really only a drop in the bucket, though, so you may want to do a little searching of your own.

## Table 16.2—A few typical gaming services

| *Service* | *Type* | *URL* | *Cost* |
|---|---|---|---|
| The Zone | Matchmaking, plus exclusive content | `www.zone.com` | Free for matchmaking. Costs vary for exclusive content. |
| Mpath | Matchmaking | `www.mplayer.com` | Free. |
| HEAT.NET | Matchmaking, plus exclusive content | `www.heat.net` | Free for matchmaking. Costs vary for exclusive content. |
| Everquest | Massively multiplayer roleplaying game | `www.everquest.com` | $50 for boxed set; $9.95 per month (special prices for extended purchases). |

*continues*

**Table 16.2—A few typical gaming services** Continued

| *Service* | *Type* | *URL* | *Cost* |
|---|---|---|---|
| Ultima Online | Massively multiplayer roleplaying game | `www.ultimaonline.com` | $50 for boxed set; $9.95 per month. |
| GameSpy | Matchmaking | `www.gamespy.com` | $20 one time fee. |

# Small World

It used to be that finding someone to play with was difficult at best. With Internet gaming, even the most isolated gamers can find someone to play with. Whether your tastes run to massively multiplayer roleplaying games or merely a bit of Bridge on a slow night, you no longer have to be content with playing alone.

See you on the Net!

# Part 5

# Building Your Own

# Chapter 17

# Tools of the Trade

## Loyd's Nifty Perfect Toolkit

Building a personal computer from parts is no more difficult than putting together a medium-sized jigsaw puzzle or wiring a home stereo system. It does take patience, perseverance, and care, but it's not rocket science by any means. With the right tools and a place to work, you should be able to piece together an ultimate game PC using the parts you prefer. Then, maybe, your friends will think you're a rocket scientist.

In this chapter and the three that follow it, we'll walk through the process of building a typical system, using a slot-one motherboard in an ATX case. The principles are the same in other types of systems as well.

When people think about building a computer, they think of one of two things: long assembly lines, with people in lab coats and funny hats, or someone with very thick glasses and an enormous array of arcane tools, oscilloscopes, and soldering irons. Neither is completely accurate. Given the standardization of interfaces and the plug-and-play nature of today's hardware, you really only need a few tools (see Figure 17.1).

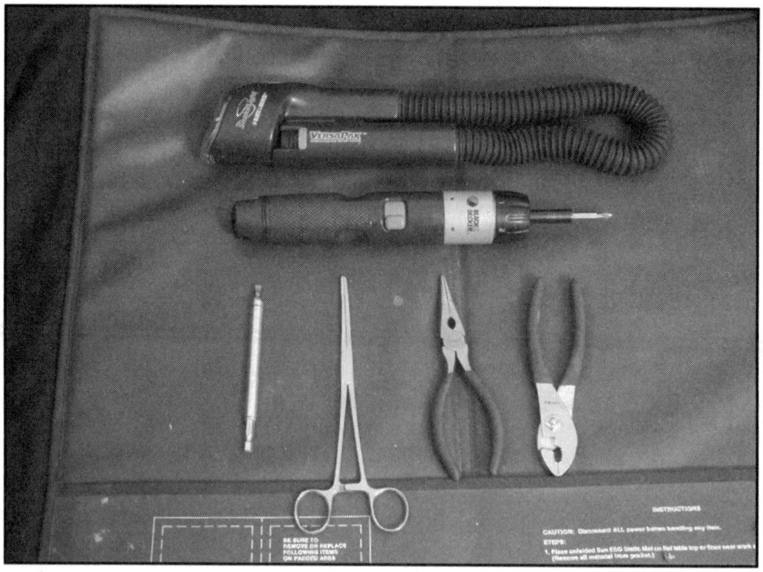

**Figure 17.1**

This is really all you need to assemble a PC. Note that the screwdriver and flashlight use the same type of rechargeable batteries. The tools are resting on an antistatic mat.

The tools are:

- **An electric screwdriver, with rechargeable batteries.** Keep a spare battery or two around. Get the long, cylindrical type, rather than the kind that looks like a small power drill—it's easier to get into tight spaces. The model I use has an adjustable clutch, which enables me to avoid over tightening screws. Note that I do have a screwdriver bit extender for easier access to tight spots.
- **A long pair of forceps.** You can get them at medical supply stores or certain electronics supply stores. I got mine at Radio Shack. They're very handy for inserting or removing jumpers in close quarters, not to mention retrieving dropped screws.
- **A flashlight.** Although any type of flashlight will do, I use one with the light mounted on a long, flexible neck. Called a snake light, it can hang off the side of a case or stand up by itself—very useful when you need that third hand. The inside of a PC case can have some pretty dark spots, especially after you get all the cards and drives installed.
- **Standard pliers and needle-nose pliers.** The standard pliers are for tightening down small nuts. The needle-nose pliers, which are spring-loaded, are useful for holding a nut in a tight place while you use the screwdriver.

- **An antistatic mat.** One of the hazards of computer gear is that it can be damaged by a stray jolt of static electricity. An antistatic mat of some kind minimizes this possibility. Note that for best results, it does need to be grounded by attaching the supplied grounding wire to a ground source, such as a metal edge on the computer case (assuming the power supply is plugged in). You should also use an antistatic wrist strap, which is not pictured.

That's really all you need. A couple of items might be a long, very fine, flat-bladed screwdriver and a very small nut driver that's the right size to turn those ubiquitous hex nuts used in a lot of connectors. I get by most of the time without those, however.

# Where to Start

## Creating a Workspace

Creating your dream machine requires a fairly sizable workspace. You may also need to leave everything set up for a day or two. Although a kitchen table is sufficient space, your spouse may not care to share the dinner table with PC components.

### Caution

Also, you should childproof your work area to the extent possible, and you should never leave computer hardware components where small children can get into them. Never mind the fact that little ones have a unique ability to quickly break things, all those small screws are a serious choking hazard.

Make sure there is adequate lighting. An additional lamp, on an extensible neck, is handy too.

## Static Electricity

Modern semiconductor components—memory, CPUs, graphics chips, and so on—are susceptible to damage from accidental discharge of static electricity. The problem is much less severe than it was a few years ago, due to improvements in chip packaging. Even so, you should take care to avoid static electricity discharge. Just walking across a nylon carpet on a dry, cool day can generate static discharges from your fingertips in excess of 10,000 volts. (The actual current is very low, which is why you don't fry someone when you touch him or her.) Touching the metallic slot connector on an $800 Athlon CPU after shuffling across carpet will net you an $800 paperweight.

The problem is really simple to avoid. If you think you'll be working on PCs frequently, invest in an antistatic mat and a grounding strap that fastens onto your wrist. However, an equally easy thing to do is to frequently touch the chassis of the PC while working on it. Note that this works best if the PC is actually plugged in. Touching the center screw on a wall outlet will ground you as well.

### Note

Although grounding yourself by touching the chassis discharges any static electricity built up in your body, an antistatic mat and wrist strap are the best precaution.

If you have to work in an exceptionally cool, dry place (say, Alaska in the winter), the danger of static discharges increases dramatically. In a case like this, you need to take extra measures, such as running a humidifier in the room while you're working—and turn the thermostat up a bit.

## Gathering the Pieces

The temptation is very strong just to pile everything next to you and unpack the boxes as you install components. That's likely to cost you more time, especially if you have to go off searching for odd little items, like that bag of screws to mount the floppy drive.

Instead, after you've set up a workspace, take a little time to carefully unpack everything first. Check the motherboard box and make sure everything is there: CPU retention bracket (if it's needed), drive cables for both floppy and hard drives, and spare jumpers.

The PC chassis usually ships with an I/O shield. This is a thin metal sheet with cutouts for connectors like keyboard, parallel port, and so on. Your chassis should also have come with either mounting screws for the motherboard or plastic standoffs.

Unpack all the other components and check to make sure they have all the various parts that you need, including the vital driver disks or jumpers for the hard drives. You may also want a second IDE cable (for an IDE system) because it's a good idea to connect the CD-ROM drive to the second IDE port. (Your system will perform better if the CD is on a different IDE port than the hard drive.)

Be sure you have all the software you need for installation, including a Windows CD. One last, but extremely important, item to remember are all those pesky serial numbers you'll need to type in during software installation.

Now that you've a space to lay everything out, and all the various pieces of the puzzle gathered in one location, the next three chapters will walk you through the physical steps for building your dream gaming rig.

# Chapter 18

# Case and Power Supply

## Give Me More Power...

People will spend $40,000 for a sport utility vehicle, or $500 for a new DVD player. Those same people will begrudge spending more than $50 for a computer chassis *and* power supply. As the old adage goes, you get what you pay for. Spending a few more dollars for a case will pay dividends. It will be easier to work inside, the I/O shield and drive cage assembly edges will be rolled so you don't bleed all over your components, and it will run cooler. Similarly, spending a few dollars for a rock-solid power supply will ensure fewer system glitches and longer component life.

It's also true that many off-the-shelf systems from companies like Dell and Compaq come with power supplies that are adequate for the system as bought. But woe be to he who drops in several additional peripherals. Many of these systems come with power supplies rated at 200W or less.

Newer CPUs and graphics cards draw more current than in the past. Some graphics cards will draw up to 6A from the AGP port. A borderline power supply may not be able to handle the current draw, even if the motherboard is up to snuff. This can translate directly to system instability. Your games will crash more often, Windows will generate strange errors, and sometimes, you cannot even boot immediately after you power down.

# Cooling, Cooling, Cooling

Modern PC components run hot—that's just the way it is. If you've ever held your hand over the heat sink of a Voodoo3 model 3000, you'll quickly remove it—the heat sink attached to the chip can run as high as 95 degrees centigrade, or 5 degrees C cooler than the boiling point of water.

You want a case and power supply that can help in the process of keeping components cool. Begin with an ATX case.

### Note

ATX 2.01 is a specification that defines the rough layout of a motherboard and how it mounts into the case. It also defines how the power supply connects to the motherboard and how it circulates air. A few years ago, an older format known as *baby AT* (after the IBM PC-AT) was common. The baby AT format suffered from relatively poor air circulation and the inability to have "soft" power switches (you always had to turn on the switch at the power supply, instead of using a switch on the front of the case).

ATX essentially rotated the motherboard 90 degrees horizontally, relative to the baby AT style boards. Air can circulate more easily in ATX format cases. The keyboard, mouse, and other I/O connectors are now mounted in a cluster on the rear of the motherboard. The power supply is now switched on by a soft power switch that's actually connected to the motherboard, not the power supply. This enables more efficient power management by both Windows and the system BIOS. The only downside to ATX is that it defines a maximum of seven expansion slots.

Pick a case that allows you to add extra cooling fans. If you do add an extra fan or two, get the kind that plug into the small, three-pin connectors on the motherboard. This avoids using up scarce hard drive power connectors, and in some cases, the motherboard can monitor the fan RPM. Most hard drive cooling fans are constructed so that the hard drive is mounted in a spare 5.25" drive bay, rather than the more typical 3.5" bay (see Figure 18.1).

## Adding Fans and Heat Sinks

The need for adding fans and heat sinks can vary from one system to the next. Systems designed as gaming rigs from the outset from companies like Falcon Northwest or Alienware Systems have extra cooling already built-in. On the other hand, systems from the major suppliers, like Gateway, Micron, Dell, and the rest, often have "passive cooling"—heatsinks.

If you look inside one of these systems, you'll typically see a heatsink that is as much as 2 inches deep attached to the CPU. Unlike Intel's own retail boxed CPUs, there is often no fan in these cookie-cutter systems. A heatsink is just a piece of metal, designed in such a way as to maximize the surface area through the use of deep fins machined into the surface. They act as radiators, sucking heat from the CPU. Unfortunately, they only work through convection. The idea is that the difference in temperature gradients throughout the case will generate natural airflow locally. Of course, the power supply always has a fan, but this is often not good enough, especially after you drop in some extra expansion cards and things start to get crowded.

**Figure 18.1**

Here are three critical components in your system's cooling capacity. The PC Power & Cooling Turbocool 300 is an ATX 2.01 power supply that exhausts air out of the case, rather than blowing hot air over the components. The 4" muffin fan plugs into a 3-pin motherboard connector. Finally, the hard drive cooler moves warm air away from high-speed hard drives, extending drive life.

If you have one of these systems, you can attempt a little surgery by removing the passive heatsink and adding an aftermarket heatsink with a fan built in (referred to as an "active cooler"). That may void your warranty, however. There are devices that either plug into a free slot or attach to the side of the case with fans built in.

If you've built your own system, always have an active cooler on the CPU. Retail, boxed CPUs come with fans. If you get an OEM (that is, a tray) CPU, you'll need to buy one separately.

If you decide you want to try overclocking, get a beefy fan. Some fans designed for slot one CPUs have more than one small fan. Also, when you buy a chassis, look inside the case and make sure there's an extra bracket or housing to add a muffin fan.

## Note

The graphics card is kind of a special case. Most high performance 3D accelerators—except those from 3dfx—come with fans. 3dfx puts enormous heat sinks on its graphics chips. Even the fans that come with some graphics cards aren't always attached in such a way as to maximize heat flow from the chip. There's now a small industry that has sprung to life around building aftermarket cooling for graphics cards. Companies like TennMax (`www.tennmax.com`) build high performance coolers for graphics cards.

# Space to Live and Work

You definitely want to have a case of adequate size. If you've ever tried to route a hard drive cable inside a minitower case, you know what I mean. I've scraped many a knuckle trying to line up a connector in a case with inadequate room. Rolled or deburred edges are also a blessing. One friend of mine believes that a PC will never work right unless you spill a few drops of blood into it when you build it, but don't you believe it.

That doesn't mean you need a huge case. Generally, a mid-tower case 17" high is good enough—provided that it's intelligently designed and constructed.

# Choosing the Right Chassis

I've walked into computer stores that literally have dozens of different cases on display. They range from pint-sized desktop cases to huge towers on wheels for servers. The newest twist, driven no doubt by the existence of Apple's new systems, have been cases in garish colors. This can help you guide through the Sargasso Sea of computer cases that seem to be out there.

As we noted above, get a case that's at least 17 inches tall. Look for rolled or deburred edges (I can't emphasize this enough). Your knuckles will thank me later.

Make sure there's enough room to lay out the motherboard and work on it. During the installation process, you'll need to get your hands inside to connect some tiny wires, so make sure there's enough room. A case that's 17" high—my minimum recommended size—may not have enough room to work in comfortably. If that's true, ensure that there are removable drive cages. Many compact mid-towers have metal cages that hold the hard drives. Most are removable, either by snapping out or by removing a couple of screws. Removing the drive cages allows you to easily install your drives outside of the case and then slide the entire cage back into the case.

Removable drive bays are handy in other ways. Even if you have a large case, it's often awkward to reach in and make adjustments, like SCSI ID changes. Yanking out the drive bay is often easier than removing a single (or several) hard drives.

Check the way the motherboard will mount to the chassis. Sometimes the actual attachment may be fine, but the back of the motherboard won't line up correctly with the slots or I/O cutout. If you plan on installing something like a Zip drive in addition to a standard floppy, make sure there are at least two 3.5" drive bays exposed to the outside. Also, count the number of drives you plan on installing, and make sure there's enough bays for all of them. In one example you'll see in Chapter 19 ("Installing Componments"), the system has three hard drives, a DVD-ROM drive, and a CD-R unit.

# Adequate Power

Don't skimp on the power supply. Many cases come with power supplies, but a lot of them are 235W or less. A high-performance gaming machine may need more power; I tend to recommend a minimum 250W; more is better, to a point. Most cases these days come with a power supply. Sometimes they're decent, but most of the time, they're afterthoughts. It may be better to remove the existing power supply and upgrade it with something better.

### Tip

I tend to rip out any power supply that comes built into a case and install a PC Power and Cooling supply. PC Power and Cooling (`www.pcpowercooling.com`) makes rock-solid power supplies, ranging from fairly economical, 235W units up to dual 600W redundant supplies for servers. My favorite is the Silencer 275. It has a "smart" cooling fan that operates when needed, and is fairly quiet even then. And it delivers 275W of stable power.

Do check to see if the power supply is UL Listed, or at least certified by the U.S. FCC or some European agency. That will ensure that it at least meets minimum specifications. Be wary of any power supply that has an easily removable case or side. Finally, count the number of connectors, and make sure there are enough for the devices you'll be installing.

### Tip

If you do run out of power connectors, there are Y-adapters readily available if you need them.

After you've chosen the case and power supply, it's time to begin the work of assembling the puzzle.

# Chapter 19

# Installing Components

## Keep a Stiff Upper Lip

Now we're to the heart of the matter.

If you've been reading along until now and using the advice I've given you on making the right hardware selections, you're probably sitting there, surrounded by boxes and hardware. Trust me, I know it's easy to feel a sense of despair. Take a deep breath, and take it one step at a time.

## Setting Up the Case

After unpacking the PC chassis from its box, you probably have a pile of strange looking parts. Cases usually come mostly assembled. Inside the box—sometimes stashed inside the chassis itself—is a package containing I/O shields, screws, slot covers, motherboard mounting hardware, and possibly, feet for the case.

Find the I/O shield that matches the layout of your motherboard's I/O connectors. If your motherboard has an unusual layout (onboard audio connectors, for example), the correct cutout probably came with the motherboard itself. Install the shield in the rectangular space in the rear of the chassis. Note that some I/O shields have metal flashing overlaying some of the connector holes (see Figure 19.1). Make sure you either remove these or bend them out of the way.

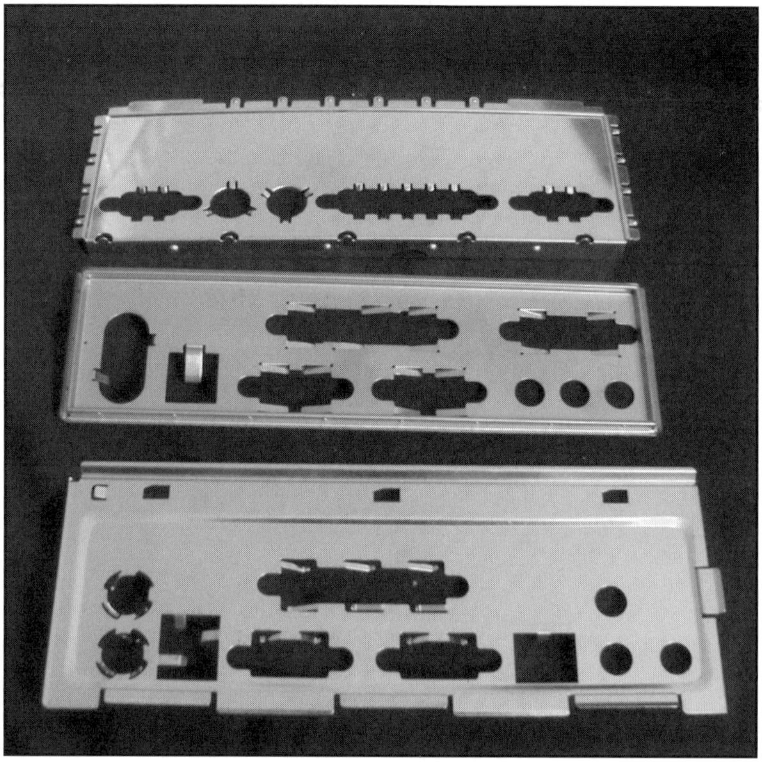

**Figure 19.1**
Three typical I/O shields. Motherboards with a single row of connectors are quite rare.

If the case requires that hardware be installed for mounting the motherboard, now is a good time. There are a variety of ways to mount a motherboard, ranging from plastic or brass standoffs to screw-downs. These prevent the motherboard from actually touching the case chassis or mounting tray (some cases include a removable tray to which the motherboard is mounted). Different motherboards often have slightly different layouts for mounting holes. Most cases have different sets of mounting points, so make sure you install the mounting hardware in the mount points correct for your motherboard (see your motherboard documentation).

At this point, if the case has removable drive cages, take them out. We want as much space to install the motherboard and its various parts as possible (see Figure 19.2).

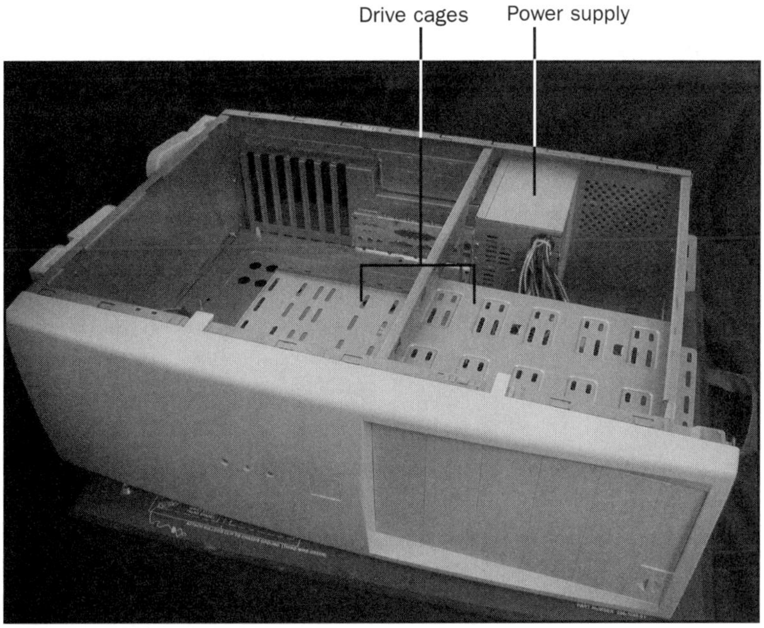


**Figure 19.2**

Here's a big tower case, almost ready to go. Note that the removable drive bay is still present, near the center of the case. If you've decided to install a different power supply than the original, go ahead and install it now. Power supplies are very easy to install—it just takes four screws. Note the orientation of the power supply's cooling fan and make sure the new one is arranged correctly.

Determine where you're going to install drives that require an open front panel (such as CD-ROM drives or floppy disc drives). Remove the drive cages by simply detaching them from the case chassis (either by snapping it out or removing attachment screws, depending on the case). Note that some cases require you to actually remove the front bezel before installing drives or unscrewing drive bays.

At this point, we're ready to install vthe hardware (see Figures 19.3 and 19.4).

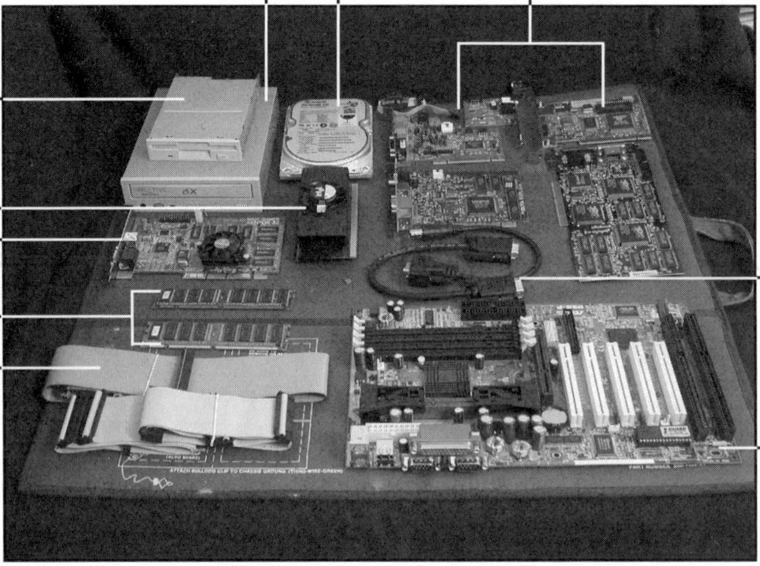


**Figure 19.3**

If you are building a PC that will use IDE devices, your basic equipment list will look something like this. Of course, your selection likely will not look exactly like this (for example, if you install a Celeron or K6 processor instead of the Pentium II shown here).

# Motherboards, CPU, and Memory

Now it's time to pop in the motherboard. Unpack the mainboard from its antistatic wrapper.

## Tip

If the motherboard is a slot-type (that is, Pentium III or Athlon CPU), check to make sure the CPU retention bracket is installed. If it's not, *install it now!* There is nothing more annoying than having screwed down a motherboard and discovering that you need to install the CPU retention bracket. If the board uses the newer universal retention bracket, you can often install it even after the board has been screwed down. Some motherboards, however, still come with the old kind. In that case, the bracket needs mounting gear to be attached from the *underside* of the motherboard.

Consult your processor and/or motherboard documentation to see how to mount this bracket. Above all, be sure that you use extreme care when installing the bracket. Push the bracket pins into the motherboard with your fingers. Don't even be tempted to use a screwdriver because you could slip and gouge the motherboard, which of course, is a very bad thing.

The good news is that all the new motherboards I've seen lately have the new retention vbracket pre-attached.

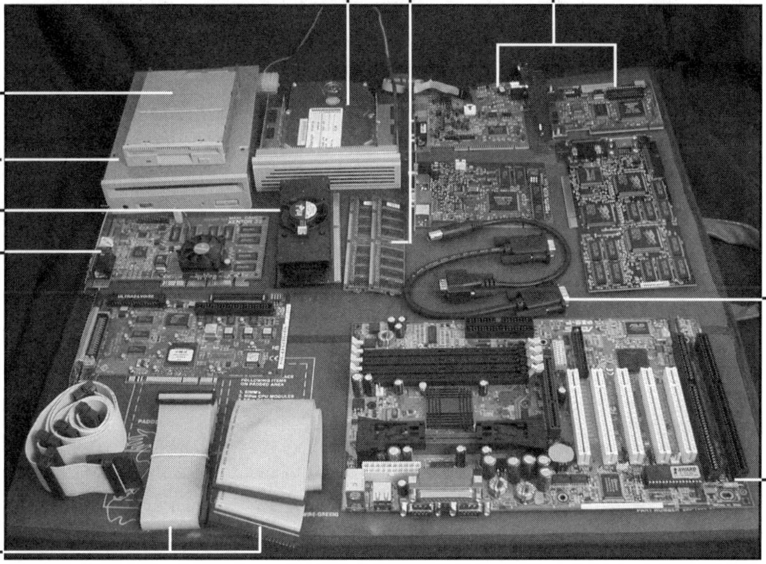


**Figure 19.4**

If you are building a gaming rig that will use SCSI devices, your hardware selection will look something like this. Of course, yours will be somewhat different, depending on the particular components you plan to install.

Some people prefer to mount the CPU and memory modules *before* installing the motherboard in the case. I am not among that number. Install the motherboard first, get it solidly in there, and installing memory and processor become a snap—literally.

# Install the Motherboard

Align the motherboard in the case and slide it toward the backplane cutouts. You may have to fiddle a bit to make sure the parallel and serial ports slide into their respective holes. I find that gently grasping the parallel port and giving the board a gentle nudge usually works—do *not* try to force it. If everything is properly lined up, the ports will pop easily into the I/O shield (and the motherboard mounting holes will line up with the holes on the mounting tray, if your case uses a tray—some do, some don't).

If the motherboard uses plastic standoffs, you'll have to also align the motherboard so it slips over the standoffs. If the case uses screws, align the motherboard holes and fasten it down with screws. With current mainboards, you no longer have to use insulating washers.

Once installed, the I/O shield should look something like Figure 19.5.

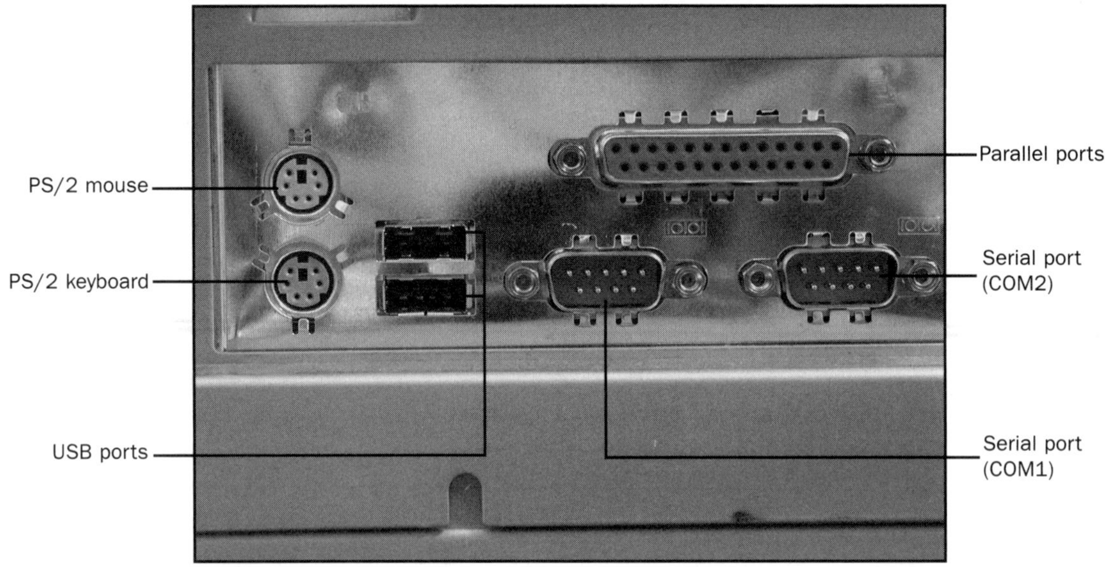


**Figure 19.5**
The back panel, with all I/O ports properly seated in the I/O shield.

# Install the Memory

If you look carefully at the memory modules, you'll notice a pair of notches. These notches line up with keys in the DIMM (or RIMM) sockets, so you install the module or CPU in the correct orientation (see Figure 19.6).

A plastic tab lies at each end of the DIMM socket. Pull the tab *away* from the slot itself. Line up the memory module so that the notches match the keys in the slot. Push the DIMM *straight down*, making sure each vertical edge lines up with small slots in the left and right tabs. If you do it correctly, the tabs will rise up automatically and the module will snap into place.

# Install the Processor

If you bought an OEM slot-type CPU, you'll need to attach the CPU fan/heatsink before you slip it into the slot. This is different from socketed CPUs, where you install the fan after the CPU is installed. There are small slots on the facing of the cartridge shell. Heatsinks have matching tabs that snap into these. Slot 1 Celeron CPUs have odd mounting brackets that snap around the CPU. Like the memory modules, the CPU has an asymmetric notch and key to line up the CPU correctly (see Figure 19.7).

**Figure 19.6**

These keys line up with matching notches in the memory module itself.

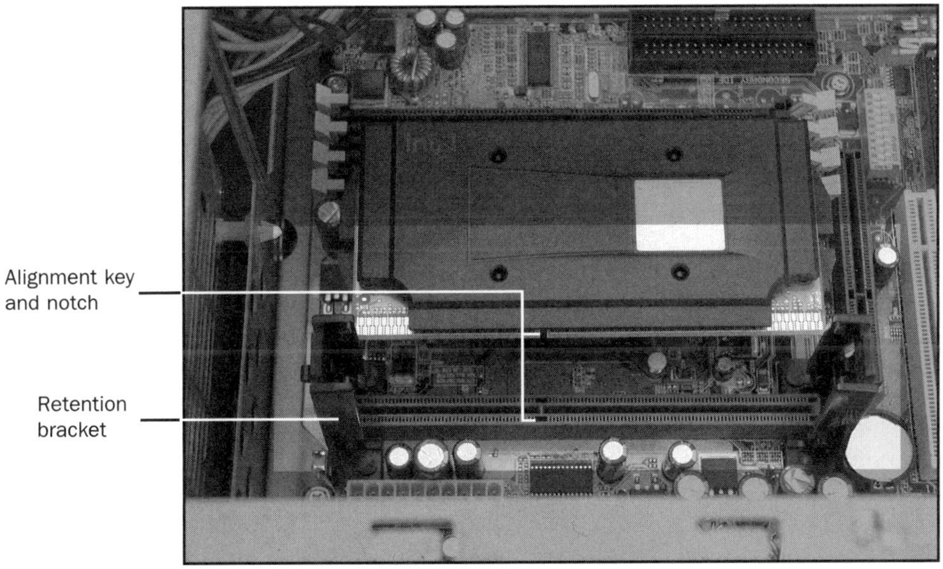


**Figure 19.7**

Line up the notches with the keys in the slot to properly insert the Pentium III or Athlon CPU. Then, slide the CPU gently down, lining up the sides of the processor with the CPU retention brackets. It should slide very easily until the edge connector of the CPU cartridge touches the slot. At this point, push down gently until it seats into place.

The latest Celerons, as well as Intel's upcoming Coppermine CPU, use a socket format. AMD K6-2 and K6-3 CPUs also plug into sockets. Figure 19.8 shows a Celeron lined up with a Socket 370. This socket happens to be on a Socket 370/Slot One adapter, but the same idea holds true for socketed motherboards (see Figure 19.8).

## Note

Intel designs adapters, called Slotkets, which allow you to use a socketed processor, such as a Celeron or Coppermine chip in a slotted board (one that was designed for a Pentium II or Pentium III processor).

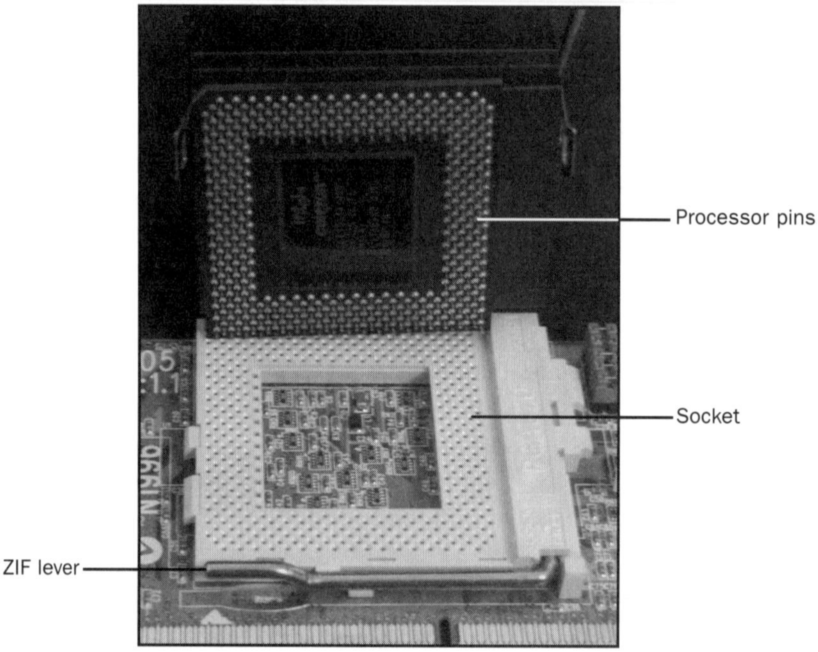


**Figure 19.8**

Socketed processors slip easily into the socket and are locked into place by depressing the ZIF lever.

Find the corners of the lines of pins that have triangular notches cut out. Line them up with the matching triangular hole formation in the socket. Lift up the ZIF (zero insertion force) lever and *very gently* let the CPU slide into the socket. It should go almost all the way in without any effort on your part. Give it just a little push to get it all the way in and snap the ZIF lever back into place.

Now that the CPU is in place, you need to attach the heatsink and fan. Most have a metal bracket whose sides protrude from the heatsink and lie parallel to the CPU. Each side of the bracket terminates in a right angle with a small slot. These slots fit over matching tabs on the socket itself. Connect the fan power to one of the 3-pin connectors on the motherboard.

# Connecting the Motherboard Power

At this point, let's connect the power supply to the motherboard (see Figure 19.9).

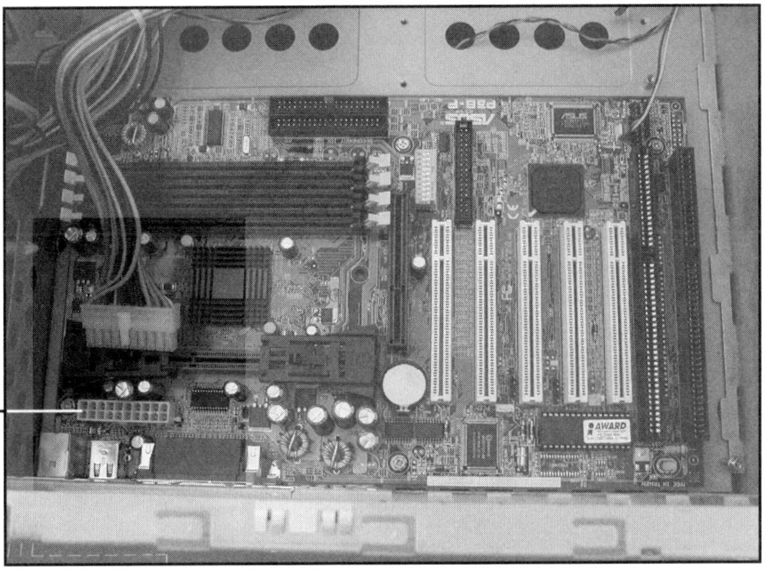


**Figure 19.9**

The ATX power connector has a snap-in tab, and can't be connected incorrectly. Note that the location of the power connector may vary from motherboard to motherboard.

## Caution

If you find yourself upgrading or repairing an older PC, be very careful when reconnecting the motherboard power. Older connectors were not keyed to prevent improper connection. Improperly connecting these plugs will result in destruction of your motherboard and attached components, and could start a fire. Most of these older connectors were actually split into two physical connectors. Make sure the two black ground wires in each connector are next to each other, which should help align it properly with the motherboard power sockets.

# Connect Accessory Plugs

The final thing to do before moving on to installing expansion cards is to make the connection to the PC speaker, power switch, and reset switch, at a minimum (see Figure 19.10).

**Figure 19.10**

These tiny plugs connect the power switch, reset switch, PC speaker, and IDE hard drive activity light.

# Installing Expansion Cards

The next step in assembling your hotrod gaming machine is to install all the expansion cards, including graphics, audio, and so on. A typical gaming PC is populated with a primary graphics card, a secondary card (generally a 3D accelerator), a sound card, a fast Ethernet NIC, and a hardware DVD decoder. You may not have so many cards, depending on what you're trying to accomplish.

First, let's scope out the slots. Figure 19.11 shows the AGP, PCI, and ISA expansion slots, in all their glory.

Naturally, the AGP graphics card goes into the AGP slot. When inserting any card into a slot, lower it gently into the slot and make sure the bracket lines up properly with the bracket opening in the rear of the case. The bottom of the bracket narrows to a small tab, which slides into a matching hole where the motherboard meets the back of the chassis.

Some cards fit very snugly, and require some force to pop them into place. If you run into one of these cards, make sure you press straight down; any sideways force may damage the card or the motherboard. A slightly easier way is to rock them into place by wiggling them in a direction parallel to the slot. Once in the slot, you'll note a screw hole at the top of the slot bracket. Make sure you screw the card down here so it doesn't wobble or pop out.

**Figure 19.11**

There are three types of slots in today's PCs: AGP, PCI, and ISA There is only a single AGP slot in a system, and it's used exclusively for graphics.

You might consider doing a quick power up after the graphics card is in place, with a monitor attached. Just fire up the system long enough so that you can see the POST (power-on self test) message on the screen, and then turn it off. Now that you know the system will boot, you can install the rest of the cards.

# IRQ Issues with Multiple PCI Cards

The limited number of hardware IRQs available in the current PC architecture has led to some creative accounting on the part of motherboard vendors. The problem is that there are multiple ways to do it. Here are some cautions as you populate your PCI slots:

- Some (but not all) boards force the AGP slot and the PCI slot immediately adjacent to share IRQs. Many graphics cards don't like to share IRQs, even under Windows 98. If you need to use that slot, make sure that the card you put in there is very friendly about IRQ sharing, or doesn't require an IRQ at all.
- Most motherboards have the PCI slot and first ISA slot share an IRQ. This makes sense because you can't have both a PCI card and an ISA card in those adjacent slots anyway; they share a common backplane opening.
- A few motherboards don't assign an IRQ to the PCI slot next to the first ISA slot. Or, they'll have that PCI slot share an IRQ with the AGP slot (see above). If there's no IRQ assigned at all, only cards that don't require an IRQ can go in that slot.

- Motherboards with four or fewer PCI slots generally don't have these problems. You may come across motherboards with more than five PCI slots. Most of these have an onboard PCI-to-PCI bridge chip, which can be the source of incompatibility with some PCI cards. One newer board, the Asus P3B-F may come with six bus-mastering PCI slots, but some juggling of IRQs takes place.

# The Home Stretch

Okay, now we've got all the expansion boards installed. Now it's on to mass storage. We're in the home stretch for the hardware setup!

Before installing the hard drive, you want to try to power up the system. This is where the rubber meets the road. Connect the monitor and a keyboard (you don't need the mouse—there's no hard drive installed). Plug in to wall power and turn the system on.

At this point, all the fans should come on, one beep should emanate from the PC speaker, and you should see the first signs of life on the PC monitor. If you don't see anything displayed on the monitor, there may be several things that could be happening, some simple, some not so simple:

- Check your power connections and make sure they're connected correctly.
- The expansion cards may not be inserted all the way. Remove them, one at a time, and carefully reinsert them. This is especially true if you hear multiple beeps in succession—that means that the graphics card is not being detected.
- The CPU or memory modules aren't fully inserted. Make sure they're snug in their respective slots.
- It's possible that there exists some kind of conflict between ,the video card and something else. Remove all expansion cards except for video and try again.
- Sometimes, at the factory, motherboards are tested at certain configurations, and those settings may still be "live" in the BIOS. Often, there's a clear CMOS jumper on the motherboard that resets the state of the BIOS to some default. Enable it, turn the system on, and then power down and switch it back to the default state.
- If the power supply fan (and other fans) doesn't even come up, you may have a defective component. Remove everything except the CPU and try again. At the least, the system should go live, including all fans.
- Finally, before you decide something is defective, check to make sure that nothing is inadvertently creating a ground fault. I once found a stray screw, wedged under the motherboard, touching a solder joint on the board. It was the only thing preventing the system from powering up.

If you've been careful, though, most of the time, you'll be rewarded by that magic POST (power-on, self test) message on your PC monitor. If you've gotten this far, it's time to move on to installing your mass storage devices, which is covered in, Chapter 20, "Installing and Setting Up IDE and SCSI Devices."

# Chapter 20

# Installing and Setting Up IDE and SCSI Devices

## (Daisy) Chain of Events

The good news is that setting up hard drives is much easier than it used to be. In the bad old days, you had to enter some arcane parameters into the hard drive section of your system BIOS. These were items like the number of cylinders, the number of heads, and so on. As drives got bigger, the BIOS makers had to play tricks because of some limitations that existed in the original PC BIOS. For example, the PC BIOS was limited to 1,024 cylinders. So, you'd enter numbers that had nothing to do with reality, like 850 cylinders and 255 heads, or other nonsense.

These days, the hard drives have become much smarter, and system BIOSes can now auto-detect all the hard drive parameters, meaning that you don't have to enter them yourself when installing and setting up a hard drive. But there are still some details you need to know as you install your first mass storage devices.

# Setting Up IDE Drives

IDE drives have steadily increased in both speed and capacity. Lately, we've seen IDE drives hit 36GB, and plummet below the penny per megabyte barrier. There are quite a number of IDE drives out now that rotate at 7,200RPM as well.

### Note

There's actually a trade-off between platter density and rotation speed. A drive with a higher bit density—say, 6.8GB per platter, but rotates at 5,400RPM—may actually be faster than a drive with 4.0GB per platter, but rotating at 7,200RPM.

Let's cover a few basics first. Each IDE port on your motherboard can support up to two IDE devices. The two ports are usually labeled Primary and Secondary IDE. If you connect two drives to a single port, you do it with a single cable, which has three connectors—one for the motherboard connection and two for the two IDE devices.

Now, the system needs to be able to identify each drive individually. Making one drive the master drive and the other the slave does this. This is usually done by placing tiny jumpers into the back of the drive. A *jumper* is a small piece of plastic with a U-shaped wire embedded in it, and two holes for mounting on small pins. Most current hard drive have the actual jumper configuration silk-screened on to the disk drive itself.

Drives are then usually identified by the connector and the drive ID. For example, a CD-ROM set as the master on the secondary IDE connector is the secondary master. A second (slave) hard drive on the primary connector is the primary slave, and so on.

### Tip

Because jumpers are very tiny, it's usually much easier to place jumpers *before* you install the drive in the case. Though you can place the jumpers with your fingers, it is generally easier to use a small pair of tweezers.

When you've attached two devices with a single cable, you've created a daisy chain. With modern, ATA/33, and ATA/66 hard drives, you generally want the master to be the last drive in the chain. This is absolutely required when using 80 conductor ultraATA cables.

If you have a single drive, it's usually configured as the master, and attached to the primary IDE connector on the motherboard.

## Note

The master drive on the primary IDE connector is the boot drive (C drive).

Many IDE cables are keyed so you can't install them the wrong way. All cables have a red stripe running along one edge—this identifies the side of the connector that must be plugged into pin 1 on the IDE connector. Usually, the location of pin 1 is silk-screened on to the drive and the motherboard.

## Caution

Some IDE cables are keyed by actually blocking one of the holes in the connector. The matching pin on the motherboard is missing, so the cable will slide in easily. Should you try to plug in the cable the wrong way, it won't go in. *Never* try to force an IDE cable—you may end up damaging the connector.

There are several simple steps to configuring an IDE drive:

- Place a jumper on the drive for the appropriate master or slave setting
- Install the drive into the case
- Attach the cable
- Boot up to test parameters

That's really about it. But, as they say, the devil is in the details.

Figure 20.1 shows an IDE drive mounted in a detachable drive bay. This particular drive is a Seagate Barracuda ATA. Note the jumper settings are printed directly on the drive—a welcome and common addition these days. This drive represents the most complex type of IDE drive to set up, due to the number of possible settings. There are separate settings for master with no slave, master with non–ATA-compatible slave, slave, cable select (rarely used), and a setting limiting the drive to 2.1GB for older systems. That's it—those are the sum total of the jumper settings.

After configuring the jumpers, the drive cage is installed into the chassis using screws that came with the case. Power and IDE cables are attached. As you can see in Figure 20.2, there is one jumper set, indicating that the drive is set as a single, master drive.

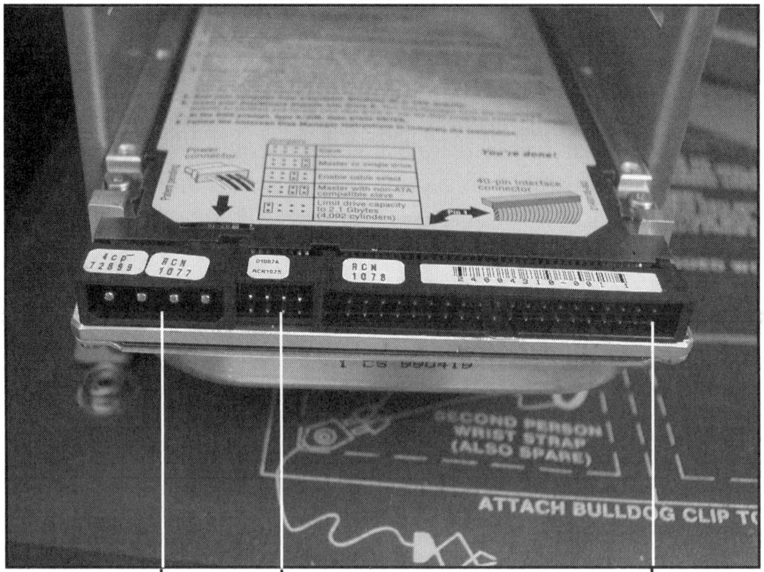


**Figure 20.1**
The Seagate Barracuda ATA. There are a grand total of five jumper settings.

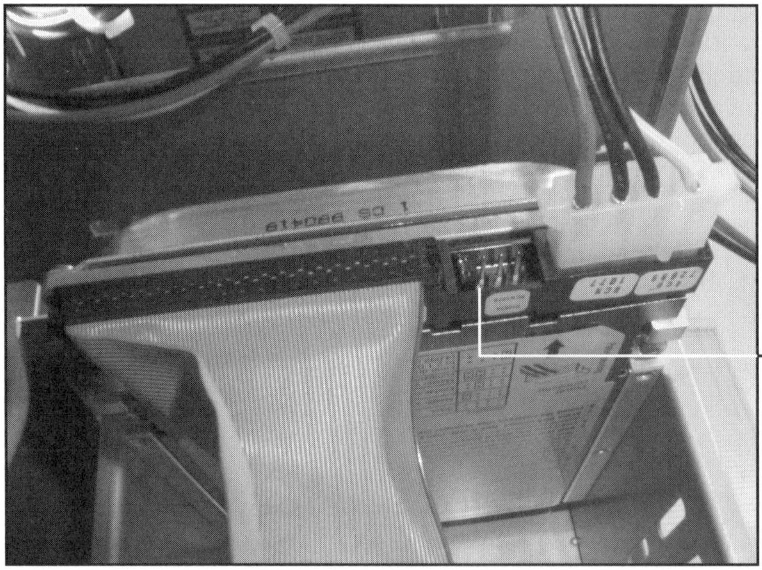


**Figure 20.2**
The drive, installed and connected. Note that IDE cables—especially ATA/33 or ATA/66 cables—should not be longer than 24 inches.

# CD-ROM and DVD-ROM Drives

If anything, CD and DVD drives are even easier to install. DVD drives that use an ATA connection typically always want to be a master—so you should always connect them to the secondary IDE port on a motherboard. After connecting the IDE cable, be sure to attach the analog audio cable from the sound card. That's all you typically need to do. The motherboard BIOS and Windows automatically detect the presence of an ATAPI CD or DVD drive (see Figure 20.3).

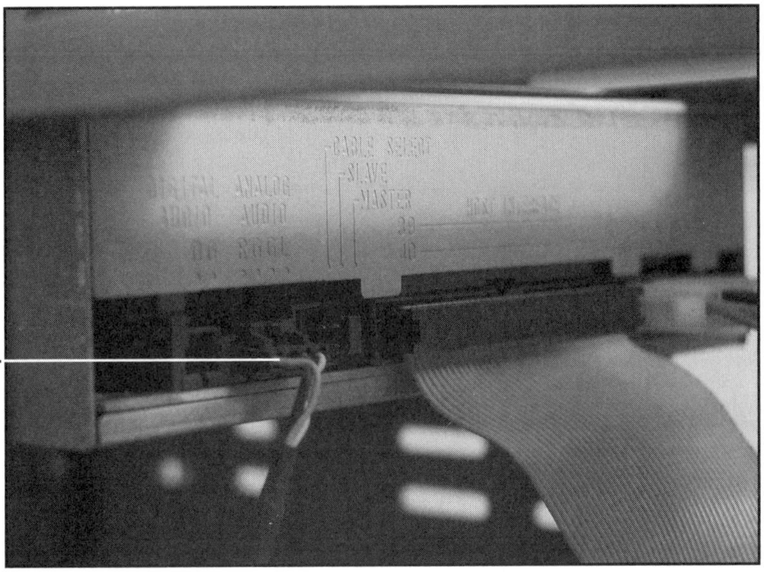


**Figure 20.3**

An ATAPI DVD drive, connected and configured. Note the audio cable, which is connected to the sound card.

## Caution

When installing a CD or DVD drive, don't forget to also connect the analog audio cable from the back of the CD/DVD to the sound card! If you forget, you won't hear audio when playing games or watching DVD movies.

When you boot the system, you should go into the system BIOS at the first boot. If the system has a Phoenix BIOS or very recent Award BIOS, it's usually set to autodetect anything attached to the IDE ports, but it's good to double-check.

### Caution

Most newer IDE drives adhere to the ATA/66 standard, the latest, fastest variant of IDE. Most of the drives I've tested run fine when attached to an ATA/33 IDE controller common to many motherboards. A few, though, have problems. One example is the Western Digital Expert series drives. However, Western Digital has supplied a utility on its Web site that can enable or disable ATA/66 operation. You can get it at `www.westerndigital.com`. If you're having problems with other ATA/66 drives, check with the manufacturer.

Most hard drive manufacturers now recommend 80 conductor IDE cables. These cables are more stable at the high clock rates demanded by ATA/33 or ATA/66. Figure 20.6, later in this chapter, shows these cables, also known as Ultra-IDE cables.

You may run into a few problems when trying to start a system with a new IDE drive:

- The master/slave jumpers may be set incorrectly.
- The cable may be plugged in backwards. Despite the increasing prevalence of keyed cables, this still happens fairly often. Usually, the system won't even start. You should be sure that the stripe on the IDE cable aligns with Pin 1 on the drive. Generally, Pin 1 is labeled.
- If you're putting multiple devices on an 80-conductor cable, make sure the last connector is attached to the master drive.

### Note

When saying that the last connector is attached to the master drive, I mean that one end of the connector is attached to the motherboard and the other end is attached to the master drive. Other drives, such as CD-ROM or additional hard drives, should be attached to the connectors between the motherboard and master drive.

# Setting Up SCSI Drives

SCSI drives are inherently more complex to set up. There are two main reasons for this:

- There are more jumpers to set, like autostart mode, and up to 15 SCSI IDs.
- There's termination of the SCSI chain to worry about. This is the single biggest cause of headaches when running SCSI hardware.

As with IDE drives, most new SCSI drives have the jumper settings printed or silk-screened on to the drive. Even so, you have to take extra care to make sure the jumpers are set correctly (see Figure 20.4).

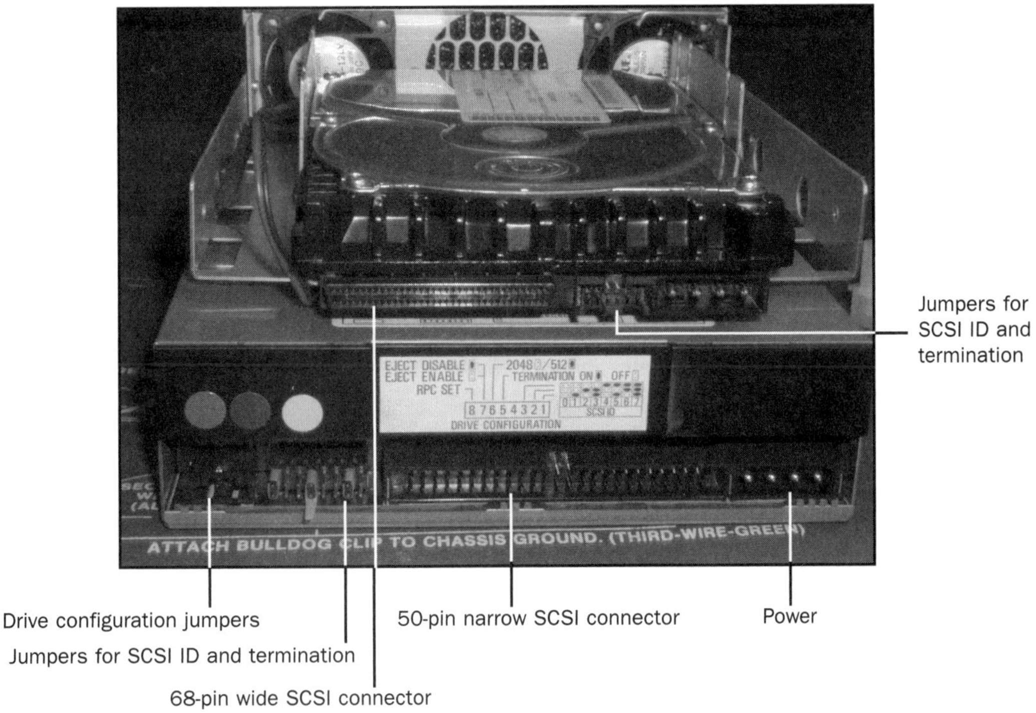


**Figure 20.4**

Here is the back of a Pioneer 6x SCSI DVD-ROM drive and a Quantum Atlas 10K Ultra2 LVD SCSI drive. Note the numerous possible settings engraved on the back of the DVD drive. If you read carefully, you'll note that *removing* the termination jumper *enables* termination. SCSI devices are full of little gotchas like this.

# Setting SCSI IDs

When you have multiple devices attached to a single SCSI adapter, they somehow need to be identified. The simplistic master/slave setup used in IDE is too limited for SCSI because a good PCI host adapter can support up to 14 devices. Instead, each drive is assigned a unique device ID—a number from 0 to 15. The host adapter itself has an ID (usually ID 7 in a PC setup).

SCSI IDs are set using small jumpers. The jumper blocks may be on the back, front, or the actual drive circuit board facing. There are normally three or four jumpers—you can set up to 15 IDs using four jumpers (see Table 20.1).

### Table 20.1—SCSI ID settings

| *SCSI ID* | *Typical Jumper Setting (x Means Jumper Attached; o Means No Jumper)* |
|---|---|
| 0 | oooo |
| 1 | ooox |
| 2 | ooxo |
| 3 | ooxx |
| 4 | oxoo |
| 5 | oxox |
| 6 | oxxo |
| 7 | oxxx |
| 8 | xooo |
| 9 | xoox |
| 10 | xoxo |
| 11 | xoxx |
| 12 | xxoo |
| 13 | xxox |
| 14 | xxxo |
| 15 | xxxx |

Setting the correct SCSI ID can be confusing. One of the two main sources of SCSI problems occurs when two devices have the same ID set.

### Note

There was a movement afoot to allow host adapters to auto-assign SCSI IDs. This concept was called SCAM (SCSI Configured Auto-Magically). Several host adapters used it, but it never seemed to catch hold, which is too bad.

## SCSI Termination

The second issue—and the chief culprit in most SCSI problems—is termination. Any electrical circuit needs to be terminated somewhere. Termination usually consists of a high resistance or impedance that identifies the end of a circuit.

SCSI cables come in variable lengths. Cables that are used inside a computer look superficially like any ribbon cable (such as an IDE cable), but may have up to eight connectors. One end is attached to the host adapter, then each connection is attached to a device, as needed. Note that you do not have to use all the connectors, and there can be gaps. For example, after connecting the end to the host adapter, the next one might be attached to a hard drive. Then, you may have several unattached connectors, with the last one attached to the CD-ROM.

External cables attach to a connector on the back of the PC—usually at the I/O bracket where the host adapter is connected. However, it is also possible for an internal connector to end in a connection to the outside. It's this ability to connect to external devices that makes SCSI interesting.

External devices usually have two connectors. You attach a cable to one connector. If that's the last device, you attach a terminator (or set a jumper). (A terminator often looks like a SCSI connector with no cable attached and a small LED that's lit when everything is powered up.) Like internal devices, you have to set an ID, though it's usually made easier with a wheel that has actual numbers on it. If you have another device, you attach a cable to the second connector instead of a terminator. This cable then runs to the next external drive, creating a daisy chain. Note that external drives usually have their own case, power supply, and power switches, though these are often quite compact. Most of the gaming rigs I've set up have had only internal drives, however.

In the bad old days SCSI drives mounted internally were terminated with *resistor packs*, small, skinny objects with eight or more pins. Drives usually had two or three of these on the main circuit board. You would install them or remove them, depending on whether termination was needed. Now, thankfully, it's just a jumper setting. You have to make sure the jumper setting is correct, though.

SCSI cabling is a little different, and confusing. In this sample SCSI setup, I installed three hard drives, a DVD-ROM drive and a CD-Recordable drive.

The new Ultra2 LVD (low voltage differential) SCSI standard has made life a little easier for system installers. The main thing is that LVD drives no longer have any termination jumpers. It's now *required* that the cable be terminated, or that you have external termination of some type (see Figure 20.5).

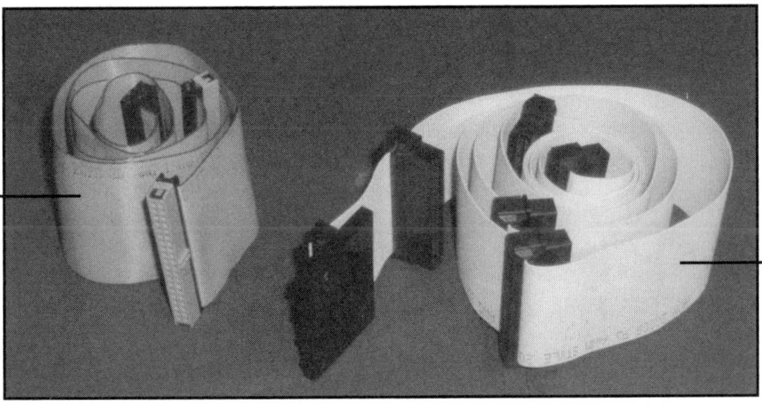


**Figure 20.5**

Here is an 80 conductor UltraATA cable and an Ultra2 LVD SCSI cable. The SCSI cable is on the right. This cable can connect to five devices, plus the host adapter. Note the terminator block at the end of the SCSI cable, on the right.

## Note

Like any long cable carrying signals, SCSI cables must be terminated somewhere. IDE drives are terminated, too, but that happens automatically. Given the wide variation in SCSI chains—including both external and internal devices—termination can get pretty complex. Most newer host adapters take care of terminating themselves automatically these days. Ultra2 LVD drives require termination on the cable. On all other devices, you either have to attach termination resistors or set a jumper. Note that *the termination must be at the end of the chain* (hence the name). If you somehow terminate a device in the middle of a chain, the host adapter will see that as the last device in the chain, meaning other attached devices will be ignored.

Although SCSI termination is typically the most common problem, there are a few other things to look for when troubleshooting SCSI problems:

- Check the SCSI IDs. If two devices have the same ID, only the one closest to the host adapter on the chain will be seen.
- Some SCSI cards cannot support connections to all connectors simultaneously. For example, the Adaptec 2940UW would support simultaneous connections to any two of the three connectors. You can connect drives to both internal connectors—and not use the external connector. Or you can use the external connector (on the I/O bracket), but not the internal connector. The newer Ultra2 SCSI 2940u2w can support connections to all four of its connectors—three internal and one external. In the case of the 2940u2w, there is a 50-pin, internal narrow connector, a 68-pin ultra-wide connector, a 68-pin ultra2 LVD connector, and an external ultra2 LVD connector (see Figure 20.6).

**Figure 20.6**
Here's an Adaptec 2940u2w, with a lot of cables attached.

- If you do have cables connected to multiple ports on the host adapter, the SCSI card can sometimes get confused, and you may have to manually set the termination in the SCSI BIOS.
- Some drives require an autostart jumper to be set before they will spin up, even if the host adapter sends a start signal.

As you can see, SCSI is more complex, but that also makes it more flexible. You can have up to fifteen SCSI devices attached to one card, using a single IRQ. With newer host adapters, you can change the boot drive—handy if you're experimenting with multiple operating systems. Some devices, like DAT tape drives and DVD-RAM drives, are only available with SCSI interfaces. Finally, the highest performing hard drives are still SCSI drives. One of Seagate's Barracuda drives comes in a whopping 50GB configuration!

# We're Done!

If you've been careful, and just a little lucky, all the hardware should be up and running. Of course, there's no way to use it... yet. We need to install the operating system. That's coming up in Chapter 21, "Installing the Operating System for the First Time."

# Part 6

# Tweaking Your Gaming Rig

# Chapter 21

# Installing the Operating System for the First Time

## Bootstrap Your World

Getting Windows 95 up and running was always a chore because the boot disc that comes with the OS doesn't properly detect half the CD-ROM drives available. So, you always spend an inordinate amount of time swapping floppies and formatting the hard drive through DOS. The capper was finding the DOS CD-ROM drivers editing the DOS startup files (CONFIG.SYS and AUTOEXEC.BAT), just so you could install Windows. It was a headache for technically astute users; for neophytes, it was a nightmare.

That situation is much less true than in the past. Recent hardware is more standardized (especially CD-ROM and DVD-ROM drives), and the Windows setup process became considerably more robust with Windows 98. So, let's dig up that Windows 98 CD and proceed!

# Windows 98 Bootable CD

If you haven't bought your copy of Windows yet, get an OEM version. You can probably get a copy from whoever sold you the hard drive, motherboard, or CPU. Don't get the retail version if you can avoid it.

There are two reasons to avoid the retail version. The first is cost. The retail version sells for $160–$190, whereas the OEM full install version goes for around $95–$110. The second reason is the ease of installation. Both versions come with a boot floppy that's more useful than the Windows 95 boot floppy However, the OEM version goes one step further: The CD is a bootable CD.

Most newer motherboards and CD/DVD drives now support bootable CDs. If you want to boot from the CD-ROM drive, you typically have to run the BIOS setup program. Just press the F2 function or Delete key as the system is going through the POST (power-on, self-test) messages. One of the screens will allow you to specify the order of the boot devices—set it to try the CD-ROM first.

When you boot from the CD, the first thing you see is a menu asking you if the system should boot from the CD or the hard drive. Pick the CD boot selection by moving the cursor with the up or down arrow key. Then, another boot menu will pop up. There are three choices here:

- Start Windows 98 Setup from CD-ROM
- Start computer with CD-ROM support
- Start computer without CD-ROM support

If this is a new Windows install on an unformatted hard disk, pick menu choice (1). At this point, you'll be presented with a screen welcoming you to the setup program. Press Enter. If the hard drive is unformatted, your only useful choice is to pick Configure Unallocated Disk Space.

The next screen presents you with two choices: to use large drive support or not. Given the size of today's hard drives, you'd be a masochist to pick No. You'd have to deal with as many as 14 different drive letters on a big drive. Select, instead, Yes, Enable Large Disk Support.

At this point, you're asked to put the setup floppy in drive A, and then the system will reboot. You do *not* have to put the floppy into the A drive—just boot from the CD again, and SETUP will begin and format your hard drive.

### Tip

If you use this relatively friendly method for setting up the hard drive, you'll get one large partition. If that's what you want, that's no problem. If you want more than one partition, restart using the Windows setup floppy (instead of booting from the CD). On the floppy is the DOS-based FDISK program.

When you boot from the floppy, press F3 to exit Windows setup. Run FDISK. Unlike Windows setup, FDISK defaults to large drive setup. Just press Enter at the large drive query screen. Press Enter twice at the next screen; this brings you to the screen to create a primary partition. Now, if you want a second partition (I don't recommend more than two, in general), just make the primary partition smaller than the maximum. Do make one of the drives somewhat larger, but it's your call as to which one. I recommend a 2:1 ratio for a larger (more than 10GB) drive.

Finally, after this is done, you'll want to repeat the steps, except you want to set up an *extended* partition, which will be the second drive. Use all of the leftover space for this if you want only two partitions.

After this is done, you can reboot and start from the Windows CD. The Windows setup program will format the newly partitioned drives.

One last note: There are third-party utilities, such as Partition Magic and Partition-It, that allow you to reconfigure your partitions without having to reformat or lose data (if the drive isn't full). Partition Magic can also aid in creating non-Windows partitions. for other operating systems.

## Non-Bootable OS CDs

What if you don't have a bootable CD drive? Or, what if you have the retail version that doesn't contain a bootable CD?

Windows 95 or 98 come with a startup floppy. If you have the startup floppy, it's almost as easy as the bootable CD. Make sure the floppy is set up in your system BIOS to be one of the boot devices.

Put the startup floppy in the A drive and turn on the system. As the memory check runs, insert the Windows setup CD into the CD drive. The system will boot from the floppy, detect any ATA or SCSI CD drives, and then run SETUP from the CD. Then, you're off and running, as described previously.

## When SETUP Is Running

When you reboot, setup will start normally. Scandisk will run a check on your system, and then you'll be in Windows setup itself. Hang in there, we're nearly done with the basic installation.

Using your mouse or the Enter key, click the Next button until you reach the Select Directory screen. I strongly suggest you just leave the Windows directory as c:\windows. Clicking Next a couple more times will take you through a screen in which the Windows folders are set up, and then you're presented with your first real set of choices. You can

- Perform a typical installation
- Install Windows to run efficiently on a laptop computer

- Install a compact version that takes up less disc space
- Customize the Windows installation

If you just want to move on, select the Typical installation; you can always add elements later. If you're feeling a little bold, select the Customize option. That will let you do things like *not* install all the online service setup programs, install Windows games, and various other things. The choice is yours.

After a few more clicks of the mouse on the Next button, head into the kitchen for a nice cup of hot tea. A lot of files get decompressed and installed on the hard drive at this point.

When you return, you should be faced with a logon screen, asking you for a username and workgroup. Type in something appropriate, then press Enter. You'll now be staring at the Windows 98 license agreement. You *must* select the I Accept the Agreement option to continue.

Now, we reach the most onerous and annoying part of the whole Windows 98 setup process: typing in the serial number. You have to type 25 characters into five fields. Although they aren't truly random, they look random, and you'll almost always fail to get it right the first time. Windows Setup won't let you proceed until you type it in correctly.

### Tip

Find a permanent marker that can write on the Windows CD and write the serial number directly onto the title side of the CD. You'll never have to hunt around for it again.

The next thing Windows does is detect hardware and set up the drivers for any devices it knows about. This will take a little time, so sit back with that hot cup of tea and contemplate life for a bit. After the hardware detection process is done, the system reboots again. You'll need to set the clock and calendar, and then we're into the home stretch.

Windows reboots once more. When Windows starts up again, it may ask for drivers—make sure you have your driver discs handy.

### Caution

Occasionally, Windows will ask you to insert the Windows 98 CD-ROM during the first boot—but you'll find you can't access the CD drive. This is a sure sign that you removed the CD during the setup process. Make sure you leave the Windows 98 CD in the drive during the entire setup process.

After this is done (and possibly one more reboot), we're done. Well, we're sorta done—you now have to install all your drivers and applications. But you should feel proud—you've just built a computer and installed the OS.

# Copying Windows 98 to the Hard Drive

The standard installation process I've outlined works fine. However, it makes things somewhat inconvenient later on. As you install new hardware or drivers, you'll sometimes be prompted to Insert the Windows 98 CD. Even if you're a highly organized person, and can always lay your hands on the CD, it's inconvenient.

What I do instead is create the partitions and format the drive using the boot floppy. I boot from the floppy, and then press F3 to exit to DOS. Then, I use FDISK to set up the partition or partitions. Then, I reboot, get back to the DOS prompt, and type:

```
format c: /s /v
```

The /s option makes the drive bootable.

After the C drive is formatted, I reboot from the floppy once more. When you boot from the floppy, it installs the DOS CD drivers, giving you access to the CD-ROM drive. Now, create a directory on your hard drive called \DOS by typing:

```
md c:\dos
```

Now, change to the Windows 98 CD, and find the directory \tools\oldmsdos. Copy the contents to c:\dos by typing:

```
copy *.* c:\dos
```

Now, make sure the Windows 98 startup floppy is in the drive. Copy FDISK.EXE to c:\dos. Now, we can do just about anything needed during the setup process from the hard drive. The key thing was that we copied a program called XCOPY to c:\dos.

The next step is to create a folder called \win98. If you have two partitions or two physical hard drives, put this folder on the second partition or hard drive by typing:

```
md d:\win98
```

(Substitute the correct drive letter for d:)

Now, change to the c:\dos folder. Type:

```
xcopy g:\win98\*.* d:\win98\*.* /e /v
```

(G is your CD-ROM drive letter and d is your hard drive.)

Substitute the correct CD drive letter for G and the correct hard drive letter for D if they are different. This should take several minutes—you're copying roughly 170MB worth of files. After this is done, you will have all the files you need to install Windows, right there on the hard drive. You will no longer have to be prompted to insert the Windows 98 CD.

After copying the files over, run setup from d:\win98, and proceed normally. It should go a little faster because you're installing from a hard drive.

# Creating a Startup Floppy

Windows 95 and Windows 98 come with startup floppies. But one thing you should know how to do is to create one yourself, just for your system. When you install Windows the first time, it prompts you to create a new startup floppy. This is a good idea, and you should have done it. However, here's a manual process for creating your own.

1. Format a floppy, using the option to install the system files. If it's formatted from within Windows, there's a Copy System Files check box. If you format from the DOS prompt, type: `format c: /s`. The /s tells the DOS format command to make the floppy bootable.

2. Locate your DOS CD-ROM drivers. They may be on your hard drive, or on a floppy. There are two files: the actual hardware driver, and a file called MSCDEX.EXE, which is the Microsoft CD file system driver. The hardware driver may have various names, such as ATAPI_CD.SYS, OAKCDROM.SYS, and so on. MSCDEX.EXE is in \windows\command.

3. SCSI is a little different. There are usually two files you have to worry about. The first is the driver for the SCSI host adapter. This can have a name like ASPI8DOS.SYS or ASPI8U2.SYS (for Adaptec cards). You should have an install floppy for the host adapter with this file on it, or you can get it from the maker's Web site. The second driver is the CD hardware driver, which also came with the host adapter. This may have a name like ASPICD.SYS.

4. Copy all the CD files onto the floppy.

5. Now, copy the following files from \windows\command to the floppy: FDISK.EXE, SYS.COM, MSCDEX.EXE (if you haven't done it yet), SCANDISK.EXE, XCOPY.EXE, FORMAT.COM, and EDIT.COM. Then, copy \windows\HIMEM.SYS to the floppy.

6. Now, using either Notepad or Edit, create a file called config.sys. Add the following lines to this file:

   ```
   DEVICE=HIMEM.SYS
   DEVICE=ATAPI_CD.SYS /d:mscd001
   ```

   (Or whatever the correct CD-ROM driver is—but leave the /d:mscd001.)

   If it's a SCSI drive, also add a line immediately after HIMEM.SYS for the SCSI adapter driver.

7. Save this file to the floppy (making sure to call it CONFIG.SYS).

8. Next, create a text file called AUTOEXEC.BAT. Add a single line to this file:

   ```
   MSCDEX.EXE /D:MSCD001 /L:E
   ```

You now have a useful DOS boot floppy. You can use this to recover from disk problems, reinstall Windows (though you'll need to manually run SETUP from the CD), and other general troubleshooting.

## If You Have Windows 95

We've been assuming you're installing Windows 98. Because this is a brand new system, I strongly encourage you to use Windows 98, which automatically understands AGP and USB. But if you have Windows 95, here's what you can do.

First, if you only have the original version of Windows 95 or Service Release 1 (these are versions 950 and 950A), you need to get Windows 98 if you *ever* want USB or full AGP support.

If you have Windows 95 OSR2, OSR2.1, or OSR2.5, you're in better shape. OSR 2 and 2.1 both identify themselves as Windows 95 version 950B. OSR2.5 includes Internet Explorer 4.01, DirectX 5 and the USB supplement, and identifies itself as version 950C. (You can see the version number in the system control panel.)

You can tell if you have OSR2 by looking in the Add/Remove Software control panel. If you do *not* see USB Supplement to OSR2 present, you only have OSR2. You need to find and download the USB supplement. (You can just do a search on the Web—it is *not* available on the Microsoft Web site, but many other sites carry it.) You need the USB supplement if you hope to run any USB devices. In addition, the USB supplement also enables full AGP functionality.

# How Many Partitions Should I Have?

If you only have one physical hard drive, I recommend partitioning it with two partitions. There are several reasons for this:

- You can copy the Windows 98 setup files to the D drive. This makes it *much* easier to reinstall Windows should something go wrong.
- You can back up your data to the D drive. This is a little safer than keeping it all on one large partition. If a partition is going to get munged, it's usually the C drive. This is *not* as safe as backing it up off the computer, or even to a second physical hard drive. You are still relying on a single drive mechanism, after all.
- It's a little easier to keep things organized.

By far, though, the first reason is the most important one. Having a second partition that's present even if you have to reformat the C drive is a very handy thing to have. I wouldn't recommend more than two partitions, though. Keeping track of multiple drives, and where files are kept, can be a real chore.

For more detail on installing drivers, see page 293.

Okay, now it's time to install all the drivers and applications—games. Get some games installed and play them to get a feel for how your new baby responds. After you play for a bit, you'll start yearning for some human company. That means it's time for a little multiplayer action.

# Chapter 22

# Getting Your Network Running

## The Networking Experience

Prior to the advent of computer games, gaming has always been a social activity. Although solitaire style games have always been around to help while away time, getting a group of people to play Bridge or wargame miniatures creates an energizing time for the players involved. The same is true for computer games over a local area network.

Not long ago, a few of us played *Baldur's Gate*. This game supports cooperative multi-player, allowing a party of up to six people on a network to play through the storyline. It took us about six weeks of Friday evenings to get through the game. Each session was raucous good fun, with good natured shouting, moans, and laughter. People worked together to get through tough parts of the story. Later, we realized it was the closest thing to re-creating the paper role-playing game experience. The best multiplayer games are social games.

However, setting up a network can seem intimidating if you've never done it. But stick with me, and we'll uncover the secrets to setting up your own network for multiplayer games. We'll be focusing strictly on what's needed for network gaming, so I won't cover applications sharing, networked printers, or other networking applications.

# Hardware Setup

Before we move on to actual network setup, make sure your hardware is set up properly. I'm going to focus on a network that uses a hub and ethernet NIC, but the principles are the same, whether you use coax cable, USB networking, or even phone-line networking. Some networking kits automate some of what we'll discuss, but it's still useful to know what goes on under the hood in case something goes awry. Make sure the hardware is installed properly, and that the cables are attached as needed.

In this ethernet example, the twisted-pair cables have RJ-45 connectors at the end. These cables look like oversized phone jack connectors, and plug into the NIC at one end and the hub at the other. See Chapter 15, "Area Networks," for more information on the connectors used in a typical Ethernet network.

# Protocols

When people go to a business meeting or a party and introduce themselves to strangers, they usually go through a series of steps to make the introduction smooth. They'll approach someone, extend a hand to shake the other person's hand, and say something polite. This routine of having a set way of approaching another person is known as *protocol*.

Similarly, when computers communicate with other computers, they need to do so in clearly defined ways. The data must look the same to the remote system, the information is disassembled in a way that the distant computer can easily reassemble it, and so on. *Networking protocols* are the software equivalents of handshakes and hellos.

As far as computer gaming goes, there are two networking protocols that are used: TCP/IP and IPX. We'll discuss each of them, and then walk through setting them up under Windows 98.

## TCP/IP

TCP/IP stands for *transmission control protocol/internetworking protocol*. It's the native "language" for moving data around the Internet, but it's also used extensively in local area networks. Each computer on a TCP/IP network has a unique *IP address*, which takes the form of four fields, with the maximum number in any of the four fields being 255.

If you were setting up a large corporate network, you'd have to apply for a set of IP addresses. There are a limited number of IP addresses, and the supply is getting smaller each day. However, you are *not* setting up a large corporate network. Part of the TCP/IP standard defines several ranges of IP addresses that are used for internal-only networks (networks that do not communicate directly with the outside world).

When you first set up Windows 98 without a NIC, the setup program installs the dial-up adapter, along with the TCP/IP protocol stack (see Figure 22.1). No IP address is assigned to the dial-up adapter because it's assumed that most users will be dialing in to an ISP (Internet Service Provider), who will automatically assign an IP address every time you log on to the Internet.

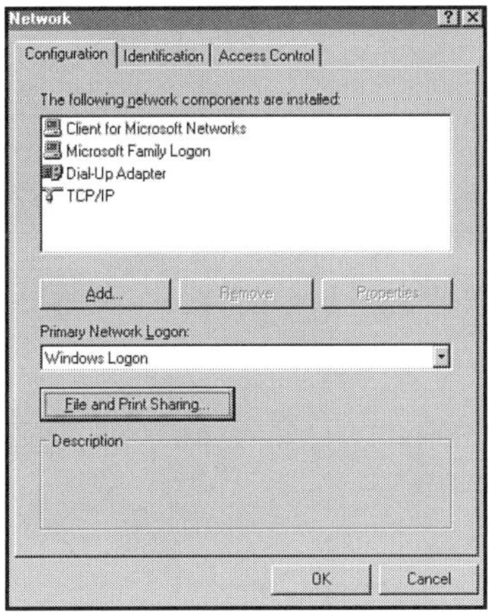


**Figure 22.1**

Here's what the network control panel shows just after a completed Windows 98 installation.

When you install a NIC, Windows *binds* the TCP/IP protocol to the NIC automatically (see Figure 22.2). However, it still assumes that you want to have IP addresses automatically assigned by a local DHCP server. (DHCP stands for *dynamic host configuration protocol*.)

The job of a DHCP server is to assign IP addresses on demand, as systems come up on a network. However, in all likelihood, you don't have a DHCP server in your home. Although Windows 98 will autoassign IP addresses itself, they will be different every time you boot up. It's better just to assign addresses yourself.

Luckily, there are ranges of IP addresses that are available for internal-only networks, called the LINKLOCAL address spaces. Microsoft suggests using the LINKLOCAL address space, which looks like 169.254.xxx.xxx. For example, if you had two systems, you'd first click Specify an IP Address, and then enter the first address as 169.254.0.1 and the second as 169.254.0.2. Set the subnet mask for 255.255.255.0. Figure 22.3 shows the TCP/IP Properties dialog box with the IP and subnet mask entered.

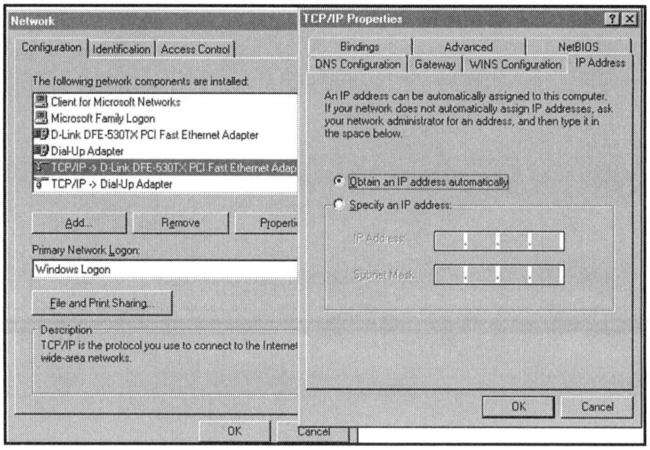


## Figure 22.2

If you click on Properties for TCP/IP, this is what you'll see. Windows assumes that an IP address will be automatically assigned.

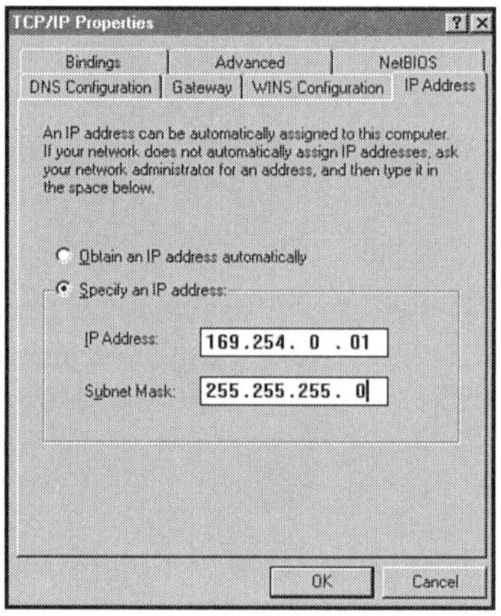


## Figure 22.3

Here's the same window with the IP address now assigned.

## Tip

There's another range of IP addresses available also for internal-only networking, starting with 192.168.xxx.xxx. Either set of addresses should work fine.

Now we have an IP address assigned. The next step is to install file sharing. Click on the File and Print Sharing button, and then click on the check box labeled File Sharing. (You can turn on print sharing, too, if you want.) File sharing enables us to move files back and forth between computers. With file sharing on and an Internet connection, you may never use a floppy disc again. Although it has no effect for games, it makes life much easieras when you want to move that 15MB patch you just downloaded from the Internet from one computer to another computer on your network.

Note that you may want to assign passwords to the file sharing capability if you have a cable modem, DSL connection, or other "always-on" Internet connection. It is remotely possible that an outside user could snoop around your system.

The last step is to check your system identity. You probably gave your system one during the Windows setup process, but just in case, click on the top tab labeled Identification. Give your system a name. You can leave the workgroup name as WORKGROUP, which is the Windows default, or you can give your workgroup a pithy name. However, all your systems need to have the same workgroup name.

Now, click OK. If you've installed from the CD, Windows will ask you to insert it into the CD drive. After a few files are loaded and configured, reboot.

Now you've got TCP/IP loaded. The next step is to install the IPX protocol.

# Setting Up IPX

The IPX protocol .was originally developed by Novell Corporation for use in its local area networking operating system, NetWare. It's a simple protocol, well suited for network gaming on local area networks.

At this point, I'm assuming you got TCP/IP running on your home network, and you can move files back and forth between the two computers. Now, bring up the network control panel, click Add, and then select Protocol. The Select Network Protocol dialog box appears (see Figure 22.4). Under company name, select Microsoft, and find the selection for IPX/SPX-compatible Protocol, select it, and then click OK. Again, you may be prompted for your Windows CD.

After a few files are installed, your network control panel should show the IPX protocol being bound to both the NIC and the dial-up adapter. I usually delete the binding to the dial-up adapter, as it's useless for our purposes.

If you bind file sharing to multiple protocols, you may actually see networking performance decline, even in games. I generally uncheck all bindings to IPX and leave only TCP/IP to be used for file sharing and logon. When you do this, you'll get an error message that asks you if you want to assign bindings. Just click No (see Figure 22.5).

You don't have to configure the workgroup again because you did it during the TCP/IP setup. We now have the two main networking protocols used for computer gaming. Now, you're ready for combating the ultimate game AI: your next door neighbor....

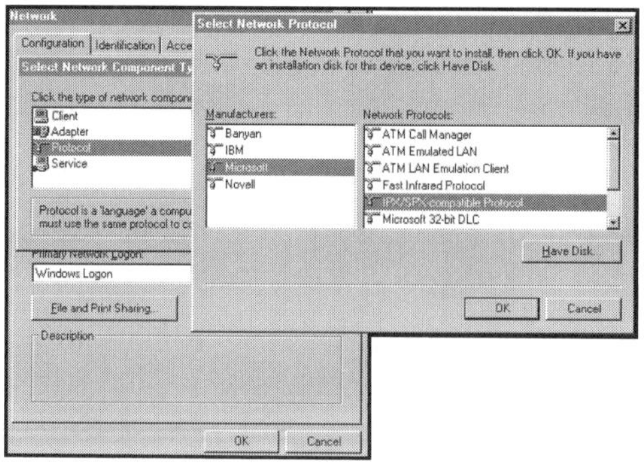


**Figure 22.4**
Installing the IPX protocol.

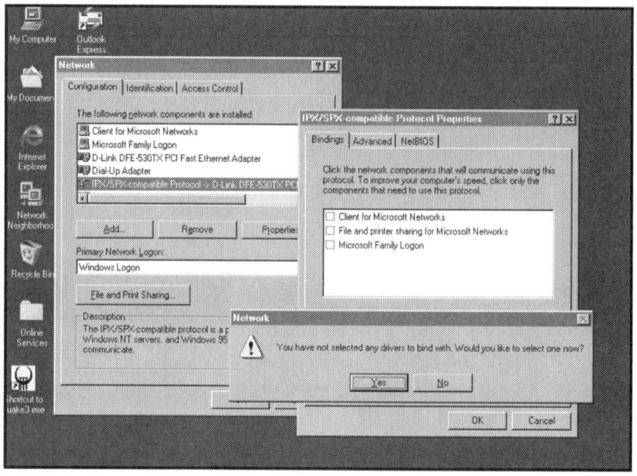


**Figure 22.5**
Uncheck the protocol bindings for IPX. This should smooth out networking performance a bit.

# Troubleshooting Your Network

A home network is one of the simplest possible networks. There's only one hub (if that), no name servers to worry about, no routing tablesjust a handful of PCs connected together. Still, things can go awry. Here are some typical problems and possible solutions.

- You can't see any other system in Network Neighborhood. Check to make sure that the workgroup names are the same. Check also to see if both systems are configured with identical sets of protocols.

## Caution

If you've installed a PCI networking card adjacent to the AGP graphics card on certain motherboards, you may not be able to see other systems in Network Neighborhood, yet connect with network games. The solution is to either disable PCI steeringnot something for the faint-heartedor simply move the NIC to a different PCI slot.

- You can move files back and forth all day long, but network games can't see each other. First, check to see if the systems really are configured for the same protocol. There are settings for both IPX and TCP/IP that can alter how the data is transmitted. Check the protocol's properties and make sure they're the same. Also, simply see if the correct protocol is loaded at all.
- Network games frequently crash, with multiple systems freezing up. This is a tough one, but the culprit is more often the game than the network. The art of writing networkable computer games is not an easy one, and many are buggy when they first come out. Check with the game's publisher to see if a patch is available or forthcoming.

With a little perseverance, some sweat, and a systematic approach, you should be able to get your own LAN running smoothly. After using it a bit, you may wonder how you ever lived without one.

# Chapter 23

# Tweaking Windows and DirectX Installations

## Recipe for Disaster

There are literally millions of different combinations of PC hardware. Toss in multiple versions of DirectX, beta software, and demo downloads from the Internet, and you have a recipe for potential disaster. Here are a few tips that can help you when you run into trouble.

## Removing and Reinstalling DirectX

According to Microsoft, the only way to remove DirectX is to reformat the hard drive. That strikes me as a rather drastic solution because I got into trouble once after installing a beta version of DirectX 6.0 (don't ask). After a lot of digging, I uncovered a procedure for uninstalling DirectX. Note that this is only guaranteed to work for DirectX 6.1, and not necessarily any future version.

### Caution

Only do this if you are having problems that a DirectX reinstall or update cannot fix.

Last Warning: We are about to edit the Registry. Do this at your own risk. Deleting the wrong Registry entry can seriously foul up your system. Make a backup of the Registry with the REGEDIT Export command from the REGEDIT file menu before hacking into the Registry.

There are three main steps to removing and reinstalling DirectX:

1. Delete references to DirectX in the system Registry.
2. Delete all the files associated with DirectX.
3. Reinstall DirectX.

Before we start, make sure you have a copy of DirectX 6.0, 6.1a, or 7.0 to install. There's usually a copy on most game CDs. Otherwise, download a copy from `http://www.microsoft.com/directx`.

### Note

Windows 98SE comes with DirectX 6.1a integrated. You should *not* have to uninstall this, unless you've installed the DirectX 7 beta.

## Delete References to DirectX in the Registry

The Registry is a database that, among other things, holds configuration data for Windows. Run REGEDIT, the Windows Registry editor. Pull down the File menu and export the Registry to another location.

Now that you've backed up the Registry, you need to delete some Registry entries (see Figure 23.1).

Now, locate the following Registry entries:

HKEY_LOCAL_MACHINE/Software/Microsoft/Direct3D
HKEY_LOCAL_MACHINE/Software/Microsoft/DirectDraw
HKEY_LOCAL_MACHINE/Software/Microsoft/DirectMusic
HKEY_LOCAL_MACHINE/Software/Microsoft/DirectPlay
HKEY_LOCAL_MACHINE/Software/Microsoft/DirectX

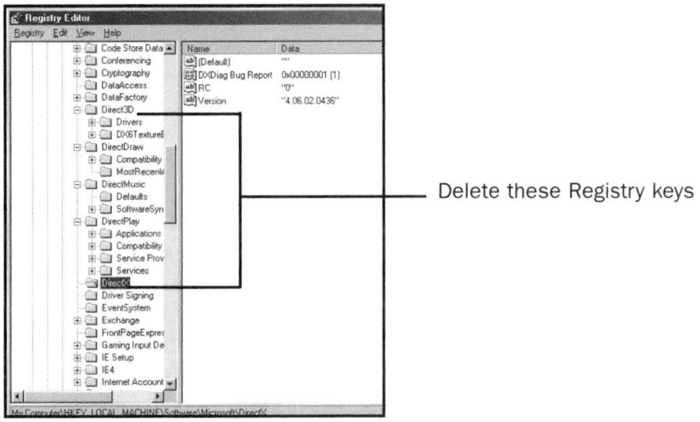


**Figure 23.1**
These Registry keys need to be removed in the first step to uninstalling DirectX.

# Delete DirectX Files

After you've deleted the Registry keys for DirectX, reboot to the DOS prompt. Remove the following files in \WINDOWS\SYSTEM:

Do this by typing each line followed by the Enter or Return key:

```
DEL ddraw*.*
DEL dsound*.*
DEL dmusic*.*
DEL dinput*.*
DEL d3d*.*
DEL dplayx.dll
DEL dpmodemx.dll
DEL dpwsockx.dll
DEL ddhelp.exe
```

Next, change to \WINDOWS\SYSBCKUP. Then, delete the following files by typing each line followed by the Enter or Return key:

```
DEL ddraw*.*
DEL dsound*.*
DEL dinput*.*
DEL d3d*.*
DEL dplayx.dll
DEL dpmodemx.dll
DEL dpwsockx.dll
```

The DOS DELTREE command can remove an entire directory. Be very careful to type in the correct command, as below, so you don't inadvertently delete the wrong folder. Using the DELTREE command in \windows\command, delete the DirectX folder in \program files:

```
C:\windows\command\deltree c:\progra~1\directx
```

That's it. DirectX is now removed. Note that a few files may still be around, like the joystick control panel, but it's not necessary to remove them.

## Reinstall DirectX

Now, reboot into Windows and reinstall DirectX. You can do this just by reinstalling a game or using a downloaded version of DirectX. If you have inadvertently deleted the joystick control panel and vjoyd.vxd, you will also probably need to reinstall your sound card drivers.

Removing DirectX is the equivalent of radical surgery, and should only be done as a last resort. Should you get into trouble, the only thing left to do is remove the Windows folder and do a clean reinstall—but that's another topic.

# Certified Drivers

One issue you may run into, especially when contacting tech support, is that of certified drivers (see Figure 23.2).

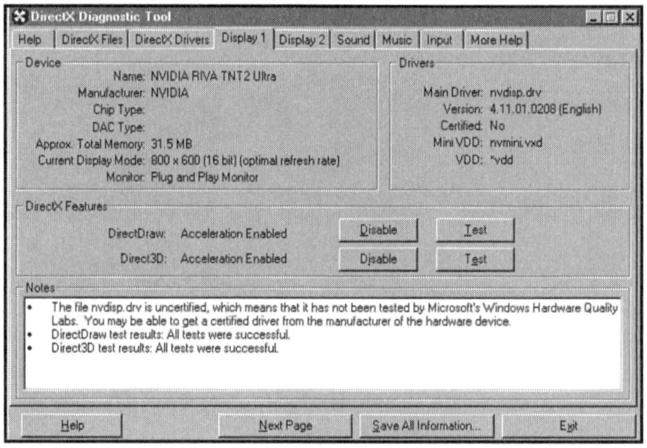


**Figure 23.2**

Note the "driver not certified" message in the list at the bottom of the DirectX control panel. You really shouldn't be worried.

Driver certification is a process where a driver goes through a series of functionality tests. Both Microsoft and the hardware vendors can run the certification tests. In fact, there's a process called *self-certification*, in which a hardware manufacturer can certify its own drivers, though Microsoft can always audit the drivers. You'll sometimes see a driver on a graphics cardmaker's Web site that has been *WHQL-certified*. This is a Microsoft-certified driver. WHQL stands for Windows Hardware Quality Lab. However, the WHQL drivers will often leave out driver "tweaking" functions that are frowned on by Microsoft.

People tend to think that driver certification is a magical process that will ensure bug-free drivers. I'm sorry to report this, but certification doesn't guarantee a lack of bugs. What driver certification does is ensure that the driver will pass a set of tests.

In addition, Microsoft won't allow certification of drivers that enable some features they consider problematic. For example, if your driver set has a check box to disable vsync, they are uncertified. Microsoft frowns on some features because they tend to generate support calls. So although driver certification is a useful tool,. it is no panacea.

## OEM Drivers

When you get a system from a major system manufacturer, like Dell, you may get a high-performance 3D graphics card. These cards are often very close to the ones you've read about in the reviews—but the glitzy control panel is often removed. The OEM versions are often much more sparse. You can be sure, though, that the drivers are certified. You can, if you like, download the drivers from the graphics card vendor's Web site, but it's a trade-off. You may pick up some additional features, but the system manufacturer won't give you support unless you install its drivers. And the graphics cardmaker won't support you in either case.

# The Clean Reinstall

There comes a time with any Windows-based PC that you have to reinstall Windows. No matter how faithfully you've used a third-party uninstaller, if you play a fair number of games and install demos you've downloaded from the Internet, the system will start to bog down. DLL files clog up the Windows system directory, residual files from old drivers linger on, and the remnants of uninstalled applications chew up disc space. It's time to reinstall.

Usually, if you're reinstalling to fix a problem—some key Windows file got munged, for example—a refresh install can fix a lot of problems. The Windows 98 setup program is much smarter than the Windows 95 installer. No longer will it overwrite newer drivers, for example.

Eventually, though, it will be time for a full install. There are two approaches. The first is to drop a thermonuclear weapon on your system—in other words, completely reformat the C drive. This is a drastic measure that should only be used if you've completely lost control of the contents of your hard drive and just want to start over.

The more common method—and the one we'll cover—involves removing Windows and it's key components in \program files and running SETUP from the DOS prompt. There are nine steps, which I quickly run down here, and then cover each in more detail:

1. Back up your critical data.
2. Uninstall all applications you won't be immediately reinstalling.
3. Write down key items, such as passwords and Internet service provider information.

4. Gather up all the applications and drivers you'll need to reinstall.
5. Create a folder on your hard drive for DOS commands, and copy the contents of \windows\command to the new folder.
6. Copy the \win98 folder to your hard drive from the Windows setup CD.
7. Boot to the DOS prompt and delete \windows and key directories in \program files.
8. Run setup from the \win98 subdirectory on your hard-drive and set up Windows.
9. After installing, run Defrag on the hard drive.

## 1. Back Up Your Critical Data

Whether it's homework, the spreadsheets you brought home from the office, or your save game files, back them up to another location. This can be floppy discs, another partition or hard drive on the computer, or a CD-R disc.

There are a couple of important things that are easy to overlook:

- If you use Outlook or Outlook Express, export the mail files to another location (using the export to .PST script). Your email, contacts, calendar, and journal information may be stored in \windows and you don't want to lose that.
- If you use Internet Explorer, back up the \windows\favorites folder.
- If you use Word in the course of your work, chances are that you've saved custom macros, styles, and shortcut keys in your Normal template. Be sure to back up this template. It's located in Program Files\Microsoft Office\Templates\normal.dot.

## 2. Uninstall All Applications You Won't Be Immediately Reinstalling

If you don't do this, you'll get confused about what applications are really set up and which aren't. I do. So remove them now and free up some disc space.

## 3. Write Down Key Items

These include: your logon password for your ISP or other online accounts, the DNS server information for your ISP, and the phone numbers you use to dial in to your ISP.

## 4. Gather Up What You Need to Reinstall

This includes all the drivers and applications. If you have more recent drivers or application patches you've downloaded, make sure those are available.

Also, make sure you have any and all serial numbers within easy reach—especially the Windows 98 serial number. If some of the applications are upgrades, make sure you have the discs for the older apps available and their serial numbers as well.

## 5. Create a DOS Folder

After you've done this, copy the contents of \windows\command to this folder. Also copy himem.sys and smartdrv.exe from \windows if you want to use them (but this isn't absolutely necessary).

## 6. Copy \win98 from the Install CD to Your Hard Drive

This comes under the heading of "making life easier." Running the Windows 98 setup program from your hard drive will make the install go much faster, and you won't get into a situation where you might need something from the CD, but the CD drive hasn't been made available in Windows yet.

## 7. Boot to the DOS Prompt and Do the Deed

The best way is from a clean DOS boot. After you've performed the initial steps (you did back up, right?), then click the Start button and click on Shutdown, Restart. Just as the system is getting past the BIOS messages, press the F8 key. You'll see the Windows startup menu. This will enable you to boot to the command prompt.

### Tip

The Windows Start menu is hard to get to, but can be a handy troubleshooting tool any time. After you're done installing Windows, find the hidden system file on your hard drive called MSDOS.SYS. Change the properties so it's not write-only because we're going to edit it.

MSDOS.SYS is just a text file. The first and only rule is: Don't delete anything you have not added yourself.

Add the following lines under the [options] header:

```
BootMenu=1
BootMenuDelay=10
```

Save the file. Now, whenever you start the system, you'll see the boot menu for 10 seconds. You can choose the command prompt, safe mode, or the step-through mode, which is handy for troubleshooting.

Now that you're in DOS, change to the DOS folder by typing:

```
cd c:\dos
```

Now, take a deep breath and type:

```
deltree c:\windows
deltree c:\progra~1\common~1
deltree c:\progra~1\plus!
deltree c:\progra~1\directx
deltree c:\progra~1\intern~1
deltree c:\progra~1\frontp~1
deltree c:\progra~1\outloo~1
deltree c:\progra~1\window~1
```

You just nuked Windows. Betcha it felt good.

# 8. Run SETUP

Now, change to the \win98 folder (on whichever disc or partition you copied it) and run the SETUP program. Set up Windows normally. This behaves much like a first-time setup.

For a walkthrough of how to set up Windows, see page 261.

# 9. Run Defrag After Installing

Install all the applications and games you want to reinstall. Copy back \favorites and restore your email, and then set up your Internet connection. After all that is done, run Defrag and defragment your hard drive.

There, you're done. If you've been efficient, it's only about four hours. But you'll be amazed at how much more responsive Windows and your games suddenly become.

# Chapter 24

# Taking Control: Making Your Joystick or Controller Work

## Taming Your Joystick

Game controllers take a myriad of forms ranging from the weird to the exotic and everything in between. Getting these controllers to do anything useful—control a fighter aircraft in a simulation, for example, can be a snap. On the other hand, a controller that isn't properly set up or calibrated can make your gaming experience very frustrating, indeed.

Game controllers can add a serious dose of realism or fun to many games. Making a game controller, particularly a joystick, work the way you want it to work can be irritating at best. The good news is that this chapter will arm you with the skills you need to tame your game controller.

# Sound Card Game Ports

Even in today's USB-happy world, most game controllers connect via a sound card game port. Sound cards can range in price from $9.95 Sound Blaster knockoffs to $1,200 cards more suitable for studio musicians than gamers. Most of these have a game port that doubles as a MIDI connection.

For more detail than you ever imagined about the inner workings of game ports, see page 138.

The adage "you get what you pay for" generally holds true with sound cards. The more expensive, PCI sound cards seem to do a little better than the cheap SB clones. Audio integrated onto the motherboard might be more problematic—you might need to get a dedicated game port card if the onboard game port isn't sufficient. You might also want to consider a USB controller instead.

# USB Issues

The game controller companies—those people who give us the controllers we love to abuse—are still learning about USB. It's very disconcerting, for example, to have to calibrate a supposedly digital USB joystick. At some point in the not-too-distant future, we'll have multiaxis, digital controllers that are rock solid—or so I fervently hope.

Normally, when you plug in a USB controller, Windows 98 recognizes it automatically and installs a generic HID (human interface device) driver. Despite its inherently digital nature, some USB devices do require calibration, but with a HID device, you don't have to specify a custom setup.

Some USB controllers also come with drivers that bring additional functionality. For example, the Microsoft Sidewinder Gamepad Pro acts as a generic HID device if you simply plug it in. If you install the Sidewinder software, you get the ability to create custom profiles for each game.

## Windows 95 OSR2.1

This version of Windows ostensibly supported USB, but it did so with some ineptitude. If you have this version of Windows, and can't possibly upgrade to Windows 98, be careful about buying a USB controller. If the box says "works under Windows 95 OSR2," then it probably comes with a custom driver and *might* work. Then again, it might not.

# The Joystick Control Panel

Setting up and configuring joysticks in Windows revolves around the joystick control panel. Let's uncover how the joystick control panel works with a couple of different sticks, one generic, and one which comes with custom drivers. Note that any other device—game pads, steering wheels, and so on—behave pretty much the same way.

## CH Gamestick 3D

The Gamestick 3D, from CH Products, is a fairly low-cost stick distinguished by a twist handle that can be used to act as the rudder for flight games or just as another axis in games like *Descent 3*. It's a purely analog joystick, but is solidly built, with good-quality potentiometers.

Although you can actually get a driver from CH, the stick is simple enough that we can easily customize it in Windows 98 using the joystick control panel. Let's connect the stick to the game port and bring up the game controller control panel (see Figure 24.1).

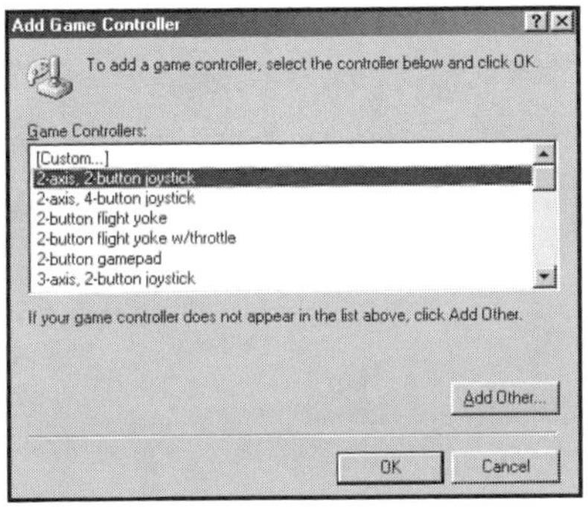


**Figure 24.1**
We begin customizing the stick here, in the Game Controller control panel.

Click on the Add button, and then select Custom. A new dialog box will immediately pop up (see Figure 24.2).

Let's assume we want to use this stick as a flight controller. The Gamestick 3D has four axes: x, y, the rudder, and a throttle axis. That means we'd want to configure it as a four-axis controller, right?

Not necessarily—we want to use it as a flight controller, remember? Bear with me for a moment as we configure it as a *three* axis controller. The stick has four buttons, so make sure that's checked. Finally, the Gamestick 3D has a four-way hat switch at the top of the stick, so we click on Has a Point of View Control. Now, let's give it a name, and then click the OK button.

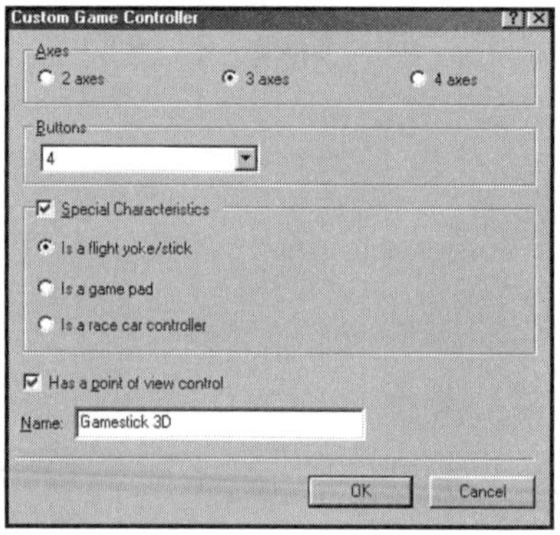


**Figure 24.2**

Setting the right parameters in the panel.

Remember how we specified the stick as a three-axis stick? When we actually begin the calibration process, we can then check the rudder pedal box—or not, as we choose (see Figure 24.3).

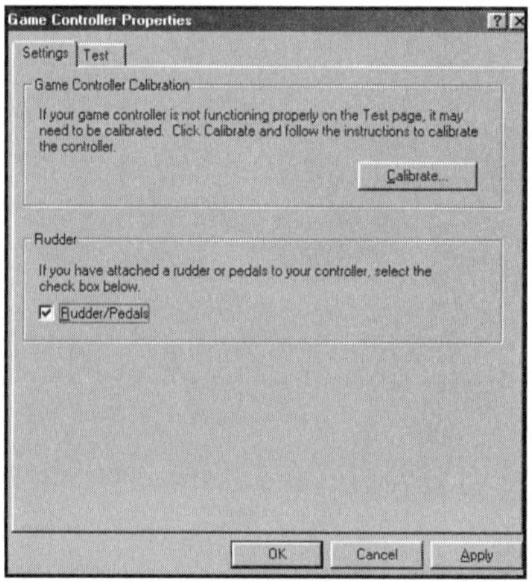


**Figure 24.3**

Here's where we define the fourth axis to behave like rudder pedals.

This is an analog stick, so we do need to calibrate it. Because this has four axes, plus the view hat, we'll need to go through a number of calibration steps. The control panel bundles them all into a single screen (see Figure 24.4).

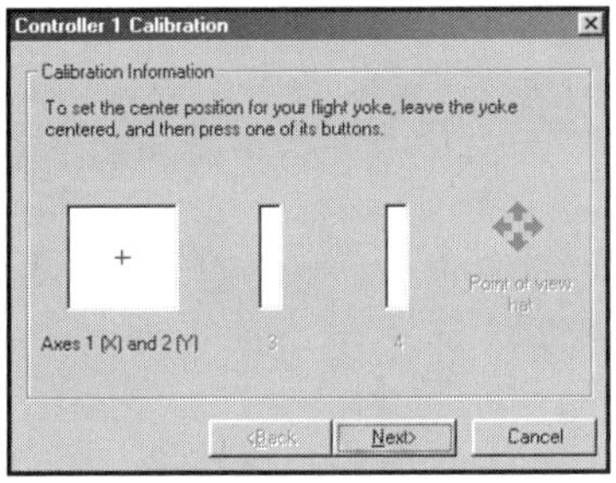


**Figure 24.4**

You should take care in each section. Move the axis slowly back and forth several times, so as to achieve as much granularity as the game port and joystick potentiometers will allow. After you've gone through the four axes plus hat, make sure to click Apply so the settings take.

The final thing to do is test your joystick setup. Click on the Test tab, and try out all the buttons and axes to make sure it's all working correctly. Typically, a rudder or throttle might not always calibrate precisely the first time (see Figure 24.5).

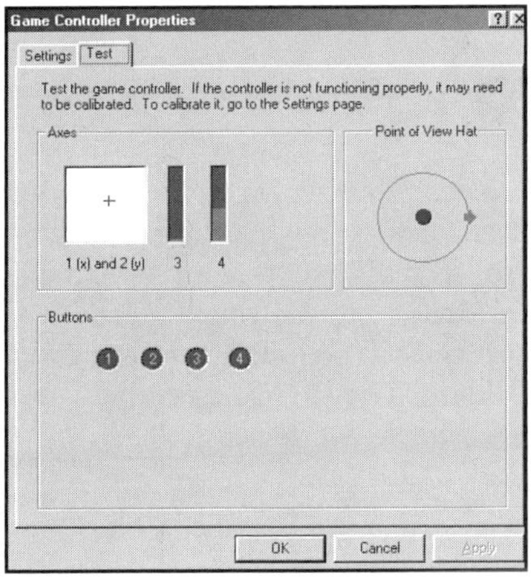


**Figure 24.5**

Test your configuration after you've calibrated to make sure the calibration "took."

### Note

Most devices that need calibration behave the same way. However, calibrating a steering wheel can be confusing. Most steering wheels only have two axes. The left-right turn of the wheel is one axis; the brake and accelerator pedals *combined* make up axis two. This last one confuses many people.

A few wheels let you flip a switch so that the brake and accelerator can act as completely separate axes. This allows simultaneous use of brake and accelerator, but only a few hard core driving simulators support this functionality.

## CTFJ

If you've dropped a wad on a good analog joystick, like the Thrustmaster F22 series or a CH F16 Combatstick, joystick problems can be very frustrating. One nifty utility, written by Bob Church, is CTFJ. CTFJ stands for *center the friendly joystick* (you might substitute another word for "friendly," depending on your mood). CTFJ can seem overwhelming, but at its core, it centers the stick and helps maintain a consistent "dead zone" in the center. You can pick up CTFJ, and several other nifty utilities, from Bob's Web site at `www.stickworks.com`.

# Microsoft Sidewinder Force Feedback Pro

If you're tired of all the hassles that revolve around analog joystick calibration, maybe it's time to try a digital joystick. One expensive example is the Microsoft Sidewinder Force Feedback Pro. The FF Pro, as we'll call it, is a purely digital device. Although it plugs into a sound card joystick port, the key to the operation of the Microsoft stick is the use of pins 12 and 15 in the joystick connection. These are normally used by the sound card to transmit and receive MIDI data. The FF Pro uses these pins to facilitate the two-way communication needed for force feedback devices.

The Sidewinder requires running a setup program to install custom drivers. This modifies the joystick control panel (see Figure 24.6).

The FF pro does have other settings, such as a panel for testing forces and one to specify the maximum amount of force delivered to your hand.

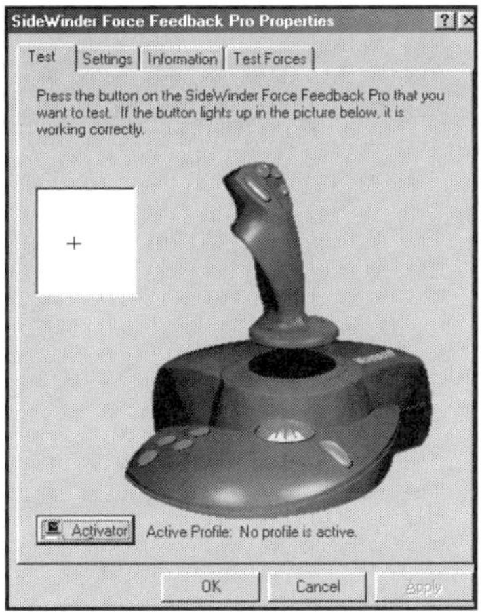


**Figure 24.6**

Note that the Calibrate button has vanished. The Sidewinder's digital operation obviates the need for calibration. You can alter some of the force feedback settings in other parts of the control panel, but this lack of need for calibration is a peek into the future of game controllers. Some day, joystick calibration will be a thing of the past. It's certainly not something I'll lament.

# Chapter 25

# All About Drivers

## Who's Driving Whom?

In the beginning, when there was only DOS (for games, anyway), drivers were of little concern to gamers. If they did run Windows for business apps, whatever shipped in the box with the graphics card was good enough, as long as it worked.

The fretting began when higher resolution (640×480×256 and above) DOS games started showing up on the scene. High resolution support in DOS games was possible due to a superset of the VGA standard developed by VESA *(Video Electronics Standards Association)*. It took some time for the card and chip makers to develop VESA-compliant hardware, so software drivers were developed in their stead. It was the first taste of what was later to become the "driver du jour" phenomenon.

When DirectX games started shipping, the issue of drivers came to the forefront. A game didn't work with your card? Download the latest driver. A new version of DirectX shipped? Download the latest driver. Can't do video overlay? Download the latest driver. It was almost a mantra. Note that a new driver didn't always fix the problem, but the presence of new drivers seemed to be something of a security blanket for support staff.

More recently, drivers have become something of a hot property on the Internet. It's become the cool thing to have the latest driver. This began with the 3dfx Voodoo2 card. The company would release reference drivers on its Web site that worked better in many cases than the one released by the cardmakers.

As profit margins have become squeezed in the card business, many companies no longer tweak and tune their own drivers. They might sometimes add useful Control Panel functionality, but the drivers these days are almost always unmodified reference drivers.

### Note

A *reference driver* is a hardware driver written by the chip company as a tool for card manufacturers. Originally, the chipmaker would give the graphics card company the reference driver and source code. The cardmaker would tweak and tune the driver and, in theory, release something faster and more robust. That's not true any more, and the chip companies (those few that don't do their own boards these days) now have significant software staffs devoted to writing drivers that require little tuning.

It's gotten to the point where unreleased drivers are leaked out on the Internet and savvy users—or the merely curious—load them up to see if anything's changed. In general, I recommend sticking with released drivers, whether they are reference drivers or from the company that made your graphics accelerator.

# How to Install a New Driver

There are generally two reasons to install a new video card driver. Either there's been a significant new release that improves stability (i.e., has fewer bugs) and is faster, or you've gotten a new graphics card as an upgrade. Though similar, the process needs to be a little different. Let's tackle the simpler example first.

## Upgrading the Current Driver

A quick look at the steps to upgrading your current driver shows that it's a pretty simple process:

- Make sure the new driver is available
- Change to VGA mode, reboot
- Uninstall the old driver, if possible
- Install the new driver, reboot
- Set up the monitor

It's pretty simple, but let's walk through it—that will prep us for the bigger challenge ahead. Note that first step, however. It's amazing how often this gets forgotten. Usually, you just forget to unzip them. Most drivers are stored on web sites as zip-compressed files, and you usually need a zip manager, like PKZip or WinZip. A few drivers, like the ones from Diamond Multimedia, come as self-contained applications that will install themselves as soon as you launch them. Most, though, are compressed. Once decompressed, you use the usual add device wizard method for installing the driver. So, after you download the latest driver you're going to use, unzip it into some folder like c:\drivers\graphics. Keep the folder name simple since you'll have to browse to find this folder during the upgrade.

First, let's change to VGA mode. You want to do this to guarantee that the current driver is overwritten. If you don't switch to VGA mode, parts of the old driver might remain, which can cause major headaches. This is done in the display Control Panel. You can run the display Control Panel by either launching it from the main Control Panel, or by right-clicking on the desktop and selecting "Properties". Select the "Settings" tab. Then, press the "Advanced" button, followed by the "Adapter" tab. The Update Device Driver wizard opens as shown in Figure 25.1.

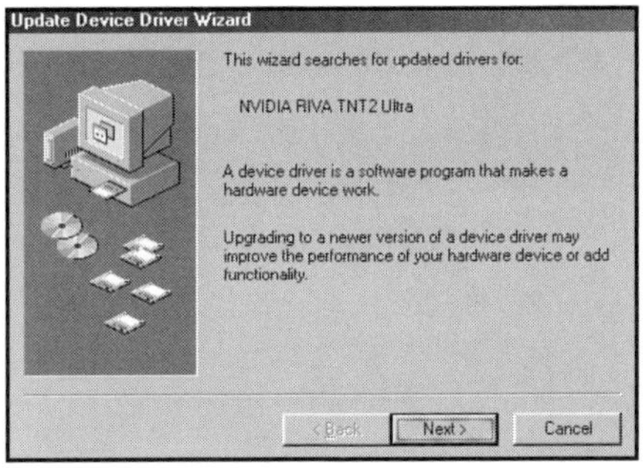


**Figure 25.1**

This is what you should see after clicking the "Advanced" button in display settings, then clicking the "Adapter" tab.

In this example, we'll be switching from a generic reference driver to a later revision directly from the card manufacturer, in this case, Guillemot. Open the Display Control Panel and click on the "Change" button. The Update Device wizard should now pop up as shown in Figure 25.2.

After pressing the Next button once, you'll have to choose between Search for a Better Driver and Display a List of All the Drivers. Click on the second selection to display a list of all possible drivers.

Now, you'll see a short list, with perhaps only a single entry. That won't do, so click the button at the bottom labeled Show All Hardware. Now scroll up and find Standard Display Types. Pick Standard PCI Graphics Adapter (VGA) as shown in Figure 25.3.

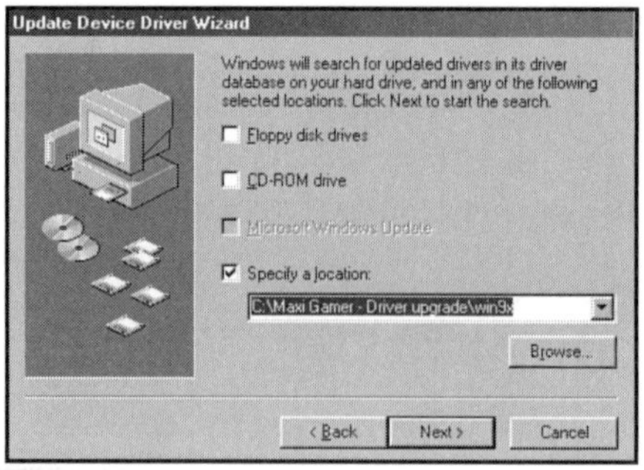


**Figure 25.2**

Pressing the Change button should launch the Update Device wizard.

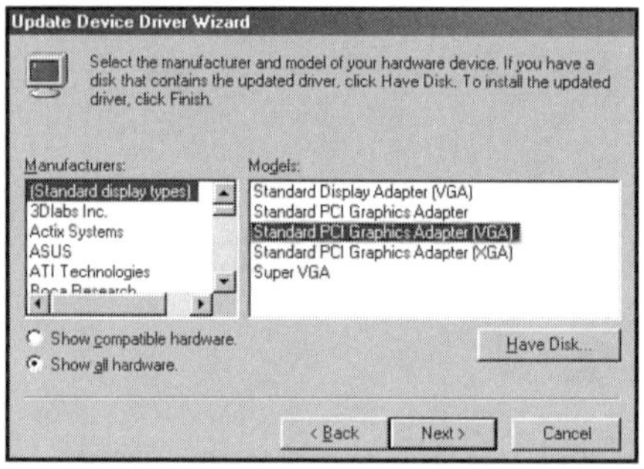


**Figure 25.3**

If you don't pick the standard PCI VGA adapter, you might get odd results and unexpected errors.

If the graphics card isn't more than two years old, this is the choice you want. Choosing one of the other standard types will generate some strange error messages, and might even result in an unbootable system in some cases.

Now, click OK several times. You'll be asked if you want to reboot the system. Select No. Instead, shut down the system to the DOS prompt. The next step is to delete a couple of pesky INF files. INF files are used by the Device Update Wizard to tell it where driver files are located. Because we're installing a completely new driver, it would be unfortunate if the old one was automatically loaded.

## Caution

The step of deleting INF files isn't always necessary. Most of the time, after choosing the PCI VGA adapter, Windows happily reboots into VGA mode. But occasionally, the old drivers will automatically reinstall themselves on bootup, and you have to start all over again.

Once in DOS mode, change to the Windows INF folder by typing: `cd \windows\inf`. Look for the INF file for your old drivers. There might be two different ones, one in \windows\inf and the other in \windows\inf\other (see Figure 25.4).

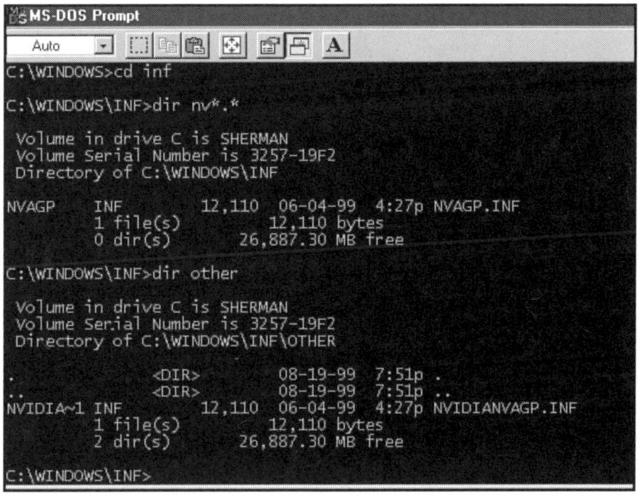


**Figure 25.4**
Get rid of those pesky INF files!

If you don't know which one is the correct one, you can open it with the DOS text editor by typing `edit`. The INF files are just text files, and the early part of the file usually has the name of the device you're updating. If you type `dir /od`, the file list will sort by date—your device was installed after the dates in all the Windows default INF files, so it will likely be near the bottom. There are typically only a few files in \windows\inf\other, so anything you need to remove shouldn't be too hard to find.

After removing the INF files, boot normally. The system should boot into straight VGA mode: 640×480 with 16 colors—pretty ugly, isn't it?

Now, you do have the driver, and it is decompressed, right? If the driver is a self-contained setup program, like Diamond Multimedia drivers, just launch it and sit back. Most drivers now retrace your steps to get to the Add New Hardware Wizard. However, this time, select Search For a Better Driver (see Figure 25.5).

It's likely that the Floppy Disk Drive" box is checked—uncheck it. Most drivers today are too big for floppies anyway. Instead, check the Specify a Location box and either type in the location or browse for it. Find the folder where you unzipped the new driver. After you find the correct location, click the Next button, and you're off and running.

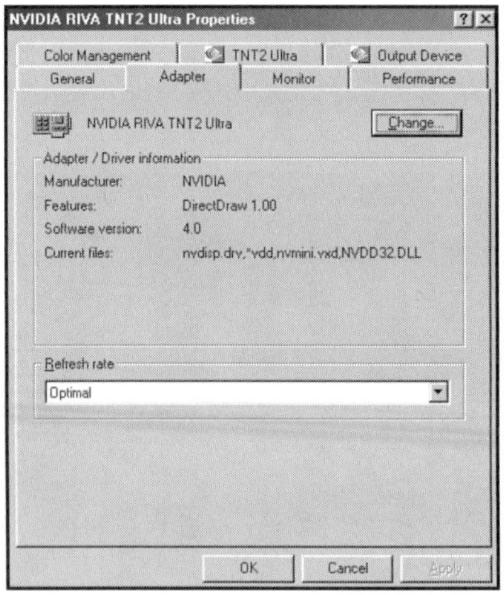


**Figure 25.5**
Choosing the new driver.

## Caution

One odd thing that might occur, depending on how the install script was constructed for the driver, is that you might be prompted for the Windows CD. (If you've installed Windows from the hard drive, you might be staring at a dialog box showing the Windows 98 setup folder.) Just browse or type in the correct folder name for the driver update.

The last step is to set up your monitor. Bring up the Display Control Panel again. Click the Advanced button, and then look under the tab labeled Monitor. If it says Unknown, you definitely have to set up the monitor. If it says Plug-and-Play Monitor, you might be okay. However, if you have a specific monitor driver (and INF file, really), for your monitor, you should install it now. Usually, you just pop the floppy or CD into the drive, click the Change button on the monitor property sheet, and point the dialog towards the location of the INF file. If you have a monitor that's over a year old, Windows might actually have it in its list of monitors. Check under the Display a List of All the Drivers" option in the Hardware Update Wizard.

Some monitors support very high refresh rates at various resolutions. If you want to get the most out of your monitor, and if it has a driver, you should install it.

That's it. You've now updated a driver. If you've followed the steps carefully, you should have no problems using the new drivers.

# Upgrading Your Graphics Card

The process for upgrading your actual hardware is similar, but there are a few additional steps:

1. After you've switched to VGA mode and removed the old INF files, uninstall any drivers and utilities that exist for your current card. Most manufacturers these days supply you with an uninstall script. Just use the Add/Remove Programs Control Panel to do this. If there is no uninstall, you're probably okay.
2. After you've uninstalled the old software, remove the old card and insert the new card into the AGP slot.

For more detail on how to install the graphics hardware, see page 242.

3. Reboot and install the new card's drivers.

### Caution

Windows 98 is pretty forgiving. If you absent-mindedly rip out the old card, put in the new one and power up, you'll *probably* boot into VGA mode, and be able to install the new drivers. However, if you're replacing one card with another that uses the same graphics chip, you might find that the drivers for the *old* card are automatically installing themselves. If this happens, just follow the steps above for installing a driver update.

# Installing a Sound Card Driver

Windows has significantly standardized the driver installation process, so installing a sound card driver is really very similar to installing a graphics card driver. Some sound cards, like those from Creative Labs, will often supply you with an installer program, which makes life much easier.

If you do have to manually install the driver, you begin the process in a slightly different way. Instead of using the display Control Panel, launch the system Control Panel. Click on the sound card (or Multifunction Parent in the case of some cards) and select Properties (see Figure 25.6). There will be a Driver tab as well. From this point, the driver install process launches the Update Hardware Wizard, and you're off and running.

Depending on how the update script was structured, updating the multifunction parent will update all the other components as well (sound driver, MIDI, and so on). In other cases, you might have to repeat the previous steps for each component of the sound card.

### Caution

Sometimes, during the install process, a dialog box pops up telling you that you're replacing a newer version of vjoyd.vxd. It then asks you if you want to keep the newer version. It defaults to Yes. Instead, say No. You want the joystick driver that comes with your sound card.

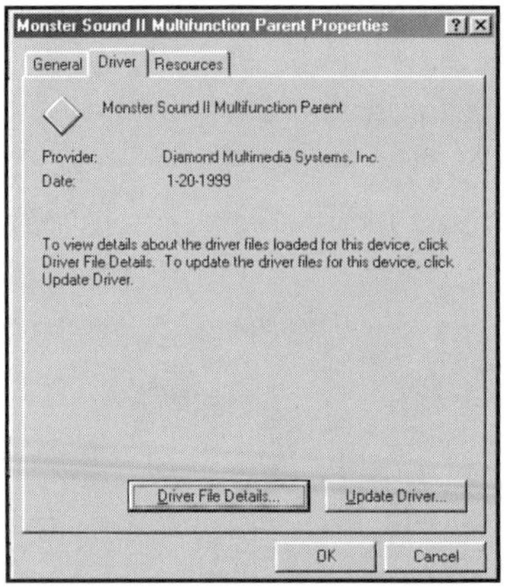


**Figure 25.6**

With some sound cards, you begin the task of updating the drivers in the system Control Panel.

# Graphics Configuration Tips

After you have the card and drivers you want up and running, it's time to do a little additional configuration:

- Refresh rates. I generally run at 85Hz. Many current cards, and most newer monitors, can run higher. But in those cases, Direct3D games often try to run at that refresh rate. A very high refresh rate will cut into the graphics memory bandwidth. It's often better to run a little lower. Some users advocate running at 60Hz within games, but I haven't found that necessary. A refresh rate of 75–85Hz works pretty well. You can change the refresh rate under the Adapters tab in the display Control Panel.
- Keep your desktop at least in 16-bit color. A number of games will pick up the color depth of the Windows desktop, and run the game at that color depth. This is especially true of games that use the *Quake I* or *Quake II* engines; *Unreal* also does this. *Quake* engine games often do not support anything other than 16- or 32-bit color. They will only run in software mode at 8-bit or 24-bit color. Be careful about running games in 32-bit color, unless both your graphics hardware and system performance are up to it.
- Some graphics cards, like those from Matrox and Diamond, come with very handy utilities that create cool pop-up menus, allow you to change resolution and color depth on-the-fly, and other useful things. Be aware that you might have to unload them when installing or playing some game titles. Some games just don't like resident utilities that affect graphics.

## Some Useful Utilities

There are a few tools that help you in either streamlining graphics performance, or just make life easier.

- **3D Control Center (3DCC).** This tool allows you to specify which graphics card is the primary Direct3D accelerator. This is very handy if you have a secondary card, like a 3dfx Voodoo2 card. You can pick which one you want Direct3D games to use. You can find it in a variety of locations on the Internet—just do a search on 3DCC in any search engine.
- **Powerstrip.** You can get this somewhat complex, but often useful, tool from `www.entechtaiwan.com`. It lets you change a startling variety of settings, as well as set default resolutions and refresh rates for Direct3D and OpenGL. It will also let you alter the clock rate of your graphics card—use this feature with care.

# Audio Configuration Tips

Configuring audio also requires an understanding of the Windows mixer. It usually appears as a speaker icon in your system tray. You typically use it to adjust sound volume for the various audio subsystems, like line out, line in, CD audio and so on. The best thing to do is start up audio, and play with it for a bit. Some sound cards expand the mixer with utilities like multiband equalizers.

- If, for some reason, CD audio isn't playing, check the mixer first. Sometimes, CD audio volume will mysteriously be reset to zero for no apparent reason.

### Caution

Some older Windows games do not like sound cards that accelerate DirectSound. If you've got a newer PCI audio card, and a game keeps crashing mysteriously, or with apparent sound glitches, check the Multimedia Control Panel (see Figure 25.7). Click the Advanced button, and then check under the Performance tab. You might need to slide the hardware Acceleration slider left a couple of notches.

- Note that some speakers will go into a standby mode when no signal is present. Sometimes, they don't come out of standby mode. If that's the case, you might have to turn them off, and then on again.
- When you attach four speakers to get four-speaker DirectSound, make sure you tell the multimedia Control Panel. There are numerous settings for speakers, including quadraphonic. You might also need to set this in a separate Control Panel installed by the sound card.
- Be careful about wiring speakers. If they're the type with two wire leads (like home stereo speakers), you want to make sure that the positive is connected to positive at both ends. If you don't you risk reversing the polarity. The result is muddy sound, with no stereo imaging.

**Figure 25.7**

To fix some sound problems, reduce the level of audio acceleration. Don't forget to push it back up with most games!

- If you have a microphone hooked up for voice communication, make sure the Mute box is checked in the *playback* part of the mixer (but not the *record* section of the mixer). Otherwise, you'll hear yourself speaking, and some very annoying feedback can occur. You switch between the record and playback mixers by pulling down the options menu in the mixer and selecting Properties.

With just a little fine-tuning in speaker placement, you can end up with a killer audio setup that can create a wonderfully immersive sound field during gameplay.

# Index

## Symbols

## A

## B



## C

## H

## J



## K

## Q-R



## S

## T

## W

## X-Z